THE TROUBLE WITH TOM

Banvard's Folly: Thirteen Tales of People Who Didn't Change the World
Sixpence House: Lost in a Town of Books
Not Even Wrong: A Father's Journey into the Lost History of Autism

The Trouble With Tom

*The Strange Afterlife and Times
of Thomas Paine*

Paul Collins

BLOOMSBURY

To Bramwell

First published in Great Britain in 2006

Jacket images:
Top: Washington Crossing the Delaware River, 25th December 1776,
by Leutze, Emanuel Gottlieb
Metropolitan Museum of Art, New York

Bottom: The Execution of Louis XVI (1754–93) 21 January 1793,
by Danish School
Musée de la Ville de Paris, Musée Carnavalet, Paris.

Bloomsbury Publishing Plc, 36 Soho Square, London W1D 3QY

A CIP catalogue record for this book is available from the British Library

ISBN 0 7475 7768 4
ISBN-13 9780747577683

10 9 8 7 6 5 4 3 2 1

Typeset by Hewer Text UK Ltd, Edinburgh
Printed in the United States of America by Quebecor World Fairfield

CONTENTS

But who knows the fate of his bones, or how often he is to be buried? Who hath the oracle of his ashes, or whither they are to be scattered? The relics of many lie like the ruins of Pompey's, in all parts of the earth; and when they arrive at your hands these may seem to have wandered far, who, in a direct and meridian travel, have but a few miles of known earth between yourself and the pole.

—Sir Thomas Browne, *Hydriotaphia,*
or Urne-Buriall (1658)

HERE

The End

A TAXI SPEEDS through the rain, dashing water up onto the sidewalks of Bleecker Street like a flume ride. I run around the corner up to Grove and duck under the awning of number 59. It's a handsome building—devilishly handsome. If it were a man, and if I were gay, I'd have a crush on it.

Open its door and a swell of piano chords roar out into the downpour: "*Raindrops on roses!*" comes the cry from within. Creaking wooden steps descend into a low-ceilinged room packed with a mass of men and women—but mostly men—and twinkling over the bald and balding heads, as well as some immaculately groomed ones, there are glittering strings of electric Christmas tree lights. The swelling chorus of drunken voices bellow at a trim, dapper fellow banging away on a ploinkety old red piano:

> *. . . and whiskers on kittens,*
> *Bright copper kettles and warm woolen mittens,*
> *Brown paper packages tied up with strings—*
> *These are a few of my favorite things.*

The squeeze through the crowd toward the bar takes several minutes, and I catch a tiny squall of conversation between just

about the only two men not belting out in their best baritone voices.
"I was innocent back then," one stirs his drink.
"Yeah," the other snorts. "Right."

Cream-colored ponies and crisp apple strudels;
Doorbells and sleigh bells and schnitzel with noodles;

I finally reach the polished wooden bar.
"What can I get you?"

Wild geese that fly with

"I'll have . . ."

the moon on their wings—

"What?"
"I'll . . ."

These are a few of my favorite things.

"Can't hear you."
I resort to telegraphing between syllables of singing, yelling:
"I. Want."

Girls in white dresses with blue satin sashes,

"A. Hein. Eh. Ken."
"Oh. Kay."
He takes a couple more orders, and my beer arrives as the song
ends in a final crashing chord and a cacophony of applause.

"Thanks." I hastily count out from my wallet. "Hey, I'm trying to find out a little about this building. Its history."

"It's got plenty of that."

"Yeah. I . . ."

"There's a plaque out front, and . . ."

I get no kick from champagne!

He finishes his sentence soundlessly beneath the barrage and gives a helpless shrug at the music. I ford upstream through knot after knot of men, drinking my beer wide-eyed. It's like one of those festive bar crowds you only see in old black-and-white movies: men hanging off each other and raising glasses and warbling. I'm probably the only guy here who doesn't know all the lyrics being sung, and the place keeps filling impossibly with even more people.

Several songs later I've drained my beer, and half trip over a stranger's shoes, out into the cold night air. It's stopped raining; a few stray drips shake down from the awning in a gust, and I crouch in the darkness to squint at the brass plate bolted into the brick wall of the ancient building.

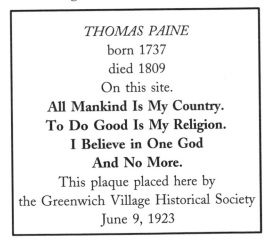

THOMAS PAINE
born 1737
died 1809
On this site.
All Mankind Is My Country.
To Do Good Is My Religion.
I Believe in One God
And No More.
This plaque placed here by
the Greenwich Village Historical Society
June 9, 1923

It stares out into the darkness, as if to really say: *what strange ends we come to.*

It's a bar called Marie's Crisis now. Who'd imagine this as the place where his life came to a halt? There might have been so many other endings for the firebrand *Common Sense* rebel of 1776, the radical on the run from execution in London, the senator of revolutionary France. Paine alone claims a key role in the development of three modern democracies. He was a walking revolution in human form—the most dangerous man alive. But dead? The plaque here could be for anybody, anybody at all: a forgotten minister, perhaps, or long-dead mayor.

The letters of the sign drip with the windblown remains of the rain. *My Country.*

I turn and survey Grove Street in the darkness. Around here is the old Greenwich Village, a vision of New York in respectable brownstone, brick and wrought iron, the city you imagine from faded lithographs. And yet even here, things quietly change. All sorts of businesses have been housed in this building over the centuries; before this plaque was attached to 59 Grove Street, the place was a delicatessen. Imagine that: Edwardians buying ham sandwiches and deviled eggs where a Founding Father once fell. It's almost as strange as belting out show tunes over the spot.

But this is indeed where he died. It wasn't for a lack of trying at other addresses. I guess you could say that Thomas Paine has died over and over. He has died innumerable times in effigy at gatherings in the English countryside; he had the visage of his corpse stamped into British coins; his imminent death predicted among bloodthirsty French mobs, foreseen in the apartment of James Madison and in the back room of a New York baker, and witnessed in the boarding rooms of Grove Street. Some people have lived everywhere, but Thomas Paine is altogether more rare. He has died everywhere.

The old man sat by a front window in Greenwich Village, visible from the street, watching the world and the country he had created passing him by. Here he sat: he who was the first to coin the phrase *United States of America*; who made from his own pocket the first deposit in what became the Federal Reserve; who shivered at Valley Forge, using a drumhead as a desk, penning the words *These are the times that try men's souls*. He who had made the country, and baptized it. The most hated man in America.

The country's rebellion eventually ended, but Paine's never did. After the Revolution he'd moved back to London to work as an entrepreneur, only to find that he could no longer view his old country in the same light. He wrote to George Washington in 1791: "I began to feel myself happy in being quiet; but I now experience that principle is not confined to Time or place, and that the ardour of seventy-six is capable of renewing itself." The monarchy chafed at him still, and so he rubbed the royal nose into *The Rights of Man*—a new *Common Sense* to prod the English into overthrowing their king. This time the troublesome Paine was chased to the Dover docks, and carried aloft at the other side of the Channel by the cheering revolutionaries of France.

But then he attacked the wrong sort of king.

He'd been in poor health for years, ever since nearly dying in a French prison at the height of the Terror. And now the old man was suffering from a series of strokes. He was arthritic, abscessed, tired. Tired of being attacked by gout, tired of being attacked by the slow rot of sores and ulcers, tired of being *attacked by everybody and everything all the time*. Of all the books and pamphlets he'd written, it was really just one that had done the damage: *The Age of Reason*.

He wasn't attacking every God in it, he always hastened to point out to enraged evangelical Christians—just *their* God. "Belief in a cruel god makes a cruel man," he explained. He'd been raised a Quaker, after all: like many Friends, he simply sought a gentler and more rational moral system of good works. But Paine returned to America in 1802 to find roads placarded with portraits of him being seized by the devil. Back at his farm in New Rochelle, Paine was denied the vote by a county registrar who contemptuously informed him that he was "not American." The registrar clearly had a fine sense of irony, seeing as how he himself had been a Tory during the war. Renting out his upstate farm for desperately needed cash, the ailing Paine began staying with sympathetic friends in the city in 1805— and perhaps had taken to, as one friend grieved, looking for "consolation in the sordid, solitary bottle."

Well, not so solitary these days: I hear a slipped glass smash on the floor inside the bar, followed by mocking applause and a rim-shotting *blorp* off the piano. This house at what is now 59 Grove Street—there was neither grove nor street back then—this was merely the final deathbed of many. When he first arrived and was casting about for a place to stay, Paine helped himself to the guest room at the home of local religious reformer Elihu Palmer. Palmer was delighted to have his hero as a guest. But Paine, the reformer warned a mutual friend, was not long for this world—"His health I think is declining."

Palmer died six months later. Paine kept living.

As reformers are prone to do, Palmer died nearly broke; his widow had to sell off their furniture, and joined Paine to cram into the house of an old acquaintance over on 36 Cedar Street. Paine was lonely and needed nursing, as the widow Palmer scrawled in a September 1806 letter: "He says I must never leave him while he lives he is now comfortable but so lame he cannot walk nor git into bed without the help of two men."

He did still have some visitors to break up his loneliness, though. His old friend John Stewart was in the city for a while, and—how time was changing him! Strange to think of all that had passed since their days together in London, reading the day's papers and philosophizing until the wee hours of the morning at the White Bear coffeehouse on Piccadilly. Back in 1790, Stewart had been perhaps the only man in London who could draw more stares than Paine himself. Tall, muscular, and exotic, Stewart had lived the kind of life found only in adventure fiction. He'd shipped out to Madras as a young clerk for the East India Company in 1763, only to decide that—as he announced brusquely in a letter to company directors— he was "born for nobler pursuits than to be a copier of invoices and bills of lading to a company of grocers, haberdashers, and cheese-mongers." And he was right: joining an Indian prince as a secretary, he rose through the ranks to become an army general and a prime minister—before, incredibly, throwing it all over to walk on foot through the mountains of Persia and Turkey, the deserts of Arabia and Egypt, deep into Ethiopia and into the terra incognita of central Africa, and then back around the Adriatic and Mediterranean to Paris. When he reached London, he was dubbed by the incredulous press "Walking Stewart." Never was there a more apt name; for he later hiked through Lapland and down into central Asia, and after sailing to New York walked all the way down to Paraguay. Walking Stewart became, as his friend Thomas De Quincey put it, the first circumambulator of the globe. Stewart attributed his survival to two things that struck anyone else back then as incomprehensible: a vegetarian diet, and an utter refusal to ever carry a weapon.

Yes, they'd made quite a pair back then. Paine, a failed grocer and customs officer who had moved to America and overthrown the monarchy, and Stewart, who paraded through Piccadilly in Arme-nian garb, his mannerisms mixed with those of all the exotic lands

he'd walked through, and his speech and accent now a mélange from the innumerable languages he'd learned. It was muttered among onlookers that Paine had become some sort of inventor, going about trying to sell iron bridges—and Stewart, well, nobody knew quite what to make of him at all. The man wouldn't talk of his fantastic travels; instead, he was always distributing bizarre pamphlets he'd privately printed, bearing titles like *The Roll of a Tennis Ball Through the Moral World*. The few who could read past their strange diction and publication date—for Stewart had invented his own calendar—found all sorts of curious ideas inside. Stewart found it incomprehensible that women put up with child care, and believed the state should establish daytime nurseries so that mothers and fathers might work or improve their minds. He saw nothing wrong with prostitution, and considered it a typical city business like lamplighting or driving a taxi, indeed, he saw little wrong with sex, and so believed that there should be "promiscuous intercourse . . . that the population might not become redundant."

And now, as they sat aged in Manhattan, Paine and his old friend still warmly disagreed on many issues: Walking Stewart had always been dubious of Paine's cries for overthrowing kings, and he thought Paine's support for voting rights was absurd. *What would it come to*, Stewart scoffed—*giving the vote to women and apprentices as well?* And while Stewart was a confirmed atheist, Paine still believed in a God—in an animating moral force, if you will—he just didn't believe in the Bible or in clergy.

But they were both misunderstood geniuses of a sort; Paine found his books banned in England and despised in America, and Stewart brooded over the fate of his own pamphlets as well. He had a notion, he said, of preserving them for posterity. Stewart bid his readers, when done reading him, to bury his books in their gardens at a depth of seven or eight feet. They were to tell no one else of the

location; but then, on their deathbeds, they were to breathe the secret to a trusted few. These fellows would keep the secret burial place until their deathbeds years later, and would communicate it again—down through the centuries, and the millennia, a secret society of philosophers passing down at death the sacred memory of the locations of Stewart's writings. *Oh*—the Circumambulator then feared—*but what if someday my works prove unreadable because the English language itself has moldered away by then?* He thereupon decided that first his readers should translate the works into Latin, *then* bury them.

Paine watched his strange friend return to England. Poor John! A traveling ascetic whose only real pleasure had been in music—the man was going deaf now. Their times were drawing near . . . too near, in fact. Word came back from across the ocean months later that Stewart's ship had been dashed to pieces on its way to Liverpool. It sounded like he hadn't survived, hadn't even had the chance to pass on his secret burial spots to his brotherhood.

Paine waited and gazed out the windows of Cedar Street. *When?* When would it be his turn? He had his usual modest supper of bread and butter, and then climbed the weary stairs yet again, when . . . when . . . he had the sensation of a bullet passing through his head: his body crumpled and toppled down the stairs, and he lay lifeless on the floor, with neither pulse nor breath.

Not yet.

Death came: but then it went away. He resumed breathing, and his brain—struck not by a bullet, but by a stroke—began to register sights and sounds again. What was curious about the whole experience, Paine marveled afterward, was how calm he felt.

His host felt rather less philosophical about it all. Instead of dying like a gentleman, Paine was lingering on and on. By the time the old rebel left in November 1806, his former friend was so irritated that he dunned Paine for twenty-two weeks of back rent.

If you wanted to transport yourself back to a precise time and place for the birth of American culture—that is, of North American art distinct from that of Europe—you might find yourself passing the ailing Paine on these streets one cold Saturday afternoon in 1807. On January 24 of that year, the first issue of a brilliantly insouciant new magazine hit the streets of Manhattan: *Salmagundi*, its title page read. It immediately declared on its first page that it would give no hint of its staff's identity. "It is nobody's business," it proclaimed, snapping its fingers in readers' faces. No matter: few had heard of the puckish young Washington Irving anyway. His subscribers read delightedly about the doings and sayings of nearly everyone of note in Manhattan, and the first number wasted no time in skewering the fashions of the season. "I was, however, much pleased to see that red maintained its ground against all other colors," the fashion column dryly commented, before wickedly explaining: *"because red is the color of Mr. Jefferson's *****, Tom Paine's nose, and my slippers."*

As the founding smartasses of American literature came gloriously alive that winter day, the elderly subject of their derision was slowly dying. His nose grew ever more red and disfigured with a skin condition that gossips ascribed, only half unfairly, to brandy. Local children running underfoot sang:

> *Tom Paine is coming from far, from far;*
> *His nose is like a blazing star!*

But Irving could hardly resist having a bit of fun at the old fellow's expense. Their orbits were not far removed now, since that winter Paine had moved into the bachelor digs at 85 Church Street of portraitist John Wesley Jarvis, an impeccably bohemian acquaintance of Irving's. Paine had already known Jarvis for a while—but then, there was hardly a fashionable or artistic person in the city who *didn't* know Jarvis. You couldn't miss him: sweeping down Manhattan streets dressed "in a long coat trimmed with furs like a Russian prince," and walking two enormous dogs at his side, he seemed the very personification of the dashing artist. Naturally, he was delighted to have the most vilified writer in America sleeping in his art studio; it was a great lark. But the young painter had a genuinely tender feeling for the old man's needs; his guest was, he explained, "perfectly manageable by art, patiently and assiduously applied." If Paine woke up troubled with gout, and inclined to eat without first washing up, the dapper Jarvis would gently nudge him into keeping up his appearances via indirect instructions to the house servant.

"Take the coffee away," he'd gently remonstrate, "give Mr. Paine a little time; he is a gentleman; he wants to wash himself; bring him some soap and water."

Jarvis just wanted Paine to buck up and look good, and he generously preserved him at his most handsome by painting a portrait of his new guest. It was all in a day's work for Jarvis—literally, as he was in such demand that he and his assistant Joseph Wood often cranked out six oil portraits a week—though he did cut corners slightly by leaving Paine's hands out of the painting. Well, that would have been *too* generous. For anyone else he'd have charged $40 for just such a portrait from the neck up; hands were damned tricky work and cost an extra $20.

Paine felt at ease among the art studio's productive chaos of brush jars, easels, and lacquer. Jarvis would paint the portrait subject on canvas, while his indefatigable Wood painted darkly haunting backgrounds; at other times they'd switch to delicate watercolor miniatures upon ivory or card stock. Paine and the artists were all archetypal self-made New Yorkers; misfits who all hailed from somewhere else, each had found a city where they could speak freely, create freely, and reinvent themselves. Wood had been an untutored farmboy in Clarkstown obsessed with art, and ran away from home at fifteen to the big city with the dream of becoming a painter; he was now quickly becoming one of the best miniaturists in the country. And John Wesley Jarvis—a brilliant raconteur and a devotee of good wine, a man whose natural curiosity extended into scientific experimentation and anatomy—he, of all people, had been raised in his youth by his uncle John Wesley, the famously dour founder of Methodism.

Sometimes the old pieties were still visited upon them. Hearing that Paine was ailing, ministers and well-meaning folk were forever stopping by to pester him, hoping to get him to recant his heresies and to accept Jesus Christ as his savior. Jarvis was usually able to keep them out of the studio, but on one occasion let his guard down when a knock came at the door shortly after dinner. Jarvis opened it to find a very old woman, wrapped in a large scarlet cloak, and asking piteously to meet Thomas Paine.

He's asleep, Jarvis explained—*he always takes his nap after dinner.*

"I am very sorry for that," she said, "for I wanted to see him very particularly."

It seemed a shame to force a frail and elderly lady to make the trip a second time, and Jarvis relented. Leading her inside and back to Paine's room, the painter woke up the slumbering infidel.

"He rose on one elbow"—it was recalled soon afterward with some mirth—"with an expression of eye that staggered the old woman."

"What do you want?" he demanded.

"Is your name Paine?" the old woman asked solicitously.

"Yes."

"Well, then," she began kindly. *"I come from Almighty God to tell you that if you do not repent of your sins and believe in our blessed Savior Jesus Christ, you will be damned and—"*

"Pooh! Pooh!" Paine stopped her cold. "It is not true. You were not sent with any such impertinent message."

" . . ."

"Jarvis," Paine sighed, "make her go away. Pshaw. God would not send such a foolish ugly old woman as you about with his message. Go away. Go back." And then, preparing to return to sleep, he added, *"Shut the door."*

The old lady left thunderstruck. Jarvis was enough of a gentleman that he probably withheld his laughter until the woman was out of earshot of his house. He was not unsympathetic to her piety; he had been raised in a strict religious family himself, and though he had little use for them now, he thought churches served a worthy purpose for the rest of society. But as for himself—well, he was busy. He had paintings to paint and wine to drink. Late in the evenings, after Paine had had his nap, the two would philosophize over a bottle; once after a long conversation deep into the night at Jarvis's table, the painter retired for a while, only upon returning at four A.M. to find Paine still at table—or rather, underneath it.

"I have the vertigo, the vertigo," moaned Paine from the floor.

"Yes," Jarvis cracked, raising an eyebrow at the remains of the bottle. "You have it deep—deep!"

Perhaps; but to Paine it felt like another stroke. Lying there on Jarvis's floor, staring up at the ceiling, at the wooden legs and underside of the table, Paine turned thoughtful for a moment. Here he was, he wondered aloud, his mind strong and yet his body fallen.

Does it not put one in mind of the immortality of the soul? he blearily mused to the painter. *Surely . . . surely we continue to exist in a state beyond life itself . . .*

Old pop music jangles out of an unseen speaker somewhere in the dreadful fluorescence of a supermarket on Bleecker Street—"I'm a Believer"—and the couple in front of me is arguing about orange juice.

"We don't need the fancy kind," she insists.

"It's better." He shakes the little bottle for emphasis.

"No it's not."

"It," shake, "*is*."

Is—is not—is. The clerk is waiting at the register with obligatory unsmiling indifference, and I look away in the middle distance of frozen foods, into this space with the same weary feel as most every Manhattan grocery. For a supermarket named Strawberry Fields, the place is kind of a bad trip, and you would not want to be here Forever. But this is where Paine lay waiting for Forever to come— over *there*, let's say, right where the chunky peanut butter is on sale. You can't tell now, of course: it's all brick and linoleum and drywall, a squat sixty-three feet of frontage that keeps changing identity. Ten years before this it was a Gristede's; a hundred and ten years before that it was a different building altogether, two stories and wooden, and housing a billiard saloon; before then, it was the Gilded Age home of a button and trimmings importer. Go back further still, and you find a workshop for making screen windows. And perhaps next year it will be something new yet again, for the space is once again up for lease.

Jarvis had to move to a new studio in the spring of 1807, and for the rest of that year Paine lived with a baker down on Broome Street. After his rent went up, Paine moved into a miserable lodging house on Partition Street. All along he kept attacking Federalist conservatives in the *New York Public Advertiser*, but few were listening anymore; by 1808, the once-tireless pen was laid down, and he simply stopped publishing altogether.

So he packed up his trunks one more time and came here to die. His newest lodgings were on what was called Herring Street back then, and Paine struggled to pay his new landlords. A deal to sell his farm in New Rochelle fell through, and a pitiful request to Congress for reimbursement of some of his expenses during the Revolution was met with crushing indifference, then with a final no.

When? When? The end would come soon: it had to. In the dead of winter, as 1808 ground forward into 1809, Paine sat down and wrote out his will. The fate of his body troubled him, though; he fretted over it for months. He'd become acquainted with a local watchmaker and Quaker minister, Willet Hicks, and when the Friend paid a visit to Herring Street in March, Paine cut immediately to the matter at hand.

"I wish to be buried in your burying ground," he said plainly. His father, Paine explained, had been a Quaker, and he himself had been raised a Quaker: now he simply wished to return to its soil.

Well . . . it was an unusual request, you see—he'd go to the burial committee and see what they thought, of course, and . . . well, and . . . Had he changed opinions, perhaps, since writing *The Age of Reason?*

No, Paine said.

Willet would see what he could do. He, of all people, knew just how fraught Paine's modest request was. The local Quaker assemblies were already shaking themselves to pieces: a schism had been opening up between Orthodox members and a liberal faction headed by Willet's cousin, Elias Hicks. These arguments eventually became so heated that at one assembly the two sides wrestled over the property of the meetinghouse and tore a desk in half. Critics tarred Hicksites as closet Deists, and leagued them with the vilified author of *The Age of Reason*; one pamphlet charged Hicks with plagiarizing Paine. In many ways *The Age of Reason* did indeed seem like an especially blunt statement of the most liberal form of modern Quakerism—but Hicks vociferously denied the resemblance. And even if he did see any, it would be deeply impolitic to admit it.

Some days later Willet came back with the burial committee's answer, informing Paine as delicately as he could that . . . well, their answer was not *yes*. His old sect had forsaken him, and now he had nowhere else to go. The trembling old man felt himself dissolving in despair over the world's indifference to his fate.

I wish to die, he'd tell his landlord, who now sometimes found his boarder weeping. *I see no other end to my sufferings.*

"One seventy-nine," the clerk intones flatly.

I count the change out and leave. There's nothing left here: the Herring Street house survived long after they'd changed the name to Bleecker, and even after Seventh Avenue cut through part of the old block, but it was demolished in the 1930s. Nothing special: just one more building that had housed a sick old man once, same as every other building in New York.

Paine grew more feeble and helpless here, with gout, strokes, and abscesses battering his health until his landlord could hardly care for him anymore. His failing body was borne a block away to a friendly Democratic household, the Grove Street home of Aaron Burr's old law partner. His new neighbor Amasa Woodworth would stop by every day to check in on Paine, and he made for welcome company, since he was an engineer involved in the invention of a new oscillating steam engine design. It was a topic that held endless fascination for Paine, for steam engines had always appealed to his sense of progress—why, back in the day, he'd discussed steam engine design improvements with James Watt himself. Amasa began keeping Paine company late into the night too, for though the old man was not afraid of dying, he did dread dying alone.

Word trickled out from the sickroom that spring: it was true, Paine really *was* in his final days. A quiet procession of old friends came by to see Paine, to pay their respects. They found a man so weakened he could barely sit up, and who could not keep down weak milk punch without vomiting it up again. Even Jarvis, now at the top of his game as an artist, took time off from working in his grand studio at the corner of Wall Street and Broadway to visit his old friend. Gladdened by the sight of the dashing painter, Paine would turn over onto his side—gasping *"Oh! God! Oh . . . God!"* as he rolled upon his sores—and then, regaining his composure, confide in Jarvis. He had been getting harassed constantly by people trying to convert him, he said: ministers were stopping by every day now, angling for a recantation. Even the nurse, Mrs. Heddon, would wait until he was helpless with pain and then pounce upon him with the Bible and Hobart's *Companion for the Altar*.

I recant *nothing*, he told Jarvis.

The next morning, warned by his physician Dr. Manley—*you are about to die, dissolution is upon you this very day*—Paine refused yet again to accept Christ. The doctor pressed him one last time.

"Do you *wish* to believe that Jesus Christ is the son of God?" he demanded.

There was a long pause of minutes. Perhaps the patient really had died. But Paine's lips moved: words, weak but distinct.

"I have no wish to believe on that subject."

And then . . .

Then . . .

He should have been dead from the start. He'd been cheating Death almost from the beginning: at the age of nineteen, leaving his parents' home for the first time, Pain—he'd not yet added the final *e* to his name—set out for London and was recruited at dockside for service on a privateer ship called the *Terrible*, commanded by one Captain Death. Thomas's father showed up on the docks in time to save him from what was either a very good allegory or a very bad Ingmar Bergman film. The *Terrible* sailed without Pain, and Captain Death and the crew were slaughtered. And there is something curiously familiar in that account, isn't there? For we all nearly board a *Terrible;* we all look back in relief that we did not. We always slip free of Captain Death one more time . . . until, of course, we don't.

He should have been dead halfway into his life. It was in Philadelphia, on November 30, 1774, that the *London Packet* disgorged a nondescript passenger half-dead with typhoid. Pain was by then a middle-aged failure: the son of a Quaker family of corsetmakers in Thetford had left England a disgraced customs officer and a bankrupt shopkeeper. He was recently divorced from his second wife, having already lost his first wife and only child in childbirth. And after watching five other dead passengers dumped over the ship's side on the way over, it's a wonder Pain didn't throw himself overboard as well. But among his meager belongings was found a letter to Richard Bache, a prominent local merchant:

> The bearer Mr. Thomas Pain is very well recommended to me as an ingenious worthy young man. He goes to Pennsylvania with a view of settling there. I request you to give him your best advice and countenance, as he is quite a stranger there. If you can put him in a way of obtaining employment as a clerk, or assistant tutor in a school, or assistant surveyor, of all of which I think him very capable, so that he may procure a subsistence at least, till he

can make acquaintance and obtain a knowledge of the country,
you will do well, and much oblige your affectionate father.

It proved to be the best introduction to Philadelphia one could
imagine, for Bache's "affectionate father" was in fact a stepfather
with a different name altogether, a gentleman scientist and merchant who had noticed Pain's argumentative and restless brilliance
in London coffeehouses: *"Benj. Franklin"* read the signature.

How many times must progress be born, struck dead, and reborn
again, before it finally survives? It was, after all, not the first time
Franklin had been intrigued by the fiery zeal of a fellow Quaker.
Decades earlier he'd befriended Benjamin Lay, a hunchbacked
glovemaker disowned by English Quakers for denouncing slavery
and capital punishment as abominations. Exiled to Philadelphia and
dismayed to find slaveowning there too, he'd quit town in disgust
and lived as a hermit in a cave outside the city limits, refusing to
wear or eat anything that had involved the suffering of an animal.
Quaker slaveholders probably fancied themselves rid of him. They
were not: attired in a biblical beard and a flowing white overcoat,
Lay would sweep into Philadelphia meetinghouses to scourge the
Friends throughout the 1750s. *"In the sight of God, you are as guilty as
if you stabbed your slaves to the heart!"* roared the furious elder who
materialized in the midst of one meeting, wielded a knife on
himself, and showered bystanders with fake blood. For his troubles,
Lay was physically thrown into the gutter on Market Street. He
refused to pick himself up from the muck, preferring to lie there as a
reproach to the Friends as they left the meetinghouse. But he still
entertained one occasional visitor in his cave—Franklin.

And perhaps it was that same idealistic quality that the now-
elderly Franklin saw in the unemployed fellow who held forth in
London coffeehouses. Absurdly, this newest protégé simply had a

notion of going to Philadelphia to start a young ladies' finishing school. Ah, but then Franklin himself had once nearly thrown it all over to become a London swimming instructor. Pain, too, was marked out for greater things—he just did not know what yet. After a job at a local newspaper, where he reinvented himself by changing his name slightly and penning editorials that excoriated the very same inequalities Lay once had, Paine finally found his life's mission in writing a pamphlet.

The pamphlet.

In the will he'd scrawled in Ryder's house on Herring Street, Paine carefully included instructions for his tombstone, a simple headstone with his name, his dates, and an epitaph of just four words: *Author of Common Sense.* A single pamphlet, written when he was a nobody, published anonymously; of the thousands of pages he had published in his life, for all the tumult and agony he had undergone, it all came back to that one act. *Understand this and you understand my life.*

Why? True, *Common Sense* sold one hundred and twenty thousand copies in its first three months after January 10, 1776—and upwards of five hundred thousand copies in the next three years. In those days of expensive paper, each copy was passed around. America's population was only about 2.5 million, many of whom could not even read, so readership of this pamphlet was virtually universal among the literate. It was a feat unequaled by any document in the Colonies save perhaps the Bible. It brought forth a frenzied response by Loyalist propagandists, desperate to stanch the wounds he'd made, but it was already too late. Paine had changed the very terms of the debate. "Without the pen of the author of *Common Sense*," John Adams later mused, "the sword of Washington would have been raised in vain." This was no small admission coming from Adams, since he'd initially condemned

Common Sense as "a poor ignorant, Malicious, short-sighted, Crap-
ulous Mass."

But . . . Who cares now? Why should this still matter, this tax
and sovereignty polemic from centuries ago? Lots of political writers
have written lots of bestsellers, and a few have even managed to tear
the nation from its moorings. Yet we do not still read Rowan
Hinton Helper's *Impending Crisis of the South*. So why this one: what
made it special? Why make this one pamphlet the epitaph on his
grave? Perhaps the clue lies in plain sight. Though *Common Sense*
was a forty-six-page pamphlet, its animating spirit may be found
within its first sentence: "A long habit of not thinking a thing
wrong, gives it a superficial appearance of being right." Forget what
you thought was wrong, Paine says, and forget what you thought
was right: produce proof that they are so. And if there is one word
that expresses what the achievements of the Enlightenment are
about, it is that one. *Proof.*

Reader, just for the moment, let us assume that as you hold this
book open with one hand, you are holding a piece of ivory in the
other. It is two feet long, and the thickness of a man's thumb. Now,
if you were to make this piece of ivory descend with great force upon
the head of your closest neighbor, they would inform you that it is
an item possessing great hardness. Yet, were you to rest this ivory
rod between two chairs, and then sit upon it, you would find it
possessed a surprising flexibility. One might have assumed that as
this item is hard, it was therefore not flexible. Its hardness, although
not actually opposed to flexibility, seems incompatible at first
glance. This is what *second* glances are for: an assertion demands
proof through actual observation, rather than mere assumptions.

Writing in his book *Elements of Logick* in 1748, the Scottish
logician William Duncan explains:

Ivory for instance is hard and elastic; this we know by experience, and indeed by that alone. For being altogether strangers to the true nature both of elasticity and hardness, we cannot by the bare contemplation of our ideas determine, how far the one necessarily implies the other, or whether there may be a repugnance between them. But when we observe them to exist both in the same object, we are then assured from experience, that they are not incompatible.

Elements of Logick was the boning knife of the Scottish Enlightenment: it sliced argumentation clean of bloated classical artifice, tearing away its Latinate fat to reveal a Greek skeleton of Euclidian logic. Duncan wielded self-evident propositions and a geometrical progression of proofs and assertions to build arguments: his was the elevation of mathematical logic to rhetoric. *Elements of Logick* influenced revolutionary intellectuals and scientists alike—and when you realize that to be the former was also often to be the latter, you begin to understand the era of Franklin and Paine. When their fellow rationalist Jefferson fatefully claimed that "we hold these truths to be self-evident," he was laying out the destiny of his continent as a mathematical statement.

But then there is that problem with our ivory rod. Certain truths are *not* self-evident: that is why they must be examined and spelled out. They are *not* common sense. And that is why *Common Sense* itself, weirdly enough, is not common sense at all. This strange little book, so often cited as a model of plainspoken clarity, is something altogether more subtle. Only its language is straightforward: its form and aims are not. *Common Sense* is in fact at least three separate arguments, none of which many Americans in 1776 would have been inclined to entirely agree with. Yet Paine makes one argument imperceptibly slide into the next, like the telescoping segments of a collapsible spyglass. By the time you realize what he's doing, he's already folded you up and put you in his pocket.

Paine begins with his most outrageous implication: *all kings are illegitimate.* He does this by denying that most precious possession of monarchs, their noble bloodlines. "Could we take off the dark covering of antiquity," *Common Sense* dryly notes, "and trace them to their first rise . . . we should find the first of them nothing better than the principal ruffian of some restless gang." Granted, a loyal subject may say, perhaps that's true; in fact, it *has* to be true for Shakespeare's history plays to work. But an unsavory past does not always dictate reform in the present. It would not be very *practical.* The great benefit of kings in the present, one might think, is that no matter how compromised the monarchy's origins are, they have become a safe and predictable form of government.

Except that they are not. "The whole history of England disowns the fact," Paine snaps. "Thirty kings and two minors have reigned in that distracted kingdom since the [Norman] conquest, in which time there have been (including the Revolution) no less than eight civil wars and nineteen rebellions."

Very well. But eventually the present king and prime minister will both die or lose their party's confidence. The taxes for war debts against France will fade. A hopeful reader in 1776 might still believe that America's more or less peaceful relation to Britain would return. What is curious for an American to realize today is that *this indeed might have happened,* as it did in Canada. That an entire section of *Common Sense* is dedicated to arguing against making peace—"reconciliation *now* is a dangerous doctrine"—shows that peace was still thought a very real competing possibility in 1776. What made reconciliation a dangerous answer, to Paine, is that its proponents had asked all the wrong questions. In *Common Sense,* the burden of proof is not upon Americans to prove why they should be independent, but upon the British to prove why America should stay dependent. Britain only used America to its own purposes, Paine argued: why shouldn't Americans determine whether Britain served them any purpose? "Dependence on Great Britain tends to directly involve this continent in European wars and quarrels . . ." he concluded. "America goes to ruin, *because of her connection with Britain.*"

While a great many Americans were unhappy with King George, not many of them had really thought of being unhappy with *all* kings. Colonists wanted power over their own affairs, but were not overly picky about what form that power should take. Perhaps they would have their own king, or become a British protectorate; maybe they'd simply agitate until they got their own members of Parliament. But make that seemingly outrageous assertion "all kings are illegitimate" and this anchors your readers in a way that makes subsequent statements sound comparatively pragmatic: such as, say, how to raise up a navy against the most powerful country in the world. By the end of the pamphlet Paine has his green eyeshades on and his red pencil out to price various configurations of warships for Colonists—and suddenly the prospect of revolution is looking alarmingly practical, if not downright inevitable. Which, in retrospect, we probably imagine it was.

We think of *Common Sense* as being the most withering attack ever upon that favorite bogeyman of Americans, mad old King George. Yet when you read it closely, you find this remarkable fact: *not once is the name George III uttered.* What Paine wrote was an attack on all kings, all illegitimate authority, on all the great and petty brutes of the world. *Common Sense* is a pair of rhetorical bolt cutters, and it will neatly snap in half anything—the cant of kings, priests, or next-door neighbors—that is placed between its blades. It is a declaration of independence, a new kind of argument that denies

all precedence by smacking the rulebook out of an opponent's hands
and ignoring every previous thing thought or said in their favor.
Paine does not cite classical authors, or Tory opponents, or the
constitutional theories of Bolingbroke; he is not playing at polite
debate. He does not want your tradition: he wants your *reason*. The
scepter of authority is no more exalted to him than the logician's rod
of ivory, and when proof is lacking we may slap it aside. What Paine
offered America was nothing less than rebirth, independence from
the dead weight of the past: his epitaph directs you to an admonition
from the dead to the living.

"We have it in our power," he wrote, *"to begin the world again."*

And this is where it ends.

Stand clear of the . . . Doors thud shut on the number 2 express
and it roars out toward Brooklyn as I make my way through the
turnstile and up into a canyon of buildings. Wall Street at night
always feels strangely desolate, as any financial district is in its off
hours, I suppose: nobody wants to stay here unless they have to. It's
hard to imagine, looking up at the slumbering mass of law and
investment firms, that people used to live around here. Carver's
house was just a few blocks from here, as was the dreary Partition
Street boardinghouse where Paine finally stopped writing—it's
called Fulton Street now. And his room in Jarvis's studio was a
couple of blocks in the other direction, looking directly across the
street into what was once the World Trade Center.

I stop at the corner of Wall and Water streets, by the endless print
churn of a Kinko's shop: this is where the newspaper instructed me
to go. I fish the *New-York Herald* out from my backpack, its pages
browned by the passage of two centuries. It flutters slightly in the
breeze off the looming buildings:

> FOR SALE, at public auction, at the Tontine Coffee House in
> the city of New-York . . . an excellent FARM, situated in the
> town of New Rochelle, in the county of Westchester, and late the
> property of Thomas Paine, dec. containing about 84 acres . . .
> The terms of sale are one half cash; the remainder to be secured
> by mortgage on the premises—An indisputable title will be given
> to the purchasers by the Executors of Mr. Paine.

Granted, the auction gets far less space than an entire column on the
same page devoted to the felicities of Dr. Robertson's Vegetable
Nervous Cordial, but it is more than most New York papers
bothered to say about Paine himself when he died. Most had little
to say except to tartly note that he had done "some good and much
harm." The man they had no use for; his plot of dirt upstate, at least,
was worth something. A buyer coming here to the coffeehouse that
afternoon would have found the place a bustle of transactions, as it
always was: the Tontine was the precursor to the Stock Exchange,
and in its three floors of cigar smoke and bidding, you could make
political deals, pick up mail off-loaded from newly arrived London
ships, and buy entire cargos of pelts or lumber. But if you bid in that
auction for the property of the late Thomas Paine, you got just a
little more than you'd bargained for—something they had rather
conveniently forgotten to mention in the ad. For along with his
land, you also got . . . Thomas Paine.

It was a sad tale to relate. After Jarvis made one last pilgrimage to
his friend's deathbed, this time to make a plaster death mask of
Paine, he bitterly drew a caricature of Manhattan's ministers
stomping on the dead body while a Quaker turns his back and
walks away with a shovel, muttering, "I'll not bury thee." The young
men who had once shunned Benjamin Lay were now old men who
turned their backs on Thomas Paine. But a quietly defiant Willet

Hicks, at least, had come to Paine's aid. Hicks rode with the corpse as it was hauled up to the farm in New Rochelle; and there, not far from Paine's cottage, he officiated at a burial in the unconsecrated corner of a field.

A taxi passes me with a familiar image affixed to its roof—an ad with Ben Franklin's face staring out from a hundred-dollar bill. The old mentor, staring past the vanished remains of his wayward protégé.

There were twenty thousand mourners at Franklin's funeral. Tom Paine's had six. And while Franklin's grave became a place of pilgrimage, Paine's attracted a different sort of attention. Pious locals in New Rochelle would make sure to pelt his headstone with rocks whenever they passed: others kicked at the leaning stone, or chipped off pieces as souvenirs. It all became too much for Paine's old neighbor Charity Badeau, who ran a tavern across the street; exasperated by the desecrations, she saved the few remaining pieces of the stone by mortaring them into the wall of her establishment. Even these still had small nuggets pried out of them. Few gave much thought to the dead fellow now buried in an unmarked grave in the weeds, save for the local drunks idly flaking chips off Mrs. Badeau's wall with their penknives. Years passed: his memory faded.

But in the dead of night in October 1819, Badeau's son Albert thought he *heard* something outside their tavern. He peered out his window and into the darkness. It was hard to make out, but across the road there were—one, two, three men. All gathered around where the gravestone used to be. Albert squinted harder. It looked like they were . . .

Digging.

Committed to the Ground

THE MORNING OF November 21, 1819, brought a mist off the Mersey and swirling over Liverpool piers, fogging the early morning's frenetic haulage off merchant vessels: bales of cotton and tobacco from Georgia, sacks of sugar from Haiti, crates of pepper and tea from Bombay—men sweating under their loads; horses stumbling; commands punctuated by tubercular coughs of city air fouled with coal. Towering above it all at the riverside was the newly built Customs House, a commanding Regency pile of porticos and pillars capped by a mighty dome. It was there to put arriving passengers in awe of the nation's mercantile might, and in its grand yard the excise officers awaited to put them in awe of government regulations as well.

The cargo of the *Hercules* was next on their slate: it had been docked for a couple of days now, and its waiting crates were pried open and bills of lading scrutinized. But if there came to be a strange pause in the proceedings, customs officials could be forgiven for any hesitancy about the next passenger in line. "William Cobbett," read the name on the passenger manifest.

A middle-aged man, slightly portly and clearly brooking no nonsense, stood before them. The yard filled with a crowd eagerly craning inward to gape—they had, upon the ship's docking on

Monday, cheered Cobbett from the dock and through the streets of Liverpool, all the way to the inn where he was lodging. Now they watched as his numerous trunkloads of heavy luggage were examined by the officers. Clothes, personal effects, books, papers . . . yes, yes. Plant cuttings? Well, that was to be expected, as the fellow was also a noted author on horticultural matters. But then the officers arrived at a wooden box. The passenger watched gravely and closely as the excisemen pried it open and reached inside. And then, from within its depths, the crowd saw an object emerge into the cold winter light.

A human skull.

Cobbett gazed upon it, and then upon his inquisitors.

"There, gentlemen," he announced, "are the mortal remains of the immortal Thomas Paine."

This place is utterly dead. Brit Rail's diesel rattle builds up and shudders the train out of Wanborough Station, leaving me to regard an increasingly silent landscape of trees, hedges, and English gardens. Wanborough's not *much* of a station. In fact, I'm the only person here at all. The last ticket-window clerk left in 1987, and now the doors to the station house are locked: peering in through a gap in its blinds, I can see that its two doleful rooms are emptied out and covered with dust, shredded wires dangling grimly out of the walls. OFFICE TO LET, announces a sign.

If you lay down right here on the platform and took a nap, it might be a very long while before anyone noticed you. This part of Surrey, just past an isolating ridge known as the Hog's Back, has some of the quietest and most thickly forested expanses in all of Southern England. And yet modest country places like these can hide a great deal: Saxons left barrows here, and Romans dumped sacks of gold coins in the ground. During the war, an engineer died when a Luftwaffe pilot bombed this stretch of the railroad tracks, but he was not the first to go; two other men were killed here in 1891, building a little railway station that there was no real need for in the first place. The tenant of nearby Wanborough Manor, as it happens, was the private secretary of Prime Minister Gladstone, and the cabinet thought it'd be jolly convenient to put a station near his house. And so it is that we are outlasted by our impulsive acts: the secretary is gone, but his station and its ghosts remain.

Though the station is named after the local manor, the train actually serves the tiny hamlet of Normandy. It's a quiet and ancient place, quite possibly one of the smallest villages in Britain to still have a working rail stop. I make my way up Glazier's Lane past inoffensive new brick bungalows—one, inevitably, is called Wisteria—all built atop parish plots that once housed inoffensive old stone cottages. In between them, I can see ancient farmlands peeping through. Across these fields is an incongruously tall brick smokestack attached, as best I can tell, to absolutely nothing at all. But all else here is cozily domestic; the road crookedly leads onward past an intersection with the A323, past Normandy Common and a little pub, toward the old neighborhood known by the quaint name of Christmas Pie.

No Pie for me, thanks: I tramp onward down the A323, letting Vauxhalls whiz past me as I walk on the verge. Odd little local businesses, washed up like flotsam from faraway towns, appear at irregular intervals along the road. A karaoke and PA shop, which surely must be doing its business by mail from this location. A glazier, inexplicably not based back on Glazier's Lane, advertises itself with the rather dispiriting motto *"Probably the Best Window Installers in Your Area."* Soon even these curiously misplaced shops disappear, and the once-hidden farmland stretches out on both sides. The side of the road becomes a ditch, filled with brackish water and hubcaps; growing in and around it are a wild profusion of winter-wilted daffodils and tulip stalks awaiting the return of spring, and wildly capillary trees; for the trees here are, for lack of a better word, very *branchy*. And then for long stretches come the hedges.

Ah, the hedgerows: I *am* in England. It's hard to imagine a time when the rural landscape was not thus. Hedged-in country lanes are so utterly English, indeed so utterly *this* latitude of England. Up northward, in the rough tracts of Scotland and the Yorkshire dales, the fields are bounded with piled stone walls and stiles; but here in Surrey the road is hemmed in by dense greenery. I walk slowly along the verge, squinting my eyes at one stretch of the endless miles of twisting and gnarled foliage, peering in at the interlocking branches and trying to count. *One . . . two?* Two species here, I think. Hawthorn, of course—there is always hawthorn in these hedges—but there also looks to be some blackthorn growing in there.

There's an old rule of thumb for dating hedges, commonly known as Hooper's Rule. It goes like this:

Age of the hedge = [(No. of species per 30 yards) × 110] + 30

For two species, then, that works out to about 250 years. So take away the cars, take away the glazier's shop and the karaoke, take away the cat's-eyes in the road—take away the road itself. And imagine a gentleman walking along this muddy lane those two centuries ago, back when these old hedges were still young. In his arms, he bears a box of bones.

William Cobbett was born into the life of a farmer's son: a world that in the 1760s was small and circumscribed, with age-old tasks to keep the boy busy. "I do not remember the time when I did not earn my living," he later mused. "My first occupation was driving the small birds from the turnip seed, and the rooks from the peas. When I trudged afield, with my wooden bottle and my satchel over my shoulders, I was hardly able to climb the gates and stiles, and, at the close of day, to reach home was a task of infinite labour."

His childhood in Surrey was one of relentless work and simple pleasures: for amusement, he and his brothers would shove each other down a steep slope, "rolling down the hill like a barrel or a log of wood" and laughing uncontrollably as they got dirty and torn up. He had little formal schooling, and for the rest of his life considered that hillside—where he and his brothers bled in and breathed in the dirt, where he covered himself in it and picked it out of his mouth and nose—as *his* schooling. "It is impossible to say how much I owe to that sandhill," he later claimed. Upon hearing that the king kept magnificent gardens in Kew, he eagerly ran away at the age of eleven with nothing but thirteen half-pence in his pocket. From Kew, Cobbett eventually drifted onward into a miserable apprenticeship in a London law office, then back to his native farmland, and finally into a marines enlistment that sent him to the New World just as the Revolution ended.

Cobbett found little left worth defending: "Nova Scotia had no charm for me other than that of novelty. Everything I saw was new: bogs, rocks, mosquitoes, and bullfrogs . . . In short, the most villainous piece of waste land." Even his eventual promotion to sergeant major did not allay his general dismay, for after blowing the whistle on military embezzlement and writing a pamphlet on it, Cobbett was drummed out of the service and nearly charged with sedition. But in writing his pamphlet, Cobbett discovered his two true vocations: righteous fury, and writing furiously.

Wherever he went, Cobbett found trouble—and when he

couldn't find it, he made some of his own. Moving to Philadelphia in 1794, he took up the apt counterrevolutionary pen name Peter Porcupine, and enraged locals by plastering his bookseller storefront with pictures of King George. Then, for good measure, in his window display he coupled the likeness of the bloodthirsty Jean-Paul Marat with that of revered city father Ben Franklin—who was also, Cobbett helpfully explained, "a whore-master, a hypocrite, and an infidel." He called Tom Paine a wife-beater—such accusations were nothing new to Paine, as another Tory writer had already accused him of raping a cat—and in the pages of his newspaper *The Porcupine* he gleefully eviscerated the "malignant philosopher" Jefferson. Rather more prosaically, he also accused Declaration signer and local physician Benjamin Rush of killing his patients.

"Honour the King: Fear God," read the motto on *The Porcupine*, but soon Cobbett had quite a few others to fear. "There were, in Philadelphia, about ten thousand persons, all of whom would have rejoiced to see me murdered," he wrote. He was not far wrong, and when Dr. Rush finally slapped the would-be Peter Porcupine with a crushing libel judgment, it sent the nettlesome scribbler fleeing the country.

But back in his beloved Britain, Cobbett fared little better. He loved the *crown*, not the government that had surrounded it. And so he started an immensely popular newspaper, the *Political Register*, to record the speeches of Parliament and the court. This unprecedented exposure of their machinations was duly resented by politicians, and eventually Cobbett was thrown—thrown quite enthusiastically, one gathers—into Newgate on a trumped-up charge of treason. Cobbett was left incredulous: "Having lost a fortune in America, solely for the sake of England, I was sent to prison in that same England!" Perhaps, he wondered, the problem was that it wasn't that *same* England. He brooded over how it was no longer the land of his youth.

And then, as always—he wrote.

If his two years in jail were meant to shut Cobbett up, it didn't work. "During my imprisonment," he boasted, "I published 364 Essays and Letters upon political subjects." He still managed to keep his *Political Register* going every week, even during a spell as a farmer back to America from 1817 to 1819. In the midst of this, he also became the great agricultural author of his era, writing on *Cottage Economy* and the popular guide *The American Gardener*, which remains in print today. The man sold *seeds* in his spare time. It seems hard to reconcile the notion of a seed merchant and garden writer with a political firebrand today; you don't exactly go to the Burpee rack at the hardware store to get riled up about anything. But soil *was* political in Cobbett's time. And these hedges before us? They were harbingers of perhaps the greatest upheaval England had ever known.

A farm truck rumbles past me, heading toward Guildford, sweeping by a weedy graveyard of rusting tractors and plows. I bend down and examine the leaning sign jammed into the ground nearby:

EGGS
hens
duck
goose
HAY
MANURE

People still work their land here. But what, exactly, do we mean by *their* land? Many years ago, a rector named Augustus Jessopp pondered just this question. "If I take my handkerchief out of my pocket I show you something which certainly belongs to me; I bought and paid for it," he explained. "If I please I may—*as I can*— toss it into the fire and reduce it to ashes in a few moments; in fact, destroy it, practically get rid of it, annihilate it." It was his property, after all; why not? But, ah—there was a catch—for all property is *not* the same. Look down at the plot of land that you are standing on: "I *cannot* destroy it," he reasoned. "I *may* not quite serve it as if it were wholly and exclusively mine." So we may call our friends with the hay, eggs, and manure *owners* of the land, but only for now: it was once someone else's, and it will be someone else's again. Their tenancy on the land, even if for three, five, or ten generations, is temporary. This is why any owner who rails against land-use rules has forgotten a basic tenet of common law: they are the stewards of their plot, and not its sovereign.

A thousand years ago, these lands that we see before us here on the A323—*all* land, in fact—belonged to the king. It was granted to nobility at his pleasure, and revoked at his displeasure. These lords, in turn, let their manors to local gentry, who then sublet plots to the farmers. If anyone died intestate—as a great many of them were prone to do during plague years—land would escheat back up the chain of ownership. And nobody was unreservedly *entitled* to this land: it was always the king's, and subject to his taxes and demands for military service. That's why to this day in Britain the Treasure Act requires any poor sap unfortunate enough to find a buried sack of doubloons in their backyard to turn it over to the crown. But this was part of a rural covenant, for in return every village had a commons land where citizens could graze their sheep and cows. It was far from perfect. There was a tangle of laws over how often you were allowed to graze, how much turf you could dig up to burn as fuel, or how many branches you were allowed to lop off a nobleman's trees as kindling. These land arrangements stifled mobility: they ensured that the rich stayed rich and the poor stayed poor. But everyone was indeed guaranteed *something*.

Visit the Normandy Commons now, and you'll find a pleasant sprawl of mown fields and trees; there's slide, monkey bars, a public loo, and a decent soccer pitch. What you will not find are sheep munching the grass, or anyone hoeing beans. We're expected to earn our livings in private dwellings now, a transition from public to private wealth that occurred before Cobbett's eyes. Parliamentary orders for the fencing off and sale of commons land—known as Acts of Enclosure—remade his countryside at a frantic pace. In the decade before Cobbett's birth in 1763, there had been 163 such acts: the first decade of the new century had seen 906. Once landowners possessed this land, they guarded it jealously. They'd bore holes into hedge stakes and funnel in gunpowder; any shivering impoverished soul unfortunate enough to steal a hedge stake for kindling would, upon tossing one onto a fire, be rewarded with a hearth-shattering thunderclap. In another town, Cobbett even found a self-styled Paradise Place encircled with signs warning of leg-snapping man-traps. He shook his head at the sight of it: fancy that as Paradise!

Commons lands—*wastes*, landowners now sniffed—disappeared, and private property arose in their place. This hedge in front of me—and there are now some five hundred thousand miles of them in England—arose during these years, not as quaint sidings to rural roads, but as a sentinel of newly created private property. Cobbett was outraged: "[What] could lead English gentlemen to disregard matters like these! That could induce them to tear up 'wastes' and sweep away occupiers like those I have described! Wastes indeed!"

What induced them? Why, *money*. Private owners tended their plots with greater efficiency and ingenuity, and sought out the latest agricultural improvements: over the span of the eighteenth century, the average weight of sheep shipped to London's Smithfield Market more than doubled, and average calf weight tripled. Even as its poor starved, England was stuffed with food; even as land became rich and thick with green hedges, the country's poor became landless. These quaint hedgerows are not the stuff of Old England: they are what killed it. Walled off from sustenance, the rural poor flooded into industrial cities, ripe for exploitation. By the time Cobbett arrived at that Liverpool dock in 1819, he found a country tipping into revolution.

Not of men—but of machines.

A road branches off from the A323, and it is so unremarkable that one can drive right past it, which is indeed what every car does:

COBBETT HILL ROAD
Parish
of
Worplesdon

I should think the parish name alone is worth stopping for. Just beyond its opening verge, hidden behind a thicket, there hides a pleasant little clearing. A placid brown hare gazes at me from it, twitches in the laziest manner possible for his species, and lopes off with a perfunctory, not-trying-terribly-hard-at-hopping gait. He meanders up and across the deserted back road and toward a driveway bearing a sign reading COBBETT's CLOSE.

Cobbett's close!

Oh, but is he? Is he *close*? I fear not. It's on some of Cobbett's old farmland, true, but it's hard to imagine a place that could now be further from Cobbett's heart. For Cobbett's Close is a trailer park— a gathering of prefabricated buildings, if you prefer—all plunked down like so many discarded cracker cartons in these woods. There

they sit: modern structures not really built to last, erected on privately owned property, and not a garden plot or a grazing sheep in sight.

If you wanted a repudiation of everything Cobbett lived for, this might be it. When he wrote a book titled *Cottage Economy*, he was not speaking of being economical in the modern sense of cheapness: he was talking about creating a national economy of cottages. He longed to instruct the populace in moving back to the land, back to self-sufficiency, to grow and make for themselves. But the only thing you can *grow* in boxy prefabs like these is hydroponic weed; the only thing you can *make* is microwave popcorn. Cobbett saw all this coming even in his own day. "To buy the thing, *ready made*, was the taste of the day," he mocked. "Thousands, who were house-keepers, bought their dinners ready cooked: nothing was so common as to rent breasts for children to suck: a man actually advertised, in the London papers, to supply childless husbands with heirs! In this case, the articles were, of course, to be *ready made*."

The argument he began lives on even today. Paine and Cobbett were their era's perfect expressions of progressivism and conservatism. While Cobbett hoed turnips and railed against the mill towns and the destruction of the rhythms of rural life, Paine spent his post-Revolution years suggesting improvements in steam engines, inventing smokeless candles so that people could stay up late, and hawking the newfangled cast-iron bridge he designed. Cobbett looked to the past for Britain's salvation, Paine to the future; what they shared was a profound dissatisfaction with the present . . . oh, and with each other. Paine referred to the self-styled Peter Porcupine as "Peter Skunk," while Cobbett's pet name for Paine was generally "hypocritical monster" or the snappier "Infidel."

Indeed, Cobbett went so far in 1796 as to reprint and annotate a hostile biography *The Life of Thomas Paine*—a hit job secretly

funded by the British government, it had been published under a
pseudonym in 1791, and slyly subtitled *A Defense of His Writings*, the
better to lure in and sucker punch Paine's own readers. But its
accuracy and origins did not concern Cobbett much. Unusually for a
biographer, Cobbett frankly professed ignorance of what Paine was
even up to anymore, nor did he care:

> How Tom gets a living now, or what Brothel he inhabits, I know
> not, nor does it much signify. He has done all the mischief he can
> do in this world; and whether his carcass is at last suffered to rot
> on the earth, or to be dried in the air, is of very little consequence.
> Whenever and wherever he breathes his last, he will excite
> neither sorrow nor compassion; no friendly hand will close his
> eyes, not a groan will be uttered, not a tear will be shed. Like
> Judas, he will be remembered by posterity; men will learn to
> express all that is base, malignant, treacherous, unnatural, and
> blasphemous by the single monosyllable of *Paine*.

As a thoughtful final touch, Cobbett added that he very much
looked forward to his subject being "abandoned in death, and
interred like a dog." Strange words for a man who, reporting to
British readers back home while on another American sojourn
twenty years later, now complained that "PAINE lies in a little
hole under the grass and weeds of an obscure farm in America."
And—he now added rather cryptically—"there, however, *he shall not
lie, unnoticed much longer.*" Cobbett, having gotten his old wish for
Paine to be interred like a dog, now wanted to raise a monument to
the man.

   What?

   One might question Cobbett's sanity: certainly his detractors did,
and they had no lack of apparent madness to point at. One favorite

sport of newspapers was to arrange vehemently pro and scabrously con quotes about issues of the day, where quoted verbatim for the pro side was Mr. William Cobbett. And quoted verbatim for the con side was . . . Mr. William Cobbett.

Generally, when a man is rabidly for one cause, and then is just as rabidly for another cause, it is not because he loves the causes: it is because he loves the rabies. But there was something more than that at work with Cobbett. His two years of jail time in London had profoundly changed him. A man who once loudly applauded the death penalty—"When you hear a man loud against the severity of the laws, set him down as a rogue," he'd written—now discovered that life looked different from the other side of the bars. Paine had died only months before, in 1809, a frail old man hounded to the last: now that he, too, was thrown against the wall, Cobbett viewed his hated old enemy differently. He passed his hours in prison reading Paine's 1796 pamphlets *The Decline and Fall of the British System of Finance* and *Agrarian Justice*, and realized with horror that all these years he'd been assailing a blood brother.

"This man, born in a humble life, knew more than all the *Higher orders* put together," Cobbett concluded. Though barely known alongside *Common Sense*, Paine's essays were indeed extraordinary. *Decline and Fall* decried the British government's use of unbacked paper currency to finance foreign adventurism through ever-spiraling debts; these, in turn, required more wars to shore up domestic support and foreign resources. The national debt, Paine contended, would eventually become a national bankruptcy—and strength of its financial markets could prove the country's greatest weakness. "It will not be from the inability of procuring loans that the system will break up," he admonished. "On the contrary, it is the facility with which loans can be procured that hastens the event." Paine was deeply unimpressed by the financial acumen of members of Parliament—"they only understand fox-hunting," he snapped—and he was not fooled by the smoke and mirrors the Prime Minister employed to pay down this debt: "As to Mr. Pitt's project of paying off the national debt by applying a million a year for that purpose, while he continues adding more than twenty millions a year to it, it is like setting a man with a wooden leg to run after a hare. The longer he runs the further he is off."

Instead of endless conquest and debt, Paine's sister pamphlet *Agrarian Justice* proposed that Britain turn inward and tend to its own assets. He thought it hopeless to turn back the clock on Enclosure Acts, nor was he particularly opposed to the wealth they brought—"I care not how affluent some may be," he shrugged, "provided that none be miserable in consequence of it." But the newly landless poor, Paine warned, now faced becoming a "hereditary race." The wealthy were becoming a hereditary race, too, thanks to land inheritance, and Paine proposed a novel way to make them pay for this new social order: estate taxes. After all, he reasoned, "personal property is the *effect of Society*"—so the least they could do was support the *cause*. The collected monies would provide minimum stake for everyone when they were getting a start in life, and when they were approaching its close. "Create a National Fund," he proposed, "out of which there shall be paid to every person, when arrived at the age of twenty-one years, the sum of Fifteen Pounds sterling, as a compensation in part for the loss of his or natural inheritance by the introduction of the system of landed property; and also the sum of Ten Pounds per annum, during life, to every person now living of the age of fifty years."

What Paine proposed looks astonishingly like modern state pensions and student grants, which we take for granted now without much thinking about the seismic shifts in the social order that necessitated them. Only someone like Cobbett—sent as a soldier in a corrupt regiment to defend barren land, and returning home to find his farming community destroyed—could fully understand *why* Paine was assailing military debt and the menace of rural poverty. And this was why, chastened and humbled before the grave of his old enemy, the one-time Peter Porcupine had preceded his return to Liverpool with a remarkable letter to his astonished newspaper readers back home. "Our expedition set out from New York in the middle of the night," he reported, "got to the place (22 miles off) at the peep of day; took up the coffin entire; brought it off to New York; and just as we found it, it goes to England." He'd return with Paine's bones, he promised, in a couple of months. "At any rate, I will be there, or at the bottom of the sea."

But he couldn't contain himself, and Cobbett booked passage on another boat scarcely following the one bearing his letter. Quaker passengers refused to board when they heard of its cargo, muttering about God striking the vessel down; this was not an entirely fanciful expectation, as on a previous voyage lightning had struck two passengers sitting at either side of Cobbett. But he was elated at the prospect of returning with his prize—"These bones will effect the reformation of England in church and state" he giddily claimed before leaving New York—and with him arriving at the Liverpool docks just days after his first article appeared, the crowds meeting him at the docks were still abuzz over what he'd done. And that wasn't the only surprise he had in store for them: now, he announced, he was going to raise money for a grand English tomb to Paine.

"*CAW!*" a bird yells down from a tree.

I stop on Cobbett Hill Road and look around: I am utterly alone here. This is not a place of pilgrimage. There are no monuments to Paine or to Cobbett, no tombs grand or otherwise. This is indeed where Paine's bones would be coming to rest for a spell—but first they would travel a wildly zigzagging path.

Back down on the A323, I see a bus with green phosphorescing destination on its front. I run for it, waving my arms, and it slows down and swings its doors open. In the hour between here and London are miles of farmland, of old wooden gates and tail-swishing horses; and then more miles of stubby pebble-dashed and stuccoed bungalows; and then an endless procession of city tenements: the landscape evolves before your eyes, from broad and rural to narrow and urban, from the rolling hills of Cobbett's boyhood to the sulfurous cities of his jail-cell nightmares. But it was out here in the countryside, far from the madness of London, that Cobbett was going to build a monument to his former enemy. And as his nation's greatest gardener, Cobbett even had a fitting procession planned for him: twenty wagonloads of flowers, "brought to strew the road before the hearse."

It did not quite work out that way.

Patrons shook their heads in the Fleet Street coffeehouses, holding the latest newspaper in their hands: *Digging up the fellow claiming you'll raise a monument to him? Who ever heard of such a thing!*

Actually, some of the old men had. About thirty years before, the parishioners over at St. Giles on Cripplegate had the bright idea of erecting a monument to their most famous permanent resident— John Milton. True, the old poet's *Areopagitica* kept turning up in coffeehouse and courtroom defenses of that wretched infidel Tom Paine, but still . . . surely the man who'd also penned *Paradise Lost* warranted some sort of honor. Tradition held that Milton had been buried in 1674 under the clerk's desk in the chancel. But before parishioners went to the trouble of putting up a monument on the spot, a few thought that . . . well, maybe they should *make sure* he really was there.

Workmen began digging on August 3, 1790, and soon enough they struck a corroded lead coffin lid on the north side of the chancel. Could this be it? It was hard to tell, so the industrious sextons brushed off and then washed the coffin lid in a futile effort to find an inscription. A wooden coffin was now visible underneath the lead one—Milton's father, probably—but by now the day was getting late and the workmen were ordered to cover the whole thing back up. There was a pair of likely-looking coffins in more or less the right place, and that was good enough. He could be reburied now, and the gravediggers were left that night to get back to work.

So they got good and drunk.

Why don't we look inside and see Milton? came the inevitable suggestion. A mallet and hammer were produced, and the lid smashed open.

"Upon first view of the body," reported a witness, "it appeared perfect, and completely in the shroud, which was of many folds; the ribs standing up regularly. When they disturbed the shroud, the ribs fell."

Well, now the poet's physique was ruined anyway: might as well finish the job. Sensing some fine opportunities, two fellows ran home and fetched scissors to clip off locks of the bard's hair, though their trip was wasted: upon returning they discovered the hair came out in clumps with no effort. Another laborer decided that maybe Milton's five remaining teeth would come out as easily. To his surprise, they did not, so he cleverly applied a rock to Milton's skull. Then the teeth came out. In fact, the whole jaw came out in the hand of another fellow, though he thought better of it and tossed it back into the coffin. He yanked a leg bone out, too, but once again had second thoughts and threw that back in as well. But the teeth, rather more practical as souvenirs, were happily distributed among the merry workmen.

But morning would soon come; people would want to get into the church . . . then what? Now, sobering a little, the gravediggers decided it was time to get to business. They carefully barred the doors of the church, and pious locals arriving were thereupon informed that they could enter and see *the body*, but only if they would "pay the price of a pot of beer for entrance." And so the faithful parishioners of Cripplegate dutifully lined up, paid the cover charge, and filed past the coffin of their poet.

They left with an awe born of Milton's mortality. Also, they left with his ribs, his fingers, his hair, and numerous shilling-sized pieces of skin. When those were gone, they also surreptitiously snapped off little chunks of the corroded coffin. It was a splendid business, and the workmen might have kept it going until the poet was disassembled altogether like an exploded drawing of so many machine parts, except . . . there was that *smell*. It seemed the water they used to wash off the coffin lid had gotten inside. There was, an observer noted, "a sludge at the bottom of it, emitting a nauseous smell." Well, that settled it: it was time to do the proper thing and rebury Milton—with his head whacked in, his teeth gone, his ribs snapped off, his hands missing, and bald—doomed to this day to circulate in tiny fragments across the land.

They never did get around to building his monument.

Mind you, this is what Englishmen did to writers they *liked*. But Milton was hardly the only one to suffer such indignities. A great many coffins in London cemeteries were empty or weighted with nothing more than rocks. Grave-robbing was a long-standing trade, illicit if tacitly acknowledged, though the public deeply and rather understandably resented the practice. In Cobbett's day at least ten "resurrection men" made their living supplying London medical students, and they were assisted by numerous bribed gravediggers, sextons, and churchwardens. It could be a dicey business: when one pair of resurrection men got into a dispute with a school over a five-guinea payment, they responded by dumping two extremely ripe bodies on the school's sidewalk on Great Marlborough Street. After a pair of young ladies tripped up on them, an angry mob was barely prevented by police from tearing the school apart.

What was strange about Cobbett was not so much that he'd dug up a dead body as that he'd openly admitted to having done it. The *Times*, never the greatest of friends with Cobbett, couldn't quite believe his story at all. They accused him of planning to use local body snatchers: "There is a suspicion that the whole of this is a falsehood—a trick arranged by certain people in London, who have put in requisition the aid of resurrection-men, for the production of a body which will be decayed enough by the time Cobbett has occasion for it." But the reports filtering back from Liverpool docks were awfully convincing. Aside from the box of bones, Cobbett's luggage also included a tarnished brass coffin plate, rather worse for having been dug up with pickax and spade blows. But on it a few words were still visible:

PAINE

180

aged 74 years

The *Times*, still trying to needle Cobbett, now decided that instead of planning a hoax, he'd simply made a galling mistake: "instead of bringing home the bones of Paine," it speculated, "he has brought home the remains of a negro!" But it was becoming obvious that the wild story about Paine's bones was true: he'd actually gone and done it. The news was spreading wildly across the countryside, leaving listeners variously elated, angry, or just bewildered. At Coventry,

Cobbett was surrounded by a cheering crowd, and stood atop his carriage to give an impromptu speech; while in Bolton, a town crier with the temerity to announce the news of Cobbett's arrival was promptly tossed in jail.

Publishers rushed to cash in. Three competing biographies miraculously appeared in London bookstalls within a matter of weeks, each recounting Paine's innumerable misdeeds. All had been out of print for decades until now, but they promised to deliver anew the dirt on "a man," as one summarized, "who was a compound of all that is most base, disgusting, and wicked, without the relief of any one quality that was great or good." Tom Paine smelled bad; he drank and beat his wife; he knocked up innocent girls; he was an infidel and— worse still—a cheapskate. Another publisher cleverly reprinted Cobbett's own annotated *Life of Thomas Paine*, allowing the Cobbett of 1796 to damn the Cobbett of 1819. But Paine's partisans leaped into the ring too. From his shop on Upper Marylebone Street, Paine's old friend Clio Rickman hurriedly assembled a competing *Life of Thomas Paine*, asserting that the man had been a saint, an absolute *saint*. Not that Rickman was averse to making money himself—for his printing and engraving shop, he hastened to tell readers, also sold books, music, and Rickman's own "PATENT SIGNAL TRUMPET, *For Increasing The Power Of Sound.*"

Local doggerel scribblers were even faster out of the gate. Under a picture of Cobbett bearing a coffin on his back came one broadside: "This is WILL COBBETT, with Thomas Paine's bones / a bag full of brick-bats, and one full of stones," it chanted, ". . . 'Tis Cobbett the changeling, worthless and base / Just arrive'd from New York, with his impudent face." A printer on Threadneedle Street merrily issued *Sketches of the Life of Billy Cobb and Death of Tommy Pain*, with a cover depicting both Satan and Paine's vengefully reanimated skeleton grabbing Cobbett at the graveside and choking him: "Up THOMAS jumped, (and Satan too) / And caught him by the pipe / In which the wind keeps passing through . . ."

Even Lord Byron descended briefly from his empyrean realm of poetry to take a swipe at him:

> *In digging up your bones, Tom Paine,*
> *Will Cobbett has done well:*
> *You visit him on earth again,*
> *He'll visit you in hell.*

Cobbett had not even issued his first call for donations yet, and money was already pouring in . . . to booksellers. But hanging over them all year had been the real question—the belling of the cat. It had been a quarter of a century since anyone had openly sold the treasonous books of Cobbett's martyr. Who would now dare to reprint the works of Thomas Paine?

The Bone Grubbers

JUDGE BAILEY EMERGED from the chambers, stern in his robe and wig, and sat high in his chair overlooking the defendant. The latest case in his docket had become an utter headache. Just blocks away, copies of Cobbett's *Political Register* were being hawked with news of the return of Thomas Paine. How could one have imagined such nonsense? And delivered on the day of sentencing? The awful timing of Paine's return was now threatening to turn what should have been a straightforward blasphemy prosecution into a cause célèbre. It was bad enough that the defendant was a notorious local seller of Cobbett's *Register*. But the slight and defiant-looking young man standing in the docket, one Richard Carlile of 55 Fleet Street, had done something more, something that made him a match waiting to be thrown into a tinderbox.

"The crime of blasphemy is one of the most serious offenses known to our law," Bailey began his pronouncement. "The sentence of the court upon you, Richard Carlile, is that, for publication of Paine's *Age of Reason*, you pay a fine to the king of £1000 and be imprisoned for two years in the county gaol of Dorset, in the town of Dorchester; and that for the second offence, the publication of Palmer's *Principles of Nature*, you pay a further fine to the King of £500, and be further imprisoned for one year in the said gaol in

Dorchester." The judge rambled on with his sentence—more fines, more crushing sureties required upon release—and the young man bowed his head.

It wasn't supposed to be like this. Carlile came from a God-fearing family, and his mother and older sister couldn't fathom what had brought their misguided Richard to this place. One of his earliest boyhood memories, after all, was of gathering kindling with other village children to burn Thomas Paine in effigy—"Scouring the hedges for miles around," Carlile mused, "from daylight till dark, to gather a faggot wherewith to burn the effigy of 'old Tom Paine,' my now venerated political father!"

Then again, Richard *needed* a father. He'd lost his own in 1794, when he was but four years old. "Having no father to guide me," he recalled, "I must say that, until twenty years of age, I was a weed left to pursue its own course." He learned his letters from a local schoolmistress with the delightful name of Cherry Chalk, but by age twelve he'd dropped out of school altogether. His youth was squandered in miserable apprenticeships to a druggist and then a tinsmith; they ran him ragged on minimal food and five hours of sleep a night. But any resentment that he had was vague and unfocused. He knew a few bookbinder's apprentices who, passing around forbidden books, avowed themselves followers of Paine, but Carlile never paid them much heed.

In 1811 he moved to London to get married and seek a living as a journeyman tinsmith. It was hard to make ends meet—and even harder once Britain suffered a recession. Paine's warning seemed to be coming true: by 1816, with the nation stumbling under a bad harvest and a massive accumulated debt from endless foreign wars, the economy was becoming dire. It was a year, Carlile mused, "that opened my eyes." Scores of banks failed, and wages plummeted nationwide. Worse still was the feeling of powerlessness, as voter qualifications were rigged so that a tiny and well-to-do wealthy portion of the population determined parliamentary elections. Barely employed journeymen and apprentices near Carlile's home on Holborn Hill grumbled among themselves, passing around Cobbett's *Political Register* and contraband copies of Paine's *Rights of Man*. The grinding of poverty sharpened the edge of their complaints, Carlile recalled—"In the manufactories nothing was talked of but revolution." Trapped since childhood in a rigid class system and under a church and state that he vaguely resented without really knowing why, Paine's work at last brought Carlile's inchoate anger into focus. Why *did* the government have to be like this? Why *not* reform it? When a new and vehement radical paper called *Black Dwarf* fell into his hands, it found the tinsmith ready to drop everything for the cause.

"On March 9, 1817, I borrowed a pound note from my employer and went and purchased 100 *Dwarfs*," Carlile later recalled from his jail cell. The date of his visit to the paper's publisher still stood clear in his mind. "The *Dwarf* was then at an almost unprofitable [circulation] number, and it was a question about giving it up. However, I traversed the metropolis in every direction to find new shops to sell them . . . I persevered, and many a day traversed thirty miles for a profit of eighteen-pence." Carlile stopped showing up at work much, which was easy for his boss to overlook; the economy was so dreadful that there was little to do there anyway. Within weeks he gave up any pretense of still being a tinsmith: each morning he rose and reported directly to an abandoned auctioneer's storefront at 183 Fleet Street. He was now Richard Carlile, Publisher and Bookseller.

It didn't take long for him to make his mark. Alongside newspapers urging the reform of a parliamentary election which barely any citizens could either qualify to run for or vote in, Carlile also lashed out at the clergy. Upon hearing that publisher William Hone's parody of the Liturgy had been banned by the government, Carlile hoisted placards in his shop window announcing to astonished Londoners that now *he* would publish it. Even Hone was surprised, since he hadn't given Carlile permission. But Carlile didn't care: to him, his duty was to the book, not to the government or even the author.

"I believe that I am right when I say that this was the first time that ever an individual bade defiance to the veto of the Attorney-General upon any publication whatsoever," Carlile proudly claimed. The astounded head of the local Society for the Suppression of Vice, William Wilberforce, demanded that the blasphemous bookseller be prosecuted. Scarcely five months from the fateful day he borrowed a pound from his old employer, Carlile was sent on his first stretch in prison.

He kept publishing.

To the amazement of the authorities, now *Mrs.* Carlile ran the shop at 183 Fleet Street. And she just kept on selling Hone's parodies as impudently as ever. It was so blatantly defiant that nobody quite knew what to *do*. When Jane Carlile's husband was finally let out of jail after a four-month term, the married couple simply carried on with their insolence. More indictments: more books and newspapers. They even moved into larger quarters at 55 Fleet Street. Richard Carlile just kept contemptuously laughing off the government penalties: he didn't care.

But soon he came to care a great deal about the heavy hand of the government. In August 1819, while Cobbett was still sitting in a Long Island cottage and pondering when best to dig up his old enemy, Carlile was sharing a stage in Manchester with other reformist speakers gathered together for a massive rally. Upwards of fifty thousand Manchester workers turned out on St. Peter's

Fields to hear them. It was a joyous day: noisemakers and impromptu instruments sang out as the workers marched in, carrying
aloft handsome blue and green banners reading SUFFRAGE UNI-
VERSAL and LIBERTY AND FRATERNITY. Another demanded EQUAL
REPRESENTATION OR DEATH.

The government chose the latter. Carlile watched in horror as the
cavalry made a charge upon the crowd, slashing and stabbing with
their sabers in a melee that left eleven dead and hundreds injured. A
woman in front of Carlile, clutching a newborn infant, was "sabred
over the head, and her tender offspring drenched in its mother's
blood." Carlile barely escaped with his life from what was quickly
dubbed "Peterloo"; hiding incognito in a carriage omnibus filled
with right-thinking stouthearted Englishmen, he found himself
having to pass around a flask and join in a toast heartily damning
himself, praying as he drank his shot that nobody would recognize
him. His blistering account of Peterloo, published upon returning to
London, accused the government of nothing less than cold-blooded
and calculated murder to terrorize the populace. "Every stone was
gathered from the ground on the Friday and Saturday previous to
the meeting," he bitterly reported, "by the scavengers sent there by
the express command of the magistrates, that the populace might be
rendered more defenseless."

Public outrage over Peterloo was still palpable when Cobbett
arrived back with his infamous box of bones. Like an unexploded
bomb, Paine's ideas were now newly unearthed and ready to
detonate, and they had to be kept out of the hands of the citizenry.
Carlile had been the most outrageous instigator of all—even having
the gall to read all of Paine's *Rights of Man* aloud as evidence, in a
clever attempt to be able to publish it again—yet *again!*—under the
guise of a courtroom transcript. And this from a man who by his
own admission had already sold nearly five thousand copies of this

pernicious book. Judge Bailey decided to make an example of Carlile: it was time to throw the book at the bookseller.

". . . *And that you be imprisoned until the fines are paid*," the judge said.

Carlile could be jailed indefinitely now, perhaps for the rest of his life. But the bookseller had his answer ready for the court: *I will not pay*. He was led away in handcuffs. Everyone knew what his sentence meant; and after arriving at the jail, the new prisoner received a chilling farewell note from one of his supporters:

> Yesterday, the news of the resurrection and transmission of the bones of the persecuted Thomas Paine to their native soil struck me very forcibly as an extraordinary, almost miraculous coincidence with the decree, in the same breath, that will probably bury you alive.

Carlile looked around his grim jail cell, and then—he waited.

SHREDDED LETTUCE.

Amid the mingled London smell of wet brick and soot, and a puddled tincture of rainwater and diesel, the emptied McDonald's boxes sit piled against the alleyway wall; their cardboard flaps move in the wind like the feathers of flightless birds. The narrow entrance of Fleet Street into Bolt Court is crammed between a Starbucks on one side and a McDonald's on the other, with a peppering of fast-food refuse in between. Walking back into its recesses, the light becomes dimmer and the roar of Fleet Street slightly muffled; in the emptied courtyard, cold metal scaffolding crawls up the whitewashed face of an old building. I pace around, searching for number 11. Projecting out from one wall are what might once have been old gas lanterns, now made electric; between them and an iron railing is the sign:

Workpermit.com

Registered Immigration Advisors

A fitting enough use for 11 Bolt Court, I suppose—for Cobbett
brought himself and his box of bones home to this building upon his
return from abroad. Throughout the nineteenth century this courtyard echoed with the clatter of various printing presses, and teemed
with apprentice printers and students at its engraving school; and for
many years, too, it counted Cobbett as an occasional resident in this
building. Newly arrived in London and gazing out from the entrance
to Bolt Court, Cobbett could see Carlile's shuttered bookshop just up
the street. He'd already visited Carlile in jail, where he found his
fellow radical mooning over the country Cobbett had just left.

"Ah," sighed Carlile, "had I been in America, they would not have
thrown me in prison!"

"No," countered Cobbett. "They would have tarred and feathered
you."

But Carlile's fate had indeed been harsh here. Within an hour of
the court ruling, authorities swept into the "Temple of Reason" at
55 Fleet Street and impounded £600 worth of books and cash; the
next morning, when beadles arrived to pull down rebellious placards
surreptitiously placed on the closed-down shop, they were roundly
booed and jostled by an angry crowd. But eventually the crowd
dispersed, and the shop kept locked up by authorities until, with its
rent hopelessly due a few weeks later, Carlile's remaining family and
friends had to clear out the pitiful remains of the Temple.

Cobbett had his own problems. Even before he'd arrived in
London, he found himself and his box of bones being attacked
incessantly in the press and Parliament speeches. "Was there ever any
subject treated with more laughter, contempt, and derision than the
introduction of these miserable bones?" one member of Parliament

sneered. Writing to his son, Cobbett complained how "to cry out against CARLILE, PAINE and '*blasphemy*,' was the order of day amongst all enemies of freedom." But he was ready to fight back.

PAINE'S BIRTH DAY, a notice proclaimed in the January 22 issue of his *Political Register:* "There will be a Dinner at the Crown and Anchor, in the Strand, on Saturday the 29th." Admirers of Paine, clutching five-shilling tickets for the dinner would gather at seven P.M. to watch Cobbett ring in a new era of political reform. There might even be Paine Clubs founded in various cities. In any case, the dinner would make a fine start for his efforts to raise money for Paine's grave, and it would give Cobbett a chance to hawk his latest notion in monument fund-raising: selling gold rings containing locks of Paine's hair. Cobbett vowed that the rings would be made directly under his own supervision as he handed each lock of hair to the goldsmith, and that he would personally sign a parchment of authenticity for every ring.

It was all a splendid plan—except, Cobbett wrote glumly a few days later, "Envy, hatred, malice, revenge, fear; but above all, Envy, mean black, dastardly Envy interfered to prevent the triumph of reason and of truth." And the cause of the downfall of Reason and Truth? Well . . . the *pub*. "The Landlord refused us his house," Cobbett reported. Exasperated, he moved his dinner at the last minute. But, walking down Fleet Street when the great day arrived, Cobbett might have noticed some rather bad omens. People were suddenly dressing in black; flags were lowered; church bells were tolling. And by the time he made it to the dinner, Cobbett would have known that he'd picked quite possibly the worst day of the entire nineteenth century to celebrate the birth of King George's greatest enemy. As if in one last act of spite against his old enemy, mad old King George had died *that very morning*.

It was not exactly a propitious occasion to be publicly railing at the monarchy, and attendance at the dinner was muted indeed. Instead of the saint's relics that would incite a revolution, Cobbett was quickly finding himself stuck with a dead *body* in his house. Caricatures mocked him, showing Paine's ghost hovering over Cobbett in his bedroom, demanding, *"Give me back my pilfer'd bones,"* and the *Times* now made sure to always preface any mention of their favorite villain as "the bone-grubber Cobbett." Writing to his son, Cobbett complained that "no one dared to move a pen or tongue in my defence . . . Former friends, or pretended friends, shrugged up their shoulders, and looked hard in my face, as if in wonder that I was not dismayed."

Cobbett could take some small comfort as he gazed up the street from here that at least he was not in jail alongside Paine's publisher. But Carlile's sufferings, he warned the government, would only backfire on them. "Is this the best way of checking the progress of Mr. Carlile's, or, rather, Mr. PAINE's principles?" he asked pointedly in the *Register.* "Was it ever known that man was cured of an error by punishment of any sort? . . . Punish a man for any matter of opinion and you gather round him a crowd of converts." This should have sounded like wishful thinking: after all, the government had even checkmated *Mrs.* Carlile. It might have been expected that the tenacious Jane Carlile would, just as she had done before, take up where her husband had left off. But with the loss of their bookshop's lease and stock, any prospects for another comeback were grim indeed.

Oh, and one other thing: she was pregnant.

Jane Carlile kept up a brave face with her husband in jail, but theirs was not a relationship that augured great things. The two had been growing apart, in fact. Her manic behavior around the house left him in fear of his life at times, and they'd already quietly agreed to divorce. But Jane believed in a free press as passionately as her husband did, so they decided that they would wait awhile to divorce—many years, if need be—the better to deny any satisfaction to their persecutors.

But then there was the baby. Surely she couldn't start a shop again now?

Yet that, as her neighbor Cobbett and the rest of London watched in amazement, is just what she did. Supporters rallied in every major English city, sending money in dribbles and in torrents, from a few well-to-do sympathizers with a liberal bent and from many angry unemployed working men alike. Within months, the Temple of Reason at 55 Fleet Street was back—MART FOR BLASPHEMY AND SEDITION read one sign in its windows—and rather than a temple it was now beginning to distinctly resemble a hornet's nest.

Mrs. Carlile was promptly hauled before a judge for selling *The Age of Reason* to an undercover informant. She lashed out at the court, listing egregious violations upon the freedoms of the press and electoral reformers, right down to the murders at Peterloo and the imprisonment of her husband: "If all these things do not constitute tyranny," she snapped, "then the word is but a word of sound, and Dionysus, Draco, Torquin, Nero, and Caligula, have been falsely libeled."

Did she not have a newborn now? she was asked. Indeed she did. *You were warned*, her judge ruled. *Send the baby to jail too.*

It was a sentence which, though meant to keep mother and child from being separated, proved sensational in the hands of Carlile's partisans. *A whole family sent to jail! Father, mother, and the innocent babe at her breast!* The rebellion became giddy in defiance as *another* Carlile was arrested for selling Paine at the Fleet Street shop: this time it was Richard's younger sister Mary-Anne. Volunteers flooded

in to work at the Temple of Reason as never before, and with each
arrest another stepped up to the counter. The fight had spread now
from Paine and Cobbett's generation to a new one of apprentices
and journeymen. A third, a fourth, a fifth arrest, and still they came.
Even married women stepped up: Mrs. Susannah Wright came into
the docket of unrepentant defendants, and was duly imprisoned
along with *her* infant. More ominously to prosecutors, she was
promptly followed by a clever twenty-three-year-old warehouse
worker named James Watson. He had studied Paine's tactics of
argumentation closely, and during his trial he pointedly asked the
court to produce tangible evidence for *any actual injury* his books
had caused. They couldn't . . . and sentenced him to a year in prison
anyway.

It had only been a matter of time before this happened; Watson
had long prepared for it. He'd already spent the Christmas before
his arrest visiting Carlile in jail—"as foretaste," one friend wryly
recalled, "of the course of instruction preparing for him in that
Liberal University." The *Times* found these idealistic young martyrs
too much to bear; one reporter, passing the Temple of Reason,
scoffed at their ragamuffin appearance—"squalid, dirty, and list-
less"—and inveighed the young man to report to the local soup
kitchen. The shop could be guarded in his absence, he archly
suggested, by going to Cobbett's house up the street and borrowing
Thomas Paine to hang in the doorway as a scarecrow: "Apply to old
Cobbett, the resurrection-man, and request the loan of Tom Paine's
body . . . It would require nothing short of the hardened courage of
another resurrection-man to steal either body or books."

Actually, by the time Watson took the Temple's counter, the
shop's workers had already hit upon an extraordinary innovation to
protect themselves. Arresting a bookseller for selling Thomas Paine
required an informant to go in, buy a book, and to point out the

defendant in a courtroom. What if, Carlile's shop assistants reasoned, you couldn't *see* your bookseller? Customers entering the Temple soon found themselves confronted by a sort of Automatic Blasphemy Machine: a gigantic clockwork mechanism with nary a human in sight. A dial listed the names of all the store's many illicit publications—*The Rights of Man*, say, or an issue of Carlile's newspaper *The Republican*. With the dial set to the right title, and money dropped into a slot, a book or newspaper would come clattering down into a receptacle.

It is sobering to think that the freedom of the press once depended upon a mechanism now used to vend Mars bars. But the "invisible shopman" wasn't an entirely new concept: during a crackdown on unlicensed gin in 1737, London taxmen found themselves confounded by the disappearance of gin shops, despite the streets being as full of outrageously drunk louts as ever. It took months for taxmen to discover the existence of primitive manned vending machines called the "puss and mew." A customer coming up to one whispered "Puss," whereupon a vendor crammed inside answered "Mew." A hidden drawer popped out to receive coins, withdrew, and then slid back out with a dram of the demon drink.

Like the puss and mew, the Temple of Reason's vending machine proved only a temporary distraction to authorities, rather like overturning a chair in the path of someone chasing you; soon they stepped around it and rounded up employees from behind the clockwork. But magistrates were starting to wonder about the wisdom of the prosecutions. The Temple of Reason was now a generation's training ground in idealism, their baptism of persecution, and radicals in other towns were emboldened to follow suit. In what one commentator aptly termed the "War of the Shopmen," an astonishing 150 booksellers were arrested around the country in three years for selling Carlile's wares as he sat in jail. Among those joining the rebellion was a teenaged economics prodigy in Leeds, one John Stuart Mill. Paine had always been secretly circulated, after all—"Carlile ventured to do that openly which had been done surreptitiously," Mill noted—and to persecute dissenters, the budding philosopher explained, merely created more. "A Tindal produces a Leland," he wrote, "and a Paine calls forth a Watson."

The government found itself playing a maddening game of Whack-a-Mole: every time they hammered down one bookseller, another would pop up in the next street or the next town. And Carlile himself was gleefully getting into the act again. No longer merely a publisher, he now became a prolific writer. His dispatches were published by an army of volunteers in his weekly newspaper *The Republican*, and he leaped into the fray of Paine biographers with yet another *Life of Thomas Paine* to compete with the at least four others now jostling for public attention. Writing over a byline marked "Dorchester Gaol," Carlile shook his head at how Paine's dead bones roamed free, while his living publisher rotted in a jail cell. And it was indeed Paine's own books—and not the many *Lives* of Paine—that really mattered now. "When an author has passed the bar of nature," Carlile wrote, "it behooves us not to listen to any tales about who he was, or what he did, but to form our judgments of the utility of the man, by the writings he left behind him. Our business is with the spirit or immortal part of the man . . . we have nothing to do with the body that is earthly and corruptible, and passes away into the common mass of regenerating matter."

Yet the spectacle of Cobbett—"who heaped so much abuse on him, beyond that of all other persons put together"—returning with Paine's bones struck even Carlile as wonderful in its way, as "a volume of retraction, more ample and more convincing than his energetic pen could have produced." Still, he shrugged, he didn't see why anyone else should have much to do with it: "For my own part we have his writings, I should feel indifferent as to what becomes of his bones." But that was not going to be the end of that story—not for Paine, nor for the hidden clockwork rebels within Carlile's bookshop.

The curse—and sometimes the saving grace—of jail is that it gives endless time to recall one's past, to run it over and over and to ponder what it meant. Sitting in his cell, Carlile found himself drawn to one memory: standing in a bookstall in the Plymouth Dock Market one day in 1812, long before he'd given the faintest thought to radicalism, and noticing a well-dressed maid slipping into the stall to talk in low tones with the bookseller:

"Pray Mr. ————, *have you got that book for my mistress?*" she asked.

"Yes, my dear," the bookman assured her.

Coins were produced from her person, and a book from under the counter quietly passed hands. Carlile leaned over to spy on the title as the maid cracked it open: *Aristotle's Master-Piece*, the title page read. "The girl in question looked up quite cunning," he recalled from his jail cell, "as if she had got a curious prize or a budget of something that she did not know before, and scampered away delighted."

Carlile ran into the book again in London bookstalls. It proved to be a birth control manual—a bizarre mash of folklore and nonsense that had been around since at least 1766, having gone through scores of illicit editions in port cities. Though a few of its herbal recipes actually did work for inducing miscarriages, it was largely useless—as Carlile snapped, "a mere pack of trash that has a singular name as a smuggled book and, if freely and publicly sold, would not after a time find a customer."

What kept true information out of the hands of women? Why,

the pious local Vice Societies, such as the very one that had put the Carliles in jail. As the years passed and his open-ended jail sentence lengthened—to his full three-year term, then to four, and then five years—in 1825 Carlile penned for the first time an open letter to William Wilberforce, the minister who had spearheaded his prosecution.

SINNER,

Is it not odd that I have never addressed a letter to you before, distinguished as you have been as one of my persecutors? The reason is that, meddler as you have been in all sorts of sin and mischief, profound hypocrite as you have been, you have been, really, in the aggregate, a very contemptible man . . . I have thought it time to notice you in a public letter, lest you slip through my hands, as I never follow an enemy into the next life. I hope that your body will be well and quickly dispersed, and that not two particles may keep together to form anything like a similar being . . .

To be fair, Wilberforce is remembered rather fondly today as a key figure in the abolition of slavery in Britain. But Carlile wasn't focused on that, or even on his prison time at Wilberforce's hands; what infuriated him was how the evangelical's prudishness had imprisoned women.

Jail changed Carlile, much as it had changed Cobbett. Imprisoned with his wife and infant son, Carlile turned his mind to the realities of child care, and pondered the lot women had been given in life. He'd begun to voraciously read Paine's odd old friend Walking Stewart, and his dispatches to radical newspapers began to speak of equal rights for women. Female readers were delighted, and affectionately sent parcels of hand-knitted garments addressed to his jail cell—so many, in fact, that by 1824 he joked that he was ready "to set up a museum of curious night-caps." It wouldn't have lasted long even if he had: tired of housing a martyr who had now served the longest sentence ever given for blasphemy, in November 1825 the authorities gladly let him go free. Emerging from his prison cell, Carlile had a new book planned—and it was, he vowed, the most important ever written in the English language.

I cross over Fleet Street and pause before a building at the corner of Bouverie, where a sign proclaims FUZZY'S GRUB: A MORE CIVILIZED BREAKFAST—meaning that they serve it until three in the afternoon. That *is* civilized. The smell of frying onions envelops me as I walk in.

"Sausage sandwich and brown sauce, please."

I look away as they drain the grease off my meal. Another customer stands nearby, munching his sandwich, a paperback book shoved in his jacket pocket. He has the current inhabitants to thank for the sandwich, but perhaps has the past tenants to thank for being able to read the book. For here, at this corner, was where newly freed Carlile would move in 1826 to build his most lavish Temple of Reason of all, with walls lined with banned and radical books and a nearby lecture hall of progressive reformers arguing for everything from vegetarianism to women's suffrage and atheism. Mocking the Christian Missions of William Wilberforce, Carlile lorded over what he called his "Infidel Mission," proudly watched over by a life-sized statue of Thomas Paine that one of his Fleet Street neighbors had presented to him. The sculptor, ironically enough, was actually spying on Carlile in the hope of sending him to the gallows. It amused the radical to no end to think that the government had financed his beloved statue of old Tom Paine.

But what of the *real* Thomas Paine?

"We have been repeatedly asked of late," complained the *Times*, "what Cobbett has done with Paine's bones?"

Indeed. Though he was stumping for electoral and debt reform as much as ever in his newspaper and in lecture halls across England, Cobbett had fallen curiously silent about the famous bones. They'd shown themselves to not be a particularly useful fund-raiser, and were shelved unceremoniously in Cobbett's digs at Bolt Court. There the shrunken remains of death lay hidden scarcely a hundred feet from where Carlile's life-sized Paine stood in full public view. Radical attendees at birthday dinners regularly held for Thomas Paine—or "a number of vulgar persons," as the *Times* preferred to describe them—argued among themselves whether they should press Cobbett to *do* something with the increasingly awkward relics. Cobbett had always been one for half-finished plans; he was forever proposing new funds that didn't materialize, new books and magazines that never appeared. But the bones were different; his friends and enemies hadn't forgotten them, even if Cobbett himself now wanted to.

He had quite enough to contend with already. Restlessly moving for brief stretches out of London to return to farming and home-schooling his children, Cobbett kept getting tangled in politics. An attempt at running for the House of Commons terminated in a brawl outside a polling place; kicked and punched from all sides as he left the voting booth, Cobbett had to fight his way out by improvising a sort of impromptu pair of brass knuckles—"One of the sharp corners of [my] snuff-box, which struck out beyond the bottom of my little finger, did good service. It cuts noses and eyes at a famous rate." Other Cobbett supporters, attacked by knives, fared rather less well, and by the time the polls closed their candidate found himself placing dead last.

After such misadventures, he invariably returned to his shop at

183 Fleet Street, the same former auction room where Carlile had begun his reign of sedition a few years before. Cobbett's living quarters back in Bolt Court buzzed with activity, too, as he was now hosting his friends and sometime printers Mills, Jowett & Mills. Every Friday night at 11 Bolt Court he'd repair to the office of his printer Alexander Mills, where a jovial and even raucous editorial meeting was under way. Sitting around examining and arguing over manuscripts were the house compositor, Cobbett's secretary, and three or four physicians becoming increasingly merry over a bowl of rum punch. At the center of the group was a strapping young surgeon, Thomas Wakley, who delighted in having the old rebel of the house at hand as they assembled the next week's attacks on Britain's medical establishment. Back issues littering the office bore an apt title: *The Lancet.*

It was fitting that Paine's bones, stored here in Cobbett's house, presided over *The Lancet*'s early editorial meetings, for Thomas Wakley rivaled both Cobbett's and Paine's ability to attract trouble. Almost immediately after setting up his first surgical practice on Oxford Street, Wakley was stabbed repeatedly in his hallway in the dead of night, and his house burned down around him; the doctor, covered in blood, barely escaped the flames by crawling out a skylight and breaking into the house of a neighbor. His neighbor's servant was so astonished that, instead of giving the half-dead Wakley a cup of water, he filled it with lamp oil—which Wakley, delirious, proceeded to drink.

Some thought it was a gang's assassin mistaking his target; in any case, Wakley soon had many enemies who were not mistaken at all about the threat he posed. The young surgeon was impatient with the rampant nepotism of the Royal College of Surgeons and horrified by the badly botched operations hidden behind their establishment's code of silence. Medicine, he decided, needed the same scrutiny that Cobbett's courtroom and parliamentary reporting brought to politics. Under the heading "Hospital Reports," *The Lancet* provided withering eyewitness accounts of malpractice, such as a lithotomy botched by an inept surgeon who kept his unanesthetized dying patient strapped down for three hours of useless incisions. Correspondents were barred from operating theaters, and in a near-riot Wakley was thrown bodily out of a meeting of the Royal Society. But his *Lancet* was hitting its mark and draining the profession of pustulence and corruption. Nobody else on Fleet Street could claim to have as much influence over the very bodies of Londoners as *The Lancet*. Nobody, that is, except for the radical across the street: Richard Carlile.

Not long after Carlile was sprung from jail, he and Cobbett dined together and raised toasts to each other's health; Carlile even announced that he now planned to write a biography of Cobbett. But when his would-be subject picked up Carlile's latest pamphlet just a few weeks later, he was utterly appalled to see what his friend—with some quiet help from the young John Stuart Mill— had written during his final days in prison. *Every Woman's Book*, it proclaimed. Introduced by a plate of a naked and unashamed Adam and Eve captioned "What Is Love?"—a line from a poem by Thomas Paine—Carlile's guide immediately got down to business:

> If love were made the matter of sedate and philosophical conversation, the pleasures arising from it could be greatly heightened, desire would never be tyrannically suppressed and much misery and ill-health would be avoided. Parents would explain its meaning, its uses and abuses, to their children, at the proper time; and all ignorance, and what is worse, all hypocrisy, which leads to so many disasters, would be avoided.

Sex was, Carlile insisted, clean and healthy—"of the very first importance as to the health and happiness through life." So why was it not discussed openly? Like stamp taxes on newspapers and blasphemy bans, he believed the concept of "obscenity" exerted control on an underclass: in this case, women. "Restraints, here, operate precisely as they operate in cases of excessive taxation," he snapped, "they destroy the revenues sought and produce the evils of smuggled and more disastrous intercourse as a defiance."

Carlile was going to change that. "Equality between the sexes is the source of virtue," he proclaimed. After reading Walking Stewart, he'd decided that women had surely put up with the wages of sex for long enough: "Stewart . . . stated as his opinion that a time would come when intelligent women would not submit to the pain and perils of childbirth." And yet experience showed that men and women still desired *sex*. Carlile's answer to this conundrum took only one sentence buried deep in the text, but it was one that startled the nation. "*If, before sexual intercourse,*" he wrote, "*the female introduces into her vagina a piece of sponge as large as can be pleasantly introduced, having previously attached a bobbin or a bit of narrow riband to withdraw it, it will, in most cases, be found a preventative to conception.*"

In less than fifty words, Richard Carlile had changed women's lives.

It was the first time in the English language that specific contraceptive advice had been openly published. Throughout 1826, and for years afterward, copies of *Every Woman's Book* flew off the shelves, sometimes at the rate of fifty a day; Carlile's press could barely keep up. But Cobbett was appalled by the book's popularity. "*Obscene,*" he declared in his *Political Register*—which, naturally, helped send the book's sales through the roof. Given Cobbett's reaction, one can scarcely imagine that of Carlile's enemies. *Every*

Woman's Book was burned—once, during a debate, right before the author's eyes as a crowded lecture hall applauded wildly—and he was pilloried as vile, lecherous, a corrupter of morals. But, quietly, his book hidden in women's sewing baskets and under mattresses, he was read with intense interest. One follower even suggested that he raise money for his cause by selling decks of sedition cards: the kings would be Carlile, Cobbett, Paine, and Franklin; and the queens Mrs. Carlile, her shop assistant Susannah Wright, and the feminist writers Mary Wollstonecraft and Marie Jeanne Roland.

But Cobbett no longer quite fit in with the rest of the radical deck. As the 1820s came to a close he was becoming, well, almost *respectable*. Perhaps the constant sight of Paine's bones warned him of his own fate as a writer, for Cobbett was becoming more thoughtful as he edged toward eternity. His most lasting work came from these years: *Rural Rides*, a tour on horseback with his son that elegiacally memorialized the old English countryside before it disappeared altogether. He kept running for Parliament, and though he was still mocked about Paine when he gave stump speeches—"*Old bones! Old bones!*" crowds jeered—with each election he came closer to winning until, one day in 1832, to his astonishment . . . he won.

Carlile in the meantime was frenetically spinning out ideas and reforms and sliding into incoherence. By the 1830s, amid his multitude of crusades for women's rights, he publicly separated from his wife and took up a new lover with an alacrity that scandalized his family and friends; he loudly converted to Christianity and then back to atheism again; and he began holding lectures on some strange German theories about how the shape of one's head determined behavior. His eccentricity becomes a little more understandable when you read in one of his many writings upon medical reform that "Crude Mercury approaches as near to a panacea as any thing can, or as any thing will, approach." Indeed, he recommended it heartily for children, and had become rather fond of taking it himself: "In a quantity of about 2 drachms daily, or about the ordinary size of a pill . . . [it] has gone gradually through every part of the system, unfelt other than as a stimulant, which I always feel in a balsamic glow even at my finger ends." Thus glowing and stimulated, the slightly mad proprietor of the Temple of Reason was thrown back in jail again in 1831, for a three-year stint. His crime this time was a refusal to pay local church taxes. His defense was not much helped when he exhibited an effigy of the devil in his storefront, then one of a bishop, and then—in a wry flash of inspiration—he'd linked the two arm in arm, as if out on a stroll.

Cobbett wasn't faring much better in an institutional setting. The Peter Porcupine of yore had been at his best as a reformer attacking from the outside; as an inexperienced and outnumbered MP, he flailed ineffectively. The biggest reaction Cobbett ever received was when the crusty radical inadvertently referred to "my proposed revolution" instead of "my proposed resolution"; the chamber rang out with knowing laughter from other MPs. Soon he'd had enough of London; in 1833 he had his secretary Ben Tilly pack up his belongings from Bolt Court, and he moved back to Surrey—back to that stretch of land between the Hog's Back and Christmas Pie, back to farming the soil that he'd never really wanted to leave.

The young boy was fascinated, like the old man had once been, by the soil and stones of the land. But the thoughts of a local boy traipsing about on Normandy Farm had turned to something else that had been buried in the land.

"Is it true," he asked the ailing farmer, "you keep the bones of Tom Paine, the infidel?"

The old man leaned on his cane and regarded the boy before him.

"What do you know about Tom Paine?" he snorted.

But soon he relented. Leading the boy back through his house crammed with books, and scattered manuscripts that he and his faithful secretary continued toiling on even as his health failed, William Cobbett led him upstairs in his farmhouse. The old man produced a wooden box, and as the boy watched, the lid was opened.

Inside were bones . . . human bones.

The box was put away, and the boy sent on his way to contemplate what he'd seen. Cobbett himself hardly needed a reminder of mortality; since coming home to Surrey, he'd been growing weaker and weaker, and by the spring of 1835 was wracked by coughs and suffering a throat infection that simply wouldn't go away. His faithful Ben Tilly was there to help him, though, as he struggled to keep writing. He tended to his corn when he could, and delighted in hearing the blackbirds and cuckoos whistling across his fields. But his own voice was failing altogether. At a parliamentary debate in late May on the malt tax, he struggled to speak, but went unnoticed by the House as he rasped helplessly and unheard: his words were dying in his throat. He returned to his farm enfeebled, and his condition worsened. His body weakened and bedridden, Cobbett decided he had one last wish. He asked his sons to carry him outside to his fields so that he might check on his plantings.

"As he was carried to see the fields," his son wrote, "a little boy in a blue smock-frock happened to come by us, to whom my father gave a laughing look . . . He seemed refreshed by the sight of the little creature, which he had once precisely resembled, though now at such an immeasurable distance." Cobbett was carried back to bed. And there, closing his eyes in sleep, he never opened them again.

Pigott the auctioneer was at a bit of a loss. What, exactly, was he supposed to do with this?

Local farmers and collectors poked around in the cold January air at the sorted lots sitting out on the grass of Normandy Farm; here lay the final earthly possessions of William Cobbett. They'd been sitting in the house since last spring; and now Cobbett's eldest son, William Jr., dunned by his father's shopman for a debt, was finally forced to sell off the old man's possessions. It should have been a straightforward estate auction, except . . .

I have never, the auctioneer informed him, *been a dealer in human flesh*.

It wasn't as if young William hadn't known they were in there. He'd opened the box back in October and, with his father's secretary watching, possessively engraved his own name on Paine's skull and bones. Thomas Paine now had the name of his mortal enemy—*William Cobbett*—scratched into his very substance. Admittedly, it may seem odd for any fellow to go around scratching his name into other people's skulls—rather *transgressive*, you might say—but this was something of a hobby among unsentimental Englishmen. So much so that at the massive bonepile in the Crypt of St. Leonard's over in Hythe, one sexton found it necessary to post this notice to visitors: PLEASE DO NOT WRITE UPON THE SKULLS.

But now the young Cobbett just wanted to get rid of the thing.

I will not sell human bones, Pigott insisted.

He would, Pigott decided, defer to the legal advice of the Lord Chancellor on whether a body could be used to pay a debt. This problem had come up before; just four years earlier, the head of the debtor's jail in Halifax withheld a body when next of kin wouldn't settle the prisoner's debts. Before that, the body of the Lord of Stirling had been arrested mid-funeral for payment of debts. But there'd long been a popular belief that a dead body could be seized to pay off accounts: back in 1811, when a London bricklayer died slightly in hock to a local carpenter, two collectors showed up and promptly demanded either the money or the body from his family.

The deceased's son refused to give the money, whereupon the collectors tossed the expired bricklayer naked onto their cart, hauled him over to his creditor's house, and let the body rot in the basement for a week before dumping it in Bethnal Green.

Indeed, this was not even the first time that the courts had wondered whether *Paine's* body could be considered legal tender. In 1827, William Benbow—Cobbett's old publisher and an assistant at Paine's exhumation in New York—was himself hauled into court for indebtedness to his printer and his shopman. During the proceedings, a bright idea struck the creditor's attorney.

"Pray have you not got *Tom Paine's bones* in a cellar at your house, for we are informed you have?"

"No," Benbow answered over the snickers in the courtroom, "I have not. But I believe Cobbett has."

"Mr. Heath, if the insolvent has them in his possession," the judge intoned as the court dissolved in derisive laughter, "the assignees can *have* them."

They were, alas for Benbow's creditors, not to be found in his cellar. But here they sat amid Cobbett's furniture, cookware, and papers, forlorn and neglected. By default the bones went to George West, the neighboring farmer now acting as the creditor's receiver. West gained Cobbett's adjoining farm, which was a splendid deal; but while his old neighbor was now buried, the box of bones he'd left were just sitting here. The befuddled farmer let the box sit as he waited for an instruction from the Lord Chancellor on what to do with them. He waited, and waited: no instruction ever came.

What on earth was he supposed to do with a boxful of the villainous Tom Paine?

A couple is sitting nearby on a bench getting pleasantly drunk as evening falls. Nobody is bothering them: Bedford Square is a rather quiet space for the middle of London, a private fenced-off park boxed in by Georgian buildings of respectable brass-plate architecture firms and foreign institutes. As the sun drops below the rooftops around me, I peer into number 13. Leverton House is a vacant building; a chandelier glows in its entranceway, revealing emptied bookcases set into the walls, and an empty interior yawning back into darkness. The sign outside it sounds promising enough.

> *The Bedford Estates*
> Work Smart
> Centrally Heated
> Self-Contained Building
> Approx 374.86 sq. m. (4035 sq ft.)

Look up this place with the realtor and you'll find a splendidly refurbished office building with all the mod cons. Here, I'll summarize them for you:

> *Lease £120k/yr.*
> *Gas Cnt Ht; Sec Sys; Crpt, Vc/Data Cble;*
> *Kit; shwr fac; Per. Detail; Tms Pne Bns.*

Well, perhaps the *Bns* aren't there now, but they were—one could have considered them an additional *Per. Detail*, I suppose.

I stroll back down across Bedford Square, dodging a near-invisible nighttime cyclist. This was where the bones wound up, returned to London once again. By 1844 Normandy Farm was failing, and George West forced to hire himself out as a day laborer. He decided to rent a cottage over on Glazier Lane, and with the move and the sorting through all his possessions . . . there they were. He'd been sitting on the box of bones for nine long years. His receivership had ended in 1839, but with no instruction ever given to him, the bones had simply fallen into his own lap: he was stuck with them. It hardly seemed like something he'd want to keep around in his old age.

Cobbett had always wanted Paine to have a proper burial, after all—even in 1821, when the bones had long become an embarrassment, he announced that "in due time they shall be deposited in a place and in a manner that are suitable to the mind that once animated the body . . . If I should die before this should be accomplished, those will be alive that will perform the sacred duty in my stead." But many of those who *had* been alive had died within just the past few years. Cobbett's old accomplice Benbow had been thrown in prison for sedition in 1840 and died six months later. Richard Carlile, still living across the street from Bolt Court, died there of bronchitis in 1843, making trouble to the very end; when a clergyman began to read a standard eulogy at his burial, Carlile's family and friends loudly protested against such "priestcraft" and pointedly turned their backs as the insistent reverend finished the service. And as for those Cobbetts still living? Well, Cobbett's son wanted nothing to do with the bones anymore. Didn't even want to talk about them.

But West recalled Cobbett's old secretary, Ben Tilly, from back when the fellow was at Normandy Farm. He seemed like someone who might get the bones properly buried; and so, in March 1844, West sent the bones down to Tilly at 13 Bedford Square. It was a sensible decision: a few sympathetic souls were still to be found down in this neighborhood. Soon enough after the bones arrived, Carlile's old shopman James Watson came by, wondering what would be done with them. And indeed just on this very square lived Thomas Wakley, Cobbett's old friend from *The Lancet*. Ben Tilly and Wakley were old acquaintances, and now neighbors as well.

Wakley had worked for years in close quarters with Paine's bones; he'd surely know what to do with them. Perhaps they could be donated to science! Why not? Carlile had done it: before his burial, he'd had his body dissected for science, with *Lancet* witnesses in attendance. And then, too, Wakley had recently been elected Coroner. Yes, if there was a man in London who could dispose of human remains, it was Thomas Wakley.

But no.

Tilly . . . Tilly didn't know *what* to do, really. He was a happily married, kind, gentle, perhaps indecisive fellow—not like his fire-breathing old boss had been—and with Cobbett gone he'd drifted back into work as an itinerant London tailor. And as to where to put Paine, returned after all these years . . . well . . . He was busy as it was. He was struggling just to get by. In fact, he needed some kind of stool at work, something to park himself on as he pinned up pant legs and chalked inseams. And now on top of everything else he needed a way to guard these bones. Until the idea hit him . . . that nice wooden box they were in . . .

Why . . . not . . . *sit* on it?

I think you'll agree that the sight of people hurled off the top of St. Paul's and sent screaming through the air seems an odd way to *benefit* London schizophrenics. But that is indeed what they were doing not too long ago here in Queen's Head Passage. It was a charity event, of course: they had a zip wire strung from the cathedral dome and down into the street. But long before all that, this passage was where James Watson kept his bookstore. Tilly was still over on Bedford Square fitting customers with clothing, propping their feet onto a box that—unknown to them—put their toes just inches away from the face of Tom Paine. But Carlile's old shopman kept checking in on the tailor, just to make sure the bones hadn't been lost again. Watson even put out a pamphlet, *A Brief History of the Remains of the Late Thomas Paine*, and ended it with the simple hope that Tilly would get around to burying Tom.

None of the old passage is left now, except for the perfect cross-section of the transept and dome of St. Paul's Cathedral that fills one entire end of the street. It's a modern business neighborhood now of workers leaving the BT Building and suits drinking over in the Paternoster pub. But for centuries this was a street of stationers and booksellers. In the 1850s you could find Watson over in number 3, welcoming customers to his stock of radical pamphlets and books. For years he'd lived the simple, ascetic life of a Quaker activist— running a co-op store, sleeping on a sofa in the back room behind his bookstore counter, cooking his own lonely bachelor meals, and printing and binding his publications entirely by himself. He dressed simply and still addressed people with the traditional Quaker *thee* and *thou*. But he'd become a little more domestic now, having finally gotten married well into his thirties—his honeymoon was spent in prison for selling *The Poor Man's Guardian*—and now he and his wife Ellen worked together, printing up Thomas Paine tracts and hand-stitching them. Strolling out of his shop, he'd turn and face the irony of it all: the great looming mass of St. Paul's, home of the largest crypt in Europe. And still Paine went unburied.

It was money, always money, that shook the bones loose from their owners. First the Cobbetts lost them in a bankruptcy auction to their neighbor George West. Then West, fallen on hard times and moving off his farm, had dumped them into the lap of Ben Tilly. And now . . . well, by 1853 *Tilly* was broke too. The tailor's employer had gone under and his wife had died: Tilly fell upon hard times, and at length his goods went to an auctioneer over on Rathbone Place. An onlooker in the saleroom might have noticed a curiously familiar face bidding from the crowd—a plainly dressed Quaker, his fingers stained with printer's ink and callused from folding and stitching. *Going once . . . Going twice . . . Sold!* Down came the hammer. The unassuming gentleman made his way through the crowd, paid for the wooden box, and then disappeared into the crowded streets of London.

The travels of Thomas Paine, it seemed, might finally be coming to an end. But an ocean away, they were only just beginning.

THERE

The Talking Heads

THERE HE IS!

The novelist leaned forward and looked over the crowd that packed into a Philadelphia lecture hall. They'd come out on a cold winter night in January 1852, wondering what would come next from the excitable Mr. George Lippard. His hell-raising tale *The Quaker City* was America's best-selling novel until *Uncle Tom's Cabin* came along, and it had portrayed their hometown as so wicked that the earth opened up to boil the inhabitants alive: "It withered their eyeballs; it crisped the flesh on their bones, like the bark peeling from the log before the flame." Featuring a murderous pimp who runs a den beneath a desanctified church, his *Quaker City* played like a nineteenth-century slasher flick: death, destruction, and comeuppance for the horny and greedy. And his book was, Lippard proudly claimed, "more attacked, and more read, than any work of American fiction ever published." When a stage version of this sepia-tone *manga* was to debut on Chestnut Street, an angry mob shut down the theater before a single performance by threatening to torch the place—a potent threat, given that the mob was led by the mayor.

But tonight in Philadelphia, the shock novelist had something else on his mind.

"It is my object, tonight, to do simple justice to a real hero of the American Revolution," he told the hushed crowd. He bid them to cast their imaginations only a few blocks down over the snow-covered streets and rooftops, and deep into the past, back to January 1776; to a man who now had no monument, no memorial in their city, and no friends among their respectable gentry and clergy.

"Let us look into that garret window," Lippard bid the crowd, "—what do you see there? A rude and neglected room, a little man in a brown coat sitting beside an old table, with scattered sheets of paper all around him, the light of an unsnuffed candle upon his brow, that unfailing quill in his hand."

Lippard—a man who wrote with fire and speed—paused to consider his hero Thomas Paine, whose volcanic writing hid a painfully labored process of composition.

"Ah, my friends," he continued, "you may talk to me of the sublimity of your battle, whose poetry is bones and skulls: but for me there is no battle so awfully sublime as this one now being fought before our eyes. A poor, neglected author, sitting in his garret—the world, poverty, time, and space, all gone from him . . . Go on, brave author, sitting in a garret alone at this dead hour, go on, on through the silent hours, on, and God's blessings fall like breezes of June upon a damp brow, on and on, *for you are writing the thoughts of a nation into birth*."

Three times he, George Lippard, had tried to have this man's portrait hung in Independence Hall: and three times he had been denied. Decades before, no church would bury the infidel Paine. Now no city father would recognize him either. "Who would not sooner be Thomas Paine there before the bar of *Jesus*," Lippard thundered to the crowd, "with all his virtues and errors about him, than one of those misguided bigots who refused his bones a grave? Think of the charity of Jesus before you answer." And with that stunning challenge, the most controversial novelist in the country ended his lecture.

A zealous writer on the subject of the Founding Fathers, Lippard had single-handedly created the iconic myth that the Liberty Bell cracked while ringing out news of the Declaration. Now, thanks to Lippard, it was Paine's turn for glory: he flooded back into the market in new editions, and America's most disgracefully neglected Founding Father was recalled from oblivion.

But up in New York, a much stranger resurrection was transpiring. *I had no choice in the matter,* claimed one minister from Rochester in the weeks after Lippard's speech. The spirit of the dead man had *taken control* of the Reverend Charles Hammond: "I would take my pen, and place myself in the attitude of writing, when all thought and care would be wholly abstracted from my mind. As my thoughts vanished, my hand would begin to move, and a word would be written. Then I would know what the word was." Soon customers wandering into the Fowler & Wells bookstore in Manhattan found these very same words published in a clothbound volume. For seventy-five cents, you could hear a dead man talk:

> In the progress of the mind to the unseen world, there is no wonder within the range of human perception, analogous to transition of the spirit in what is called death. I will relate the incidents of my experience . . .

An unusual promise, to say the least. And even more unusual when you saw the title page:

Light From the Spirit World
The Pilgrimage of Thomas Paine
and others,
to the Seventh Circle
in
the Spirit World.

Lippard's listeners no longer needed to imagine their Man in the Brown Coat: Thomas Paine had come back from the dead to tell his own story.

I pace Broadway, imagining the faces staring out from the storefront of Paine's newest publisher. The skulls and plaster busts were arranged in an arc so that as you walked by the window the heads were always gazing out at you, both as you came and went past the store at 308 Broadway. Look up, and you would see the building's weatherbeaten façade, cracking away to reveal bits of plaster and exposed structural ribbing; staring down from above the doorway were two more mighty faces rendered in stone. Along the top of the store, a grand sign proclaimed FOWLER & WELLS, PHRENOLOGISTS & PUBLISHERS.

It's all gone now. The whole block is gone. The immense wholesale clothier shop of Carter, Kirtland & Company; the grand sweeping staircases of the International Hotel, the white marble edifices owned by the Astors—all gone. Birds are crapping on the concrete, and plastic bags are rustling in the puny trees. What was once a thriving block of Broadway is now the Federal Plaza, an airless expanse with the brutalist monolith of the Federal Building at its center. I am utterly alone: even in these paranoid times, there are no security guards to be seen. You could imagine yourself in the empty heart of an emptied city here. Bordering one side of the plaza is a little street sign, looking impotent out here on a lonely Sunday, proclaiming itself AVENUE OF THE STRONGEST.

But 150 years ago this was an avenue of the weakest—the infirm—the doomed since birth. It was the avenue of the self-doubting and the self-seeking; where concrete bomb barriers stand now, signs once beckoned hypochondriacs inside. But it was also where you'd find America's most expansive poet pondering human destiny, and gazing upon all the varieties of Manhattan humanity. If you cared about changing the world, or simply about buying a grinning cat skull for a shiny quarter— and both pursuits had their fans—then 308 Broadway was where you went.

I walk across the plaza, trying to imagine where the store's entrance might have been in the 1850s. Skulls here; consultation rooms back there; books over here? But it's hard to picture it now. Nothing here; nothing back there; nothing over here. But I suppose the entrance would have been somewhere right around *there*. It's entombed under this slab of concrete. You'd push a door open—a little brass bell ringing to announce your entry—and inside the bookshelves and displays would stretch breathtakingly back. Hundreds of plaster heads gazed out of the recesses, their eyes closed and expressions relaxed in the calm of death. Curatorial notes and pamphlets accompanied each.

Bly, Frederick. *Blind, yet with large order and locality he was able to keep a bookstore with success . . . The cast shows very small color, as without sight that organ cannot be cultivated. Died in 1857.*

Hunt, Miss S. *Large language, number and order. She would count her stitches when knitting, and her steps when walking.*

John. *A Chinaman, the first one seen in America; brought by Dr. Parker, a missionary, in 1839.*

Wilson, George. *Colored. Hung at White Plains, NY, July 25, 1856 for the murder of Captain Palmer, of the schooner Endora Imogene, and the alleged murder of the mate, after which he scuttled the vessel at City Island, in Long Island Sound . . . he declined to tell the place of his birth, or given any history of himself. We attended the execution, and took the cast of his head.*

Some heads scarcely needed a label: there was Washington's, and over here was Napoleon's. Still others had never borne any name at all: "Excessive Digestion (Name Lost)" was all one head had to say for itself.

Here were polished plaster busts of ideal heads—*"Varnished! Easily Cleanable! Decidedly Ornamental!"*—each one dotted and phrenologically notated. Over there were skeletons, "wired and hung, ready for use" for a mere $30; over there were life-sized, gorgeously detailed French anatomical wax mannequins, each filled with a full and uncensored complement of removable organs, painstakingly colored and textured to visceral perfection, yours for a princely $950. And gazing out upon it all in the store was a curiously familiar face. It was the very plaster visage once cast by Jarvis on Paine's deathbed. Wander past it and the pyramidal display of animal skulls, and there were shelves of innumerable books for sale—fifteen-cent copies of *Elements of Animal Magnetism* and *Essay on Wages Showing the Necessity of a Workingman's Tariff*; muslin-bound volumes of *The Philosophy of Electrical Psychology* and *Human Rights and Their Political Guaranties*; ghostly octavos of *Supernal Theology* and Thomas Paine's posthumous memoirs.

I open them up in my hand. *Light from the Spirit World* is a pretty odd book, and not least because the Library of Congress dryly lists its author as "Thomas Paine (Spirit)." Dying, according to—well, let's just call him Tom^s—turns out to be fairly straightforward stuff: it passes with little fanfare. As he lies in his deathbed in New York City in 1809, the first indication that Paine's number is up is the arrival of an unnamed lost love, a girl who had died when they were both in their youth. "Nothing but the form of marriage was wanting to make us one in the sight of the world," he muses; she leads him from his bedside through the portal of death itself. There he meets William Penn and is reunited with Franklin and Washington; they pass through circle after circle of heavenly purification. Fortunately, readers of Hammond's book have some help in visualizing the seven circles of heaven, since he includes an illustration of . . . um, seven circles. Within these circles there is endless Socratic dialogue, with Paine confronted by the same issue again and again: whether the violence he helped unleash upon the country was in fact justified.

"I have seen war," one spirit snaps. "I have seen the causes of war. I never saw a cause of war equal in wrong to the war. No cause, which hitherto has produced war, has ever been so wretched for minds to bear, as the evils of war . . . Thou hast no right to wrong thy neighbor, even though he may be thy enemy." In the afterlife's absolute reckoning of sin, arguments about sovereignty don't hold much currency against the fundamental crime of violence.

Back in the earthly realm, the corporeal Tom—let us call him Tom$_c$, with subscript to indicate his burial—*this* Tom fares little better. Tom^s watches a grave dug for Tom$_c$, while listening in on a philosophical gravedigger: "Ah!" opines the fellow between shovelfuls of dirt. "There are many who respect the talents of the dead, but few who care for the living." But there is no respect left for Tom$_c$, even in death. His body is stiffening, his corpse cold and unwanted. A clergyman duly mumbles over Tom$_c$, without much enthusiasm, about how "There is hope of a tree, if it be cut down, that it will sprout again."

It had better: publishers would need the paper someday. Tom's, the Reverend Hammond claimed, already had a sequel in the works.

Set down Paine's ghostly tome and walk father back in Fowler & Wells, and a large sign directs you toward the consultation room:

> **Phrenology**
> *Right*
> **In the Rear**

If anyone sniggered at the wording, it has been politely ignored by history. But a steady stream of customers came in each day, in search of self-knowledge, in search of understanding and hope. For phrenology, as first formulated in the 1790s, claimed that the human brain grew and atrophied with use, and that *thought itself was a tangible physical process*. Phrenologists carefully mapped which mental functions corresponded with which different parts of the brain and matched them with dozens of physical parameters of the skull.

I walk toward the invisible back of the store, to where the examining room stood. Phrenological charts and heads stared from every corner and flat surface: a thousand eyes upon you. Orson Fowler might invite you to sit down and take off your hat; then, calipers in hand, he'd set to examining thirty-seven dimensions of your head. The very top of your skull down to the beginning of your nose alone comprised five separate carefully measured arcs. Sometimes he'd pause to work his hands through your hair, gently feeling your bump of Destructiveness just over your ear, and feeling at the back of your head for a depressed organ of Amativeness. When was the last time you, strange customer, had someone running their fingers through your hair? And for the purpose of self-knowledge?

"The skull," Fowler would explain, "yields and shrinks in accordance with the increase and diminution of the brain within." This brain was a constantly changing organ, with the skull simply reflecting the changes within, like the bark upon a twisting and knotty tree. "The exercise of organs absorbs the portions of the skull which covers them, so as to render them thin," he said, "while inaction, and also excessive action, reduce their size, and allow the skull to become thick." Stop exercising parts of your brain and you'd literally become thick-skulled: a *bonehead*. But an overdeveloped organ could be a problem too. Fowler would talk of a girl who received a fracturing blow to her head that dangerously inflamed the Tune organ of her brain: ever since, she could scarcely stop singing. Ah, and then there was that case in Pennsylvania: a woman, a known glutton, who proved in Fowler's postmortem to have a skull whose Alimentiveness section was paper thin

"So very thin"—Orson leaned in to listeners—"as to be *transparent.*"

And you? Why, of the thirty-seven dimensions of your skull, perhaps a few were over- or underdeveloped. Perhaps more than a few. But—there was hope! A phrenological chart, you see, was not your destiny: it was not descriptive but rather *prescriptive*, a guide to what you needed to work on in order to achieve a well-balanced brain. By conscious effort at regulating and altering your behavior, you could build up your mental organs and effect a permanent change in the very physical structure of your own brain. "Self Made or Never Made," declared the store motto. Whether people realized it or not, they were perpetually making themselves anew: the question was whether they were consciously working to make themselves *better.*

"*Improvement* is the practical watch-word of the age," Fowler would insist. The patent office was bursting each week with new smokeless furnaces, new steel temperings, new fabrics and dyes; settlers were improving the westward lands; newspapers floated grand civic schemes for rising metropolises. Why, was not the New World itself an improvement on the Old? Right here in the store were two busts of Benjamin Franklin: one as a strapping young man, one as a wise old statesman. Very accurate, as a glance at his portrait over at Peale's Museum will confirm. Now, note how *different* the two heads are! Here, in his early days of siring bastards, we see Amativeness overly enlarged; later, as he crafted treaties and bifocal lenses, we see his bumps of Benevolence and Causality both more fully developed.

Fowler's measurements would continue around your bewildered head. Did you have children, then? Indeed. Just at the back of your skull, parallel with the top of your ears, was your organ of Philo-progenitiveness, regulating one's love of offspring. Too little, and you were cold and neglectful: too large, you were liable to be a doting and ineffectual parent. Ah, but there were even worse kinds of parents than that. "Children should never be governed by *punishment*," he'd say, wagging his finger. "Because all its forms and degrees constitutionally excite and therefore enlarge those very propensities you would subdue. No chastisement can ever be in-flicted without the exercise of Combativeness and Destructiveness in the punisher, and therefore without increasing them in the punished." Thrashing a child really did hurt you more than it hurt him: you both eventually ended up with bad, criminal-looking skulls. But even the worst skull could be reformed with enough effort. Self-knowledge was but the first step. All in time—all could be fixed. The utterly ineffable thought, our very cognition, was coming within the reach of science.

"Man is just *beginning* to think—is just learning the great truth that laws govern all things," he'd rhapsodize.

With the caliper measurements completed, Fowler would finally note down the readings in a thick brown clothbound book—your book, included in the price of your three-dollar exam. *Fowler's Phrenology*, its spine declared, and by the time you left 308 Broadway your copy would be personalized with your measurements written into the first few pages, your name written into the very title page:

THE CHARACTER AND TALENTS,

of

_____

as given by:

_____

There, in the final blank, the author of *Practical Phrenology* would neatly sign his name. Your head had now been officially measured and judged: you could now leave, secure in your newfound self-knowledge, walking fearlessly past 308 Broadway's pantheon of staring faces, the endlessly scrutinized and scrutinizing heads of eminent men.

I sit down and open my little brown book; just as, at one time, customers emerging back on to Broadway would have stopped and paused to look over their newly inked charts, pondering the secrets locked within their own skulls. Actually, this particular copy of *Practical Phrenology* wasn't even bought here in New York, or in the United States. An ancient purple bookseller's stamp testifies to its true origin: "*M. Shewan & Co., No 1 Arcade, Toronto.*" It could just have easily been purchased in London, San Francisco, or Paris. Every city had phrenologists by mid-century. What began as one

doctor's odd notion in Vienna became a national and then international movement led by Fowler. *Practical Phrenology*, his distilla-
tion of road lectures and innumerable pamphlets, went through at
least sixty-two printings in the nineteenth century.

There were phrenological children's books, phrenological alma-
nacs, and a monthly *American Phrenological Journal*, largely written
by Orson himself; you could piously peruse *Phrenology and the
Scriptures*, or you could examine the heads of your favorite celebrities
in *Popular Phrenology*. Hundreds of such titles burst forth from the
press of Fowler's Manhattan shop. You could even study the
phrenology of wild animals in guides copiously illustrated with
grinning cat skulls, hollowed-out sparrow heads, and macerated
monkey mandibles. Indeed, one of Abraham Lincoln's first employ-
ers, Denton Offutt, was for many years more famous for authoring *A
New and Complete System of Teaching the Horse on Phrenological
Principles* than for mentoring the gangly young manic-depressive
he'd kept in his law office.

It would have been unimaginable to many Victorians that Fowler's books would be utterly forgotten today; some probably deemed
him the only author of their era truly worth keeping in print. Now
the only copies of Fowler are a century old, browned by sunlight
shining in through attic windows, their pages marked up with the
measurements of skulls whose owners now have neither hair nor
skin to cover their bumps of Amativeness. These measurement
pages resemble nothing so much as Ben Franklin's famous self-
improvement grid, in which he listed his weekly progress of all his
faults and qualities. Here some long-dead Toronto resident has
helpfully marked up the measurement section of my book, working
toward *his* little bit of perfectibility: I don't know his name, but I do
know that his head had freakishly overdeveloped Agreeableness and
very little Destructiveness. Yes, well: he *is* Canadian.

Just mere curiosities now, aren't they? The death mask, the measurements of some Canadian's head—junk for the back of a memorabilia catalogue. Except that once, of course, they were not junk at all.

Beginning in the 1830s, a curious tendency arose in fiction: authors were expected to introduce their characters with a detailed description of their physical appearance, *particularly* the shape of their heads. Rochester of *Jane Eyre* is granted a noticeably squarish forehead and "a decisive nose," while in *Moby-Dick* Melville has Ishmael declare that Queequeeg "reminded me of General Washington's head, as seen in the popular busts of him. It had the same long regularly graded retreating slope from above the brows, which were likewise very projecting, like two long promontories thickly wooded on top." These were not mere splashes of scene-painting: such descriptions prefigured the morals and actions of a character. Oddly, these detailed headscapes of jutting jaws and well-defined temples can still appear in modern character descriptions, rather like an ancient coelacanth turning up in a chlorinated swimming pool: hack authors still use these absurdly detailed cerebral topographies without the faintest idea of why such a tradition once existed. They might as well be detailing their characters' balance of the four medieval humors while they're at it. Today it is household objects— brand names—*things*—that have taken the place of heads as a writer's means of implicitly delineating character. An old Volvo station wagon and an L.L. Bean barn jacket mark out a man as surely as a high brow and a weak chin once did.

From the distance of centuries, it all seems rather amusing. Phrenology as a party trick or as historical kitsch is easy to imagine, but as a *philosophy*? Really? And yet Henry Ward Beecher—that era's leading light of American religion and ethics—had no doubt at all about phrenology's importance. "The views of the human mind, as they are revealed by phrenology, are those views which have underlayed my whole ministry," he insisted. Could we but look around this spot—we, stranded in modernity, in this empty Manhattan plaza—and still see the store that stood here, we would understand what Beecher meant. A customer browsing through Fowler's stock would find him shouting out in his book *Self Culture* that most "glorious truth" of phrenology: "Small organs CAN be enlarged and excessive ones diminished, EVEN IN ADULTS."

Once you ponder the implications of this statement, as Fowler himself did endlessly, strange things start happening. Fowler's philosophy is all about the possibility and the real hope of change. Calvinistic predestination and hellfire are swept away in an instant; if the brain and its resultant behavior is malleable throughout one's life, then nobody is fated to remain bad: they can mend their ways and their selves.

Suddenly, too, the shaping influence of one's physical development—of one's diet and exercise and behavior—become of paramount importance. "Behold, moreover, the great procuring cause of man's depravity, and consequent wretchedness," Fowler explains in his guide *Self Culture*. "Namely, a MORBID PHYSIOLOGY. An irritated or abnormal state of the body morbidly affects the brain." Bad actions become the correctable result of improper development, rather than machinations of some cloven-footed prat with a fiery pitchfork. Prayer was not the answer, Fowler snapped: "Ministers may preach, and revivals be multiplied to any extent, without laying the ax at the ROOT of the tree of vice. Mankind must also abandon flesh, condiments, narcotics, gluttony, and fermented liquors, and substitute farinaceous food, cold water, and a light diet—must learn how to EAT AND LIVE."

What Fowler holds out is nothing less than the promise of

redemption. Will it surprise you at all when, at long last, Fowler tears aside his scientific lineaments, and reveals what he has been all along: a minister leading his flock heavenward? "[Let us] redouble our efforts for . . . that high and holy destiny hereafter as such by this great principle of ILLIMITABLE PROGRESSION!" Indeed. Look carefully around this empty plaza: what you see is nothing less than the birthplace of American progressivism.

The publication of Thomas Paine's spirit-memoir in 1852 came at the apex of phrenology's fame. Their fashionable interest in the latest craze of séances and spirits, though, left some wondering just how serious the Fowlers were. Orson's much younger brother Edward had suddenly proclaimed himself a spirit medium, and held nightly conferences on electricity with Ben Franklin, who would obligingly show up with a spectral set of batteries and wires. Other poltergeists, less scientific and civic-minded, amused themselves by mysteriously moving furniture while the room's lights were out. Edward's spirit interviews were duly published by Fowler & Wells in a two-volume edition, though the tome's copious notes did not include one Fowler relative's observation that he'd seen Edward secretly moving furniture and tossing sofa pillows around when he thought nobody was looking.

No matter. Lippard's and Fowler's resurrection of Paine had occurred just as dead people themselves were making a curious sort of comeback: or as much of a comeback as dead people *can* make. People could now *imagine* being dead because they'd just gained, with the 1846 debut of ether anesthesia, the remarkable ability to sink into a temporary living death. Ether arrived to find a culture already well primed for exploring liminal states: Americans and Europeans alike had already been fascinated for decades by mesmerism's claims of being able to produce states of suspended animation; newspapers eagerly reprinted wildly unsourced stories of frogs found living eons inside geological formations, "mummy wheat" seeds that sprouted anew after millennia inside the pyramids of Egypt, and bugs that reanimated themselves from deep inside household furniture generations after the original tree had been cut down.

With the dead becoming more than sloughed-off shells of the spirit, cemeteries developed into respectable places, modeled after parks and plazas; dead children and adults had postmortem formal portraits taken by daguerreotypists, so that unseeing eyes could gaze at you in shades of silver nitrate. For a while, the mysterious realms of photography and death even had a strange overlap; some believed that corpse retinas retained their last image for forty-eight hours after death, so that photographers could capture this dying image on film. In 1857 the *New York Observer* went so far as to quote experiments on a murder victim by a "Dr. Sanford"—"[I used] a weak solution of atrophine, which evidently produced an enlarged state of the pupil . . . We now applied a powerful lens, and discovered in the pupil the rude worn-away figure of a man in a light coat, beside whom was a round stone standing, or suspended in the air, with a small handle stuck as it were in the earth . . . [perhaps] the exact figure of the murderer." So . . . dead men *do* tell tales.

Posthumous narrators made their presence felt with the infinitely reprinted and pirated stories of *Blackwood's Magazine*, and even Emily Dickinson began to toy around this same year with unnerving ghostly narrators: "I heard a fly buzz, when I died . . ." So it's little surprise that just three month's after Paine's spirit-memoirs appeared, yet another found its way into stores. The author of *A Series of Communications*, Jacob Harshman, admitted that he, too, was skeptical when he heard about those spirits writing books up in New

York, but—wouldn't you know it?—now he'd been getting them
too, swooping down upon his home in Dayton, Ohio.

A Series of Communications is a real odds and sods of the Other-
world: George Washington, James Victor Wilson, Benjamin Franklin, and . . . um, Sir Astley Cooper M.D. The latter's urgent
message from beyond the grave? Eat right, bathe, exercise, and
"avoid all noxious drugs." But the greatest revelation comes in the
book's very first paragraph. Ghosts, it turns out, have terrible
spelling. "*Let truth prevale and harmony and wisdom reigns supremly,*"
they inform us. "*Misery follows arror and ignorence.*"

Other rather dubious sequels were to follow. Paine did make his
return into hardcover fame, just as promised, a couple of years later
with the 1854 spirit-memoir *The Philosophy of Creation: Unfolding
the Laws of the Progressive Development of Nature.* This time his
earthly secretary was a New York lawyer, and his Paine is a
Transcendentalist. "God is not a person, but a *principle*, the all-
animating principle of all things," Paine patiently explains. Paine
seems to have kept up with his posthumous reading, since in later
editions he argues for Darwin's theory of evolution, for life on other
planets, and for valuable truths found in other religions. And sixty
years after *The Age of Reason*, he remains not terribly fond of
Christianity: "The tendency of religion of the day is not moral
. . . I say the religion of the day is *demoralizing.*"

By the end of the decade the same freethinking and spirit-happy
bookstores and local publishers that had stocked the first Paine
memoir now offered plenty of others by the late Founding Father.
But if his spirit resided with any of them, it was with his very first
posthumous publisher—inside the curious storefront along the very
sidewalks that the living Paine himself had once trod. A true
blizzard of publications and causes issued forth from 308 Broadway.
The American Anti-Tobacco Society took its headquarters within

Fowler's store: so did the American Vegetarian Society. Fowler and his brother Lorenzo pounded out books arguing against tight-lacing in women's clothes, and for daily bathing. Convinced that the plasticity of the brain meant that there could be no such thing as permanent depravity, Orson pestered the head of Sing Sing prison to turn prisons into reforming institutions, and "declared war on the gallows" with campaigns against capital punishment; he pointedly published a magazine titled *The Prisoner's Friend*, and vociferously argued for the educability of the retarded and insane. And if, he wondered aloud and loudly, we may all progress in our mental development, what cause was there any longer for holding back women? Or blacks?

Reformers flocked to the Fowler & Wells publishing house. Margaret Fuller became one of Fowler's authors: so did Thomas Wentworth Higginson, Horace Greeley, and Susan B. Anthony. Clara Barton, founder of the Red Cross, considered her youthful consultations with Orson's brother and partner phrenologist Lorenzo as nothing short of a conversion experience: "How can the value of the results of that month, extending through a lifetime, be put into words?" Educational titan Horace Mann went so far as to name his own son after pioneering phrenologist George Combe, explaining, "I declare myself a hundred times more indebted to Phrenology than to all the metaphysical works I ever read." As they visited the Broadway store, these enthusiasts might have even noticed one ardently idealistic Fowler employee—well, *all* of them were ardent idealists. But this one, John, was especially exercised over slavery—"as though his own soul had been pierced," Frederick Douglass marveled after meeting him. He eventually moved to Kansas, joining a wave of reformist settlers struggling to outnumber proslavery settlers. And it was that quiet and intense Fowler clerk who, armed with two hundred "Beecher's Bibles"—rifles financed by New England reformists—made a disastrous raid upon the federal arsenal at Harper's Ferry, Virginia.

John Brown's last letter before he was led to the gallows was to . . . his phrenologist.

If John Brown couldn't achieve utopia with guns, Orson Fowler would through books. Fowler readers woke up in the morning and bathed themselves according to the precepts of Fowler's *Water Cure Library*, after tending to a garden raised from seed packets sold by Fowler's Broadway store, they then ate a virtuous breakfast of porridge and cold water from *The Economy of Food: Or, What Shall We Eat* ("Without exception, both rich and poor in America eat extravagantly of animal food . . . Every family should eat beans and peas."); then they could go to the job they'd been phrenologically directed toward by the Fowler & Wells career guide *Choice of Pursuits*, and comport themselves brilliantly thanks to their Fowler *Manual of Business and Guide to Success*. After jotting a few business meeting notes in Fowler shorthand learned from his *Phonographic Teacher*, they could go to lunch on food prepared from the *Hydropathic Cook-Book*, perhaps while perusing a volume of poetry or a novel from Fowler's press. Then, once their day was done, they could work out in a Fowler-approved gymnasium, and finally arrive back home to the gigantic octagonal mansion they had built in accordance with Fowler's blueprints in *Home for All: Or a New, Cheap, Convenient, and Superior Mode of Building*.

This last book left Fowler's most visible legacy. Scattered across the United States to this day are a motley collection of half-baked gingerbread Victorians built by Fowler's disciples. They go by local nicknames like the Bandbox, the Inkwell, or—less imaginatively— the Octagon House. They are the living remnants of a vision that seized Fowler as he prepared to build his own family mansion in upstate New York in the 1840s. "In looking about for some general plan," he wrote, "I said to myself, 'Why not take our pattern from NATURE? Her forms are mostly SPHERICAL . . . What should we think of a square apple, or right-angled egg?'" Building a truly spherical house with all the walls bent like a barrel, he reasoned, would be beyond the skills of most local carpenters. But an octagon—why, that should be hardly any trouble at all.

The idea was not a new one: the Founding Fathers whose skulls Fowler so admired were all well familiar with the form. The ruling gentry in Thomas Paine's hometown had their own octagonal temple, and Thomas Jefferson had built an octagonal house for his daughter. In fact, Jefferson was so delighted with the result that he also built her a pair of octagonal outhouses to accompany it. But Fowler brought a new and nearly religious fervor to octagons. They allowed more windows and thus were lighter, healthier structures, he insisted—and his readers all knew how essential good health was to the moral improvement of the world. Fowler imagined cement and glass houses built around a strange array of new inventions—an inviting showcase kitchen that formed the center of the house, taps with running hot and cold water, a central heating system, and most shocking of all, indoor toilets. "To squeamish maidens and fastidious beaux this point is not submitted," Fowler snapped, "but matrons, the aged and the feeble, are asked is not such a closet a real household necessity and luxury?"

Home for All was a hit: the eight-sided panacea was immediately demanded by fashionable homebuilders across the country. Henry Ward Beecher built himself an octagonal house; so did P. T. Barnum. Clarence Darrow spent his childhood in one. In many towns, the builders of these homes came from the two intersecting groups of readers that Fowler's works had always appealed to: doctors and ministers. Some of the latter wryly claimed that the octagonal form was ideal because they couldn't be cornered by the devil—and, as was alleged of one minister in upstate New York, "so he could see the Lord coming from any angle." Imitators upped the ante to twelve- and even sixteen-sided houses.

Circulars distributed from Fowler's store in 1855 announced a Vegetarian Settlement Company, a joint-stock venture to create an "Octagon City" in Kansas of four miles square—or rather, almost square, as it was to be a giant octagon—in which vegetarian settlers living on octagon-shaped parcels of land would build octagonal farmhouses that radiated outward from an octagonal downtown of octagonal public buildings, culminating in one immense central octagonal structure and an octagonal public green. Octagon City was also raising capital to construct "A Hydropathic Establishment, an Agricultural College, a Scientific Institute, a Museum of Curiosities and Mechanic Arts, and Common Schools"—all octagonal, of course. It was to be a glorious vision of the progressive future, with neither slavery, meat, nor alcohol tainting its purity. Checks poured into 308 Broadway, with prospective settlers committing anywhere from $50 to $10,000 in funds toward the project.

Right here, along this Manhattan counter—this mahogany counter that no longer exists, that wind blows through—and filed in these rolltop desks that our eyes can no longer see, the letters came each day, excited and hopeful. A blacksmith from Rahway, a mapmaker from Philadelphia, a printer from Tennessee, and a whole contingent of farmers from Pontiac, Michigan; envelopes both scrawled out and finely inscribed by idealistic tradesmen and farmers rolled in from across the nation. Utopia at last!

What families transported by their Fowler magazine articles into visions of pure country life among the glorious octagons found at the end of the trail, though, was not quite what the woodcut illustrations in the *Phrenological Journal* had pictured. Settlers had been promised working gristmills, fine public buildings, and a veritable fairyland of Kansan natural beauty. What they got was mud and desolation. The splendiferous Central Octagon building proved to be a windowless mud-plastered cabin of about two hundred square feet . . . and it was *square*. The founders had promised tools for every farmer: settlers found precisely one plow provided to serve the entire city. The bewildered vegetarian pioneers contemplated these woes in wretched lean-tos and huts built of bark, shivering miserably on their dirt floors, since there were only two stoves for one hundred settlers. The promoter fled, and his eager and trusting Octagonians were quickly decimated by malaria and Indian raids. The settlement's few survivors lacked even the wood to build coffins for their dead children.

By the following spring, all trace of Octagon City was gone.

Bedraggled Octagonians returning back East found yet more death and despair. The Panic of 1857 hit Fowler's business badly, and he was forced to rent out his own giant octagonal family home as a boardinghouse. It was not a great success. His newfangled cement walls had been improperly sealed, with fecal matter from the house's cesspool seeping through the walls and into the drinking water. The tenants of his octagonal palace—the healthiest building in America—died in fevered agony, killed off in a horrific plague of typhoid.

The talking heads are all silent now. Here, where the faces of worthy men stared, and the plaster heads of even worthier men stared back—they are all gone. The heads are scattered to auctions and attics, shattered into dust or stowed in trunks. The women's rights that Fowler fought for, the slaves' rights that his assistant was hanged for, even the dietary and antidrug crusades that customers went upon, these are the ordinary tasks of thousands of federal workers in this building. The rights of women and minorities are enshrined in law; food safety laws and public health statistics are pored over here. This place that was once the fringe of head-reading oddballs now sees some of their very same notions made mundane, filled in with black ink, and submitted in triplicate. But if there are any phrenological busts, it is as the stuff of quaint decoration; all memory that this little plot of Broadway had once carried on the Founding Fathers' of belief in human perfectibility, and carried it out under the approving stares and immortal death-gazes of those Fathers—all this was lost.

Yes, here was a place of Improvement. Indeed, this *place* was improved and improved upon until there was nothing left to improve. After spending decades as Fowler & Wells, 308 Broadway was a travel agency; then it was a 1930s Automat, a shining chromium vision of the beautiful waiterless future, where pies and sandwiches were delivered to you through coin-op slots. By the 1960s, 308 Broadway was back in the business of reshaping brains, so to speak: it became a liquor store. But then one day all the tenants of this building, and the clothier's next door, and the Italian-language newspaper *Il Progressivo* farther down—and everyone, all the way down the block—received eviction notices.

Get out in eight days.

Do you see that tall, tall Federal Building, silent as the grave on a Sunday afternoon? It crept in upon little concrete feet: although it was the U.S. government's second-largest building, second only to the Pentagon itself, it opened to deafening silence in August of 1968. There was no ribbon cutting, no press release—nothing to acknowledge its existence, save for its addition to local postal routes. The whole thing was a shameful affair, and everyone knew it: the Architects Council had deemed the project an "architectural disaster" as early as 1962, long before the first piling even went into the ground. And when the first piling did go into the ground, it really *did* become an architectural disaster. See, this stretch of Broadway— the building where Fowler & Wells once stood, as well as all its neighbors—it's still supposed to be here. The buildings *behind* them were slated to get knocked down and replaced. But when the first Federal Building pilings were driven in, the ground shifted and settled all the way down the block: load-bearing walls of scores of neighboring buildings suddenly cracked and crumbled.

The spirit of Thomas Paine speaks no more here. The face that Jarvis modeled no longer gazes out upon New Yorkers: the very place itself is gone. Court orders condemning the block were issued, demolition crews came out from Brooklyn, and soon it was all gone: the luncheonette, the synagogue, the jewelry store, the clothier's shop full of summer wear. They dynamited this block's past, knocked down its present, and for all I know bulldozed its future too. This barren plain was left in its place, and what was once the shining light of Fowler's empire was carted out to the Meadowlands in lumbering dump trucks, like trash in so many giant dustbins. But every now and then, a random bit of glimmering debris shines out from all our trash: the sunlight catches it just right, and you pause and try to figure out what it could possibly have once meant to someone.

Look—here, look at this paper. Just another useless head-reading chart from Fowler's Broadway office, this one dated September 27, 1856. Large Benevolence and Philoprogenitiveness, but far too little Cautiousness in this skull.

"Rev. M. D. Conway," reads the patient's name.

Personal Effects

Tick tick tick.

A librarian, clicking a pencil against her teeth, is sitting at the head of the two long tables, watching over us like a headmistress watches children eating porridge.

Tick tick. Tick-a click-click.

I'm the only one in Columbia University's rare-book room without a laptop. I've nothing but a grubby notebook that I bought at a bodega as I walked up Broadway; I believe the stationer who produced it is the illustrious *Made in China*, these being the only words to appear anywhere on its yellowed cover.

I am also the only one looking *up* in this room: everyone else looks down, absorbed in work. Even the librarian looks down, particularly while she observes us: her eyes roll up and over her spectacles, and then back down to her own desk, all without any wasted motion. Chittering away around me are the innumerable key clicks of a dozen other scholars at long tables, picking through boxes of manuscripts and personal effects, all the while recording their findings into ones and zeroes, tip-a-tick-a-tip-a-tick-tick, like little mice gnawing through an immense Cheshire cheese. That is all you hear in this room: the quiet whoosh of humidity-control ventilation, the clicking of keys, the shuffling of papers, the whump of archival boxes, and the occasional sound of a magnifying glass being set down.

"*Ahem.*"

The book trolley arrives on noiseless casters, and I retrieve a thick green archival container from it: BOX 45, MONCURE CONWAY. I untie the string and ease open the box carefully, and a sheaf of photographs instantly spill forth like a dead body slumping out of a murder mystery closet. I look up, embarrassed, but nobody notices. They're all still looking down. The security camera hovers above in an upside-down black glass turret jammed into the ceiling, but I don't think it's watching either. I look down and see scattered Victorian and Edwardian faces, family photos of the dead and forgotten, and atop them all is an ancient monochrome view over open fields, leading the eye to a string of snow-covered houses. "Falmouth, VA," the caption reads. I stare at this one for a long time: it seems impossibly far from here, from this deadened room of clicking laptops: the smoke in the chimneys, the horses and the carriages, the crunch of snow underfoot.

Imagine, for a moment, that you are dead.

Only for the moment, please: you will have the opportunity to make it permanent at a later date. Now, imagine the contents of your desk, your bureau, and your closets, as they stand at *this exact moment*, without your having time to sort them out, imagine those drawers being emptied into fifty or sixty archival boxes and sent to a local library.

Okay. Now a *hundred years* pass. Nobody looks into your boxes because, I am sorry to say, you are not very interesting to your grandchildren. But eventually, after you have passed from all living memory, someone *does* open a box. This will be a young man you have never met, and who cannot have met anyone who ever knew you: in other words, a total and utter stranger.

Could he, I wonder, make any sense of who you were?

"Moncure Conway, box forty-four," the librarian tells me, and I carry it back to my seat. This one appears to be the vertical contents of the deceased's office: the pictures off his walls. They are still in their frames and jumbled together, as if they had been hurriedly swept aside to make space for the next tenant. And they are of everything and anything: an old 1873 *Punch* cartoon about a school board dispute; a signed Rosetti print with part of its frame ripped away; an engraving of the Harvard campus in 1850; a daguerreotype labeled "Inglewood, Our House." One is a pencil portrait of a man, without any caption or identification at all. The back simply reads:

Framed at
Goodspeed's Book Shop, Inc.
18 Beacon Street, Boston
November 1, 1849, No. 8388

There is no telling who the portrait is of, or of how the deceased may have acquired it. Eventually, the contents of some other box might reveal it—and it might prove to be of no particular importance anyway, at least not to us. Who really knows the man's importance to the deceased himself?

I suppose the first time I ever had to pick through a dead man's possessions was in San Francisco. That time I'd been trying to track down a local swindler, an Alcatraz ex-con who'd run a mining scam that had involved planting gems on worthless land, and a resulting scandal that led to a prominent San Francisco banker drowning himself in the Bay. The ex-con was a slippery customer, very hard to find . . . not least because he'd been dead since 1923. But they did have his remaining possessions in innumerable boxes at the local historical society. I looked in vain for an obvious smoking gun among his papers. Or, for that matter, an *actual* gun in one of the boxes, which wouldn't have half surprised me. And there was indeed one suspicious-looking note that read, "Meet me at 5 by the tower clock. Make sure that you are not watched." But that was all. Everything else was just folder after folder of receipts, laundry tickets, battered and folded-up pamphlets, cigar wrappers, and the like. This was the mockingly ordinary debris of a life, any life at all.

"Box Forty-six, Moncure Conway," the librarian says without moving her head.

More photos. Really, they seem terribly out of place here, these daguerreotypes and tintypes, in this room of blond-wood tables and buzzing overhead fluorescents. If I ran a library, I'd build a string of period rooms, one for each century, where you could take your materials to read. A nice fainting sofa, a damasked ottoman to prop your feet upon, some heavy velvet curtains of a phantasmal oriental pattern, and the yellow pallor of a gaslight chandelier: throw in a parlor organ and some Currier and Ives prints on the wall, and you're ready to spend the day examining daguerreotypes—or, at least, acquiring a good solid laudanum habit.

I sort through the photos. Deceased subject. Deceased subject's child. Deceased subject's deceased child. Wife. Subject again. Subject in front of apartment in Paris. In front of apartment in London. New York. Wife again. Soon-to-be-deceased baby. Child. Child. Human hair.

What?

I hold up the photograph: it is startling. It is in *color*. There were, after all, crude color processes even back then. But out of the sheaves of photographs in these boxes, in a dead world of monochrome, it is the only one in color: and it is, of all things, a photograph of a lock of human hair. Brown, with a few gray strands. It looks exactly like the sweeping off the floor of a neighborhood Supercuts. But underneath is a note, written in an ancient hand.

This bit of Paine's hair was exhibited at the Thomas Paine exposition in South Place Chapel, London, 1893, by Mr. Edward Smith, biographer of Cobbett,—who carried Paine's body from New Rochelle to England in 1819. The hair was given to me by my friend Edward Smith. It is kept in the original paper inscribed "Mr. Paine's Hair" in the handwriting of B. Tilly, Cobbett's agent—whose handwriting is well known to Edward Smith and myself.

—Moncure Conway

I read it over and again. My eyes shift between the incongruity of the faded century-old handwriting, and the living color of human substance.

If, around 1850, you were to pick the one person least likely to cross paths with the body or soul of Tom Paine, then you could hardly have done worse than to choose Moncure Conway. At eighteen years old, he was a "Young Virginia" ideologue in name and in fact: as the secretary of the Southern Rights Association, he was an ardent defender of the Old Dominion's honor against the slanders of ignorant Northerners like William Lloyd Garrison. After all, what did the abolitionists know? *Slavery* did not even really exist in the Virginia that Conway knew and loved.

"The word *slave* was not used," he later recalled. "We spoke of *free negroes* and *servants*." There were *servants* on the Falmouth estate that Moncure grew up on; it was the largest house in that city, one befitting a wealthy clan of gentleman farmers and judges that could count George Washington among its ancestors. Moncure was a bookish child who took what he read seriously—and what he read, above all else, was the Bible. Riding through the abandoned old villages of rural Virginia, where nothing remained but crumbling old chimneys of vanished houses, he came face-to-face with his own ancestral calling. "At Acquia church, weird in its solitude and desolation," he wrote, "I paused for a time, and tried to picture my great-great-grandfather, Parson Conway, perched in the little black pulpit high up a column, and his congregation gathered there a hundred years before. He was the only clergyman in our family line."

And so it was in 1850 that the Conway clan gained its second minister. Moncure became a circuit preacher, riding rural routes and raining holy brimstone upon bewildered farmers. When not in the pulpit, he could be found in local lyceums, propounding his novel new theory that he had arrived at after reading the latest work of naturalist Louis Aggasiz on the differentiation of species. Blacks, Conway helpfully explained, were not covered by the Bill of Rights. They were not covered by state laws either. Slaves—servants, rather—were not protected by any human law at all. Because, you see, *they were not human.*

Granted, he thought blacks should be allowed to read and go to schools—he was not a cruel man, after all!—and he remained attached to the memory of the black nurse who had raised him in the family mansion: "I remember the comely coffee-coloured face of my nurse, Maria Humstead, nearly always laughing, as if I were a joke," he fondly recalled. "Her affection was boundless, and her notions of discipline undeveloped." No, he was not a hateful man. He was a racist, and that was not the same thing. He believed in race: he believed it marked a natural border. On one side of that border were humans. And on the other side were . . . not *quite* humans.

This otherness was always the implicit assumption of slavery—

but to make it explicit, couched in terms of genus and species?—this was a little much even for his fellow Young Virginians. But that was Moncure Conway. He was the soul of the Southern Rights Association, and the hardest of the hard Southerners. He was the one man in Virginia who could give a roomful of slaveholders pause because he was . . . well, *too racist.*

Even amid all these labors, Conway still liked to come home for a spell, and recline in the fields of his childhood. Gathering up his hunting flintlock one sunny morning, and an old copy of *Blackwood's Magazine* to while away the hours, Moncure set out into the wilds outside Falmouth. He came to a spring by the side of the path, and cupped a broad folded leaf to gather himself a small handful of cold water. His thirst sated, he sat down and set his flintlock aside. The woods, the water, the sky above—these were elements of his native land that he happily surveyed. Suddenly two slave children came rustling out of the bushes—stark naked. They were carrying water cans, and they set about filling them, completely unashamed of their own nakedness.

"I talked with them a little," Conway recalled, "found them rather bright, and, when they had disappeared, meditated more deeply than ever before on the condition of their race in America."

Troubled as he was, turning to his magazine hardly helped. Leafing through it, he found himself drawn into a minister's essay, one musing upon the nature of the "true self." It struck unaccountably but inexorably at his heart. He suddenly looked up at the sky, and then at the ground, the innocent haunt of the young black children. Then he looked at himself with his gun, bewildered. "*What was I doing out there with a gun trying to kill the happy little creatures of earth and sky?*" he muttered, appalled. "Was it for this that I was born?"

Shaken, he went home and set down his gun, never to pick it up again. He was still secretary of the Southern Rights Association, still a preacher of dogma and damnation. But something was changing inside Moncure Conway.

Methodist itinerants lived on horseback—they had no fixed address, no set routes, and no real means of room and board except for the kindness of congregation families in each town. It was asceticism with saddlebags. Conway rode the lonelier routes of the Old Dominion, following the melancholy circuit that the moralizing historian Parson Weems had traveled decades before. Strange men and decayed villages would appear like conjured magic in the deserted woods; one day, Conway found an impoverished Corsican carrying a wheezing hurdy-gurdy, and there in the forgotten road the two men played old songs, easing their road weariness for a brief spell. And then—it was back on the path again, hastening toward the next village to warn against dancing, against immorality, against losing their immortal soul to hell.

In the course of these wanderings, he came across a fertile cluster of farms near Brookville. He stopped at their meetinghouse out of simple curiosity, and found a religious service conducted in a dignified and meditative silence; he left strangely moved, and stopped by several more times, his theological curiosity piqued. After several quiet observations, he was greeted outside of the meetinghouse by Roger Brookes, a wise and respected voice of the community. Brookes proved to be the first Quaker the young man had ever spoken to in his life.

Without even realizing it, Conway had met a leader of the most progressive of Quaker communities—the Hicksites. The term meant nothing yet to the Methodist preacher, who had never heard of Elias Hicks, Paine's *Age of Reason*, or the struggles of liberal

Quakers decades before. But what he did understand was what he could see with his own eyes: gentle people, well-ordered houses, prosperous farms. And as a Southerner, this last fact was absolutely perplexing. The Hicksites were antislavery, after all, and . . . and . . . Why were their farms so superior to others in the Virginia countryside?

Church elder Brookes regarded Conway silently for a long time. "Has it ever occurred to thee," he finally said, "that it may be because of paying wages to all who work for us?"

Their conversation politely turned elsewhere, but after leaving the Quaker settlement behind, Conway was thrown into inner turmoil. The men and women he met were cultivated, charitable, and cheerful: they were good Christians. "Yet what I was preaching as the essentials of Christianity," he wrote incredulously, "*were unknown among them*. These beautiful homes were formed without terror of hell, without any cries of what shall we do to be saved?" How could this be?

Another blow came with the death of his old nursemaid. Standing by her grave, he found himself in disbelief at his own claims about her race. *These* were the people he claimed as being something other than human—the very people who had raised him? His doubt became an abscess, and his vindictive old Christian God meting out damnation and resurrection, victory and slavery, all this now appeared crude and senseless. Conway was in spiritual agony, and each sermon became harder for him to deliver. He pondered joining the Quakers, but upon visiting them he found that grave old Roger Brookes knew better.

"Thee will find among us a good many prejudices," the elder counseled, "for instance, against music, of which thou art fond, and while thou art mentally growing would it be well to commit thyself to any organized society?" Conway knew Brookes was right, but where else could he turn? Desperate, the pious young man wrote a letter to the minister whose essay he had read in *Blackwood's*, an essay urging truthfulness to oneself and to what one knows to be just and right: "About a year ago I commenced reading your writings. I have read them all and studied them sentence by sentence. I have shed many burning tears over them: because you would gain my assent to Laws which . . . I have not the courage to practice."

When Conway looked upon his old Southern nationalism, his defenses of slavery, his bitter Old Testament God, his heart broke: he could not believe in them anymore. But what was he to believe in instead—and how could he believe in these things *here*, in Virginia? The unseen and mysterious minister made a fateful reply:

The earth is full of frivolous people, who are bending their whole force and the force of nations on trifles, and these are baptized with every grand and holy name, remaining, of course, totally inadequate to occupy any mind: and so skeptics are made. A true soul will disdain to be moved except by what natively commands it, though it should go sad and solitary in search of its master a thousand years.

Conway read the letter again and again. *This* was what commanded him: *this* was his master. He knew what he had to do. He resigned his post and bought a train ticket to Cambridge, Massachusetts— and to a new life at the Harvard Divinity School.

The elder Conway watched his son pack his books away for school with a baleful glare. "These books that you read and are now about to multiply affect my feeling as if you were giving yourself up to excessive brandy," his father said, growing visibly upset. "I cannot assist what appears to me grievous error."

And so his father turned his back on the son's new life: all the men in Moncure's family did. Only the women came to bid him a tearful farewell at the railway station. Even his own horse, as Moncure had ridden into Falmouth, was spooked and tried to leap into the Potomac. It was as if everything in his homeland was against him. Young Moncure, not yet even twenty years old, was a spiritual and physical exile—and as the locomotive belched smoke and embers in its northward path, he thought about meeting the minister whose words were now calling him up north. Before that fateful day reading the magazine essay by a roadside spring, Conway had never heard this minister's name before; and yet he now clung to his mysterious correspondent's letters like a lifeline, a rope pulling him into a new life. In his bag he kept a published volume of his *Essays*, and pondered finally meeting the man behind the letters upon its spine: *Emerson*.

Run the footage of the life of any literary luminary of the nineteenth century, and sooner or later, the grave and bearded form of Moncure Conway will invariably walk in from one side of the frame, tip his hat, and then quietly exit from the other side. Even the first day of Conway's very first job as a teenager, penning brief satirical items for his cousin's newspaper in Richmond, he'd run into another young author leaving the newspaper office . . . Edgar Allan Poe. It might seem like a noteworthy encounter, except that his *entire life* was like that.

I lay out the other photos of box 46 like the cards of a royal flush. Moncure Conway, sitting in a shady grove with a child, chatting amiably with a bearded man: Bronson Alcott, the caption reveals. Another photo: snaps of a pleasant home and writing room, sent by a good friend—Helen Hunt Jackson. Next is a portrait of Mark Twain's children, posing outside their home in Hartford, grinning for Uncle Moncure. Then there are the photos of Conway's own children; one of these is of a frowning, blond-haired baby: ELECTRO-

PHOTOGRAPH declares the red ink on the back. Another photo of the baby, now dressed in plaid, the back simply reading: "Our little Emerson Conway." It is poignant, and it has the feel of a posthumous note—for the baby died just months later. Our little child: what else can one say? But for a man who lives out the term of his life, there is much, too much to say: so much that it gets lost in the tonnage of archival memory. Whole people can get lost. People like Moncure Conway.

I set aside the photos, and turn to my little array of boxes. Deep inside an archival box of personal effects I feel another item—not photos at all. It is wrapped in gauze and tied with a thin red ribbon; it is solid and heavy. My fingers against it detect a rounded edge through the fabric.

Could it be—could it *be?*—a bone of Thomas Paine's?

"*Queeny!*" Emerson shouted from his library door.

Moncure, nervously sitting in the philosopher's library, watched upon by wall portraits of Swedenborg and Goethe, observed Mrs. Emerson gliding into the room. Emerson was clearly touched by the great theological and geographical distance that his young protégé had traveled. My young correspondent, he informed her, has come all the way to Concord just to meet me—let us prepare the house so that he may stay a few days.

Who knows the effect one person may have on another? A simple gesture, an offhand word, an essay knocked out on a deadline: these may send a life ricocheting in a new direction, and the instigator will hardly ever know it. But maybe it did not have to be *that* gesture, *that* word—maybe someone has been waiting for anything at all to send them off. And so, as Conway earnestly recounted how profoundly he'd been moved by Emerson's essay in *Blackwood's Magazine*, the author was duly modest about it.

"When the mind has reached a certain stage," Emerson assured him, "it may sometimes be crystallized by a slight touch."

But there was something kindred in their spirits: Emerson immediately took to the exiled Southerner. When Conway expressed deep admiration for a book by the late Margaret Fuller, the philosopher immediately entrusted his young admirer with the signed copy of *Woman in the Nineteenth Century* that Fuller herself had given him. After dinner, the two men went for a stroll around Walden Pond. Conway found his mentor had reached a fairly pragmatic view of religion—a minister, Emerson supposed, was still moderately useful in the world. Not for saving souls, but "to have a conscientious man to sit on school committees, to help at town meetings, to attend the sick and the dead." As Conway mused over the fine points of Divinity School curriculum, Emerson cleared away the undergrowth of conversation with one sentence: "*An actually existent fly is more important than a possibly existent angel.*"

They passed a bush, and Emerson halted.

"Ah! There is one of the gods of the wood!"

Moncure looked disconcertedly into the thicket, and saw nothing.

"Where?" he asked.

"Did you see it?"

"No, I saw nothing—what was it?"

"No matter."

"What was it?"

"Never mind," Emerson smiled, "if you did not see it."

Puzzled—had it been a squirrel? A wood sprite?—Moncure walked on with the grinning philosopher until they stopped to rest by the ruins of an old shanty. It had been built and lived in a couple of years earlier by another student of Emerson's, a pencilmaker in the village. He was, apparently, writing a book about the experience, and they decided to pay the fellow a visit.

When Emerson and his Conway arrived at the Thoreau family residence, the gawking young student was struck by the contrast in the family. The son Henry David clearly resembled his father John Thoreau, "a kindly and silent pencil-maker," and mother Cynthia, and yet "neither parent impressed me as possessing mental qualities that could account for such a rare spirit as Henry." Perhaps, as Emerson did, the student should have been carefully examining the ground during their walk around Walden. For he would have found that there are very tenacious plants that will grow in the cracks of rocks, and in the worst sorts of soil: there is no accounting for this unless you closely examine their roots. But in mature creations these are well buried; all you can see is the bloom.

What, asked Thoreau, are you studying at Harvard?

"The Scriptures," his earnest visitor replied.

"*Which?*"

A bemused Emerson saw how this would befuddle the young Christian. "You will find our Thoreau a sad pagan," he explained.

Thoreau showed the visitor his collection of Asian theology, which he had studied assiduously. And perusing what he once would have dismissed as heathen texts, here in a New England pencilmaker's home, the ardent young Southern preacher had come to a place far from his old orthodoxy. But just how far, he would not discover until the next morning.

The man was trembling, hiding, terrified: he was hunted.

Henry David Thoreau ushered Moncure inside his house; their talk the day before of a pleasant morning walk was gone now. All was urgency and guardedness inside the Thoreau house, for in the next room, being tended by Henry's sister Sophia, was human

contraband. A *servant*, in the parlance of Conway's genteel home-
stead: an escaped slave, in everyone else's.

The fugitive looked up at Conway and recoiled in horror. *He was
from Conway's home county.* And here, in his room, was the secretary
of the Southern Rights Association. He had been betrayed!—his
masters had come to take him back! It was only with much
reassurance that Thoreau and Conway finally convinced the trembling man that he was among friends. The runaway had shown up at
Thoreau's door at dawn, seeking his stop on the Underground
Railroad. By the next morning he was on his way to Canada. And
Moncure Conway had, for perhaps the first time in his life,
witnessed a federal crime—indeed, had quietly aided and abetted it.

Finally taking their promised stroll together, Thoreau gave his
visitor his own tour around Walden Pond. Their walk was filled
with long silences punctuated by extraordinary lectures on—on
anything, really—rocks, grass, the varieties of pine needles and
the sound the wind made in them. *Walden* the book was not yet
published: here, in Walden itself, Thoreau was thinking paragraphs
aloud in front of an amazed Conway, and then conjuring natural
magic. The sly naturalist had discovered that the female bream,
quite unusually, would stay to defend its eggs: it would never flee. If
your walking companion hadn't seen the fish, you could perform a
seeming miracle. The woodsman, reaching nonchalantly into the
water, would pull out a wriggling fish with his bare hand.

Clank.

Everyone in the rare book room looks up: I look down. Un-
wrapping the gauze clumsily, this is what slid out: not bones, not
teeth, not even another framed photograph of Paine's hair. No,
it's—well—*It's something from the hardware store.*

I heft them in my hand, my brow furrowed: the pieces of metal are cold to the touch, and tarnished with age. They are a bundle of old iron keyhole plate covers, the sort of rectangular flourish you'd find screwed into the wood around the doorknob in a Victorian home. What, exactly, they are doing among the personal effects of a dead man is . . .

Nope. Haven't a clue.

I examine the plates carefully, and fish out the thick magnifying glass from my pocket. It's one of those massy glass lenses they sell with the compact edition of the OED, in order to read the microscopic print, and it's an absurd thing to carry around in your pants—but you'd be surprised how often it can come in handy in a place like this. I move the lens up and down until the smooth iron surface comes into focus. There are no fingerprint tarnishes visible on the metal; perhaps I am the first in many years, in decades even, to unwrap this piece of gauze. And there are no scratches in the metal either: you would expect stray key scratches on a doorplate, perhaps a clumsy scuff mark from a signet ring. But no: these are, or were, brand-new. They just happened to be sitting in Moncure Conway's desk when he died.

A life cut off in mid-sentence would, I suppose, leave a least a few unfinished thoughts—a nonsense syllable hanging in the air, detached from the last unspoken word. So: we have keyhole covers wrapped mysteriously in gauze and tied in red ribbon. "To Do," some scrap of Conway's daily journal might have once read, "get doors repaired." But that To Do was never To Be Done.

One thing you must do, Emerson told Conway in 1855, *is read this new book.*

It was a queer volume of poetry that Emerson had just received in the mail, from a young man that neither he nor anyone else in Concord had heard of. Visiting Emerson at his house, Conway heard him sing the praises of this mysterious Manhattan writer who had been unknown scarcely days before. As he was already about to take a steamer down to New York anyway, Conway assured Emerson that he'd visit the fellow, and serve as Concord's first emissary to this newcomer.

Moncure read the book on board the *Metropolis*, where the chug of the engine and the lap of its paddlewheel kept time with the poet's cadence and meter: and as the poet spanned over vast reaches of land, Conway could see the fertile landscape of America passing by on the shore. By the time he stepped off at New York Harbor, Conway was convinced—he had to find the man who had written this. Perusing a city directory, he saw he had a long commute before him. First he rode the Fulton Street ferry over to Brooklyn; then it was on to the Myrtle Avenue omnibus until nearly the end of the line, almost into Long Island itself. He hopped down off the bus and examined a row of small wooden houses along Ryerton Street before finally knocking on a door. An older woman answered: it was the poet's mother. He's not here, she told him—go back the way you came, to Rome's Printing Office at Fulton and Cranberry. So he made the trek back, and strode into the printer's office.

"I found him revising some proof," Conway wrote to Emerson that night. "A man you would not have marked in a thousand; a blue striped shirt, opening from a red throat; and sitting on a chair without a back, which, being the only one, he offered me, and sat down on a round of the printer's desk himself . . . He seemed very eager to hear from you and about you, and what you thought of his book."

He was blunt yet friendly—blithely informing Conway that "you think too much of books," and yet smiling when telling Conway that "he had heard of his poems being offered for sale by a vendor of obscene books." The poet jauntily accompanied him back across the

East River on the Fulton Street ferry, to take a stroll around Manhattan. "He rides on the stage with the driver," Conway wrote Emerson. "Stops to talk with the old man or woman selling fruit at the street corner. And his dress etc., is consistent with that . . . He is clearly his Book."

The two men parted with a promise to meet for dinner the next day. When the poet showed up at the Metropolitan Hotel for dinner, he was dressed in a baize coat and checkered shirt—"In fact," Conway reported delightedly, "just like the portrait in his book." The book was still so new that these probably were indeed the very clothes he had posed in. And if Conway was delighted with his new friend, so was the poet with the attention he was now receiving. *You see*, he told Conway, *you are the first person to visit me about this book.*

In a sense, news of his character had already preceded him. The fellow had, after all, included his entire phrenological chart in his book of poems, convinced that to understand the one you needed to read the other. "You are in fact most too open at times and have not always enough restraint in your speech," Lorenzo Fowler wrote in a chart dated July 16, 1849. "You have a good command of language especially if excited." Atop his diagnosis was inked in the name and employment of this fateful patient:

W. Whitman, Age 29, Occupation Printer

Visiting Whitman's neighborhood again, Conway wrote, "I found him at the top of a hill nearby lying on his back and gazing at the sky." The poet was now hard at work on the second edition of *Leaves of Grass*: when Whitman made pilgrimages out to 308 Broadway, it was to go over page proofs, as the newest author signed to the fearless phrenological publishing house of Fowler & Wells.

The two walked back to Whitman's house, where they were let in by the poet's apprehensive-looking mother: once inside, Conway saw the true humbleness of the place. It was a small frame house, and Whitman's room held little more than a cot and a couple of cheap engravings. "What he brought me up there to see," Conway mused, "was the barren solitude stretching from beneath his window toward the sea." And so they went to the sea—loafing for the day around Staten Island, finding empty coves where they could swim about freely, and where Conway saw the Poet of the Body's . . . well, body. He had a farmer's tan: "I perceive that the reddish tanned face and neck of the poet crowned a body of lily-like whiteness."

As they lolled about and talked, Conway came to see Whitman as someone much like himself. They had come into their literary lives by accident, and against the odds. Indeed, Whitman had no books in his bedroom at all, and none to his name save a volume of Shakespeare and another of Homer. Yet he thirsted for knowledge, and haunted libraries. Both men had been deeply moved by Hicksite Quaker teachings. Though Walt himself was too exuberant and searching to be contained by any one religion, his parents had been Hicksites of the original stamp: Elias Hicks was still preaching when Walt was a child, and he remembered attending meetings and being deeply impressed by the man who opponents still labeled a Deist and a disciple of Tom Paine. "Others talk of Bibles, saints, churches, exhortations, vicarious atonements," he recalled later, "—the canons outside yourself and apart from man—Elias Hicks to the religion inside of every man's own nature." What Hicks practiced, Walt noted approvingly, was a "naked theology."

This was indeed what both men were now seeking for themselves. And moreover, both had been profoundly jarred loose from their social moorings by the moral crisis of slavery. Whitman told Conway that, as an old loyal Democratic editor and journalist, he'd left his party with the passage of the Fugitive Slave Law—and was thus moved to write "Blood Money," which he considered his first real poem. It was the Fugitive Slave Law that fired Whitman's poetry and, Conway later wrote, "It was the Fugitive Slave Law that began the war . . . [it] brought slavery in its most odious form to the door of every family."

Soon enough it came to his own door. Conway found himself near abolitionism's white-hot center with the capture in Boston of Anthony Burns, an escaped Virginia slave whose return had been demanded by his owner. Bostonians were having none of it: antislavery mobs surrounded the federal courthouse where Burns was imprisoned, determined to block any attempt to send him home. The square was packed: Conway, accompanied by a new school acquaintance—a droll fellow named Oliver Wendell Holmes—found that they could not get into the courthouse. There was real impending violence and revolt in the air, and after Conway and Holmes left, one federal marshal was killed as the crowd tried to rush in. The situation only worsened from there: when Conway met with other antislavery activists the next day, he noticed editor Thomas Wentworth Higginson holding his cloak across his mouth, stanching the flow of blood. "He had been wounded," Conway realized, "by a cutlass on his lip and his neck."

Events were spinning out of control, and suspicion was everywhere: indeed, Holmes, with whom he had tried to run the courthouse gauntlet, had even been wary of Conway himself, describing him in private as "Virginia-born, with seventeen secesh cousins, father, and other relatives." He was right, of course, but when Southerners at Harvard held a meeting to support slaveholder Captain Suttle, Conway infuriated them by refusing to attend.

This was no hypothetical conflict to Conway: *he knew Suttle*. He had known the captain since childhood. And Conway also knew what an escaped slave looked like. Talk of reenslaving Burns, and mob talk of stringing up Suttle—into which one group of men had quietly tried to enlist Conway—all of this appalled him. Burns and Suttle were not symbols to him: they were not mere pawns in a national conflict. They were *human beings*. Suttle was on the verge of being assassinated, while Conway heard from those tending to Burns that the freed slave was also terrified, and wanted safe return to Virginia. Both men were now in fear for their lives, of being killed by those who claimed to know what was best for the country. And both sides now looked on Conway with suspicion.

Conway was brooding in Harvard Yard when he saw his mentor walking across the quadrangle.

"I am misunderstood," he told Emerson plainly.

"To be great," the philosopher reminded him, "is to be misunderstood."

They walked together across the yard, Conway pouring out how unsure he was of his beliefs, and even of his own direction in life. Emerson turned thoughtful and a little nostalgic as they walked through the grounds of his alma mater. He confided to Conway that after graduation he himself had only aspired to be a professor of rhetoric. But some fates, some gifts, and some struggles are thrust upon one: old aspirations fall aside for new ones.

Conway did not know what to hope for anymore. He was as pained by his friends as by his opponents. At an abolitionist meeting on Independence Day, voices rose to a fever pitch with shouts of "Amen!" ringing out as Sojourner Truth and Thoreau spoke; Conway watched as William Lloyd Garrison ascended the podium, holding up a copy of the U.S. Constitution. It was, Garrison announced, a "covenant with death and agreement with hell." He set it afire and brandished the burning paper, roaring: "*So perish all compromises with tyranny!*"

Conway sickened with dread. Years earlier he had come to realize that the South was on the wrong path, but now he felt the North was too. To be against slavery was one thing, but to unilaterally abolish it implied force. Abolitionism was becoming the hellfire and brimstone that he had fled from before, only in a new guise, for both relied on demons and vengeance. "That day I distinctly realized that the antislavery cause was a religion," he later wrote. "Slavery was not death, and the South was not hell . . . I knew good people on both sides. I also believed that slavery was to be abolished by the union of all hearts and minds opposed to it." Conway was against the forcible deprivation of a fellow man's freedom, but he was also against violence—and he now lived in a country that no longer accepted that the one ethical belief must logically entail the other.

In their first walk together around Walden Pond, Thoreau had paused to pull up a peculiar blade of grass. He told Moncure to chew it.

"It is a little sharp," Thoreau explained, "but an experience."

The same could be said for Conway's own life by the late 1850s. He moved on from Harvard: graduated, married, had children, rose in the Unitarian ministry. But the same old problems dogged him. He was invited to a wealthy congregation in Washington, scourged them from the pulpit on the injustice of slavery, and was then invited to leave. He moved restlessly to Cincinnati, which proved a more genial place after the rancor of Washington. It was a city swelling with German immigrants and new Continental philosophies, where he could mingle with reverends and rabbis alike.

He found himself curiously drawn to one in particular, the undogmatic and inquisitive Rabbi Isaac Wise. Often invited to lecture and dine with various members of the synagogue, Conway slowly reached a startling realization: "The majority of Rabbi Wise's synagogue were not believers in supernaturalism at all, but simple deists." Conway had, without realizing it, stumbled into the American birthplace of Reform Judaism. Many in Wise's temple had—like Emerson and Franklin years before—quietly come to the conclusion that a house of worship was a good and useful thing, if not an especially divine thing, and that its traditions and responsibilities served as a cultural and social glue for the community. But a brooding sky-God? Received truth and divine retribution? . . . Eh.

If he brought to their community meetings his exotic knowledge of the Transcendentalists of Concord, in return they pressed two newly translated German philosophers into his hands: Georg Hegel and David Strauss. These were a revelation to Conway, as much as—maybe more than—the Bible itself had ever been. Hegelian dialectic, with its argumentative clash of thesis and antithesis merging into synthesis, argued directly against received and immutable Truth: finding any truth was a *process* of argument, a changing and fleeting thing. "We perceive in Nature tremendous contrasts, awful struggles," Strauss wrote, "but we discover that these do not disturb the stability and harmony of the whole,—that, on the contrary, they preserve it."

A reasonable-sounding premise, but it was one profoundly opposed to any religious dogma. What, then, was a minister nodding his head in agreement supposed to do? Well, not much, at first: how much would parishioners trouble themselves over German epistemology? But what Hegel's fine-sounding words *meant* soon became clear, when the latest shipment of British books reached Conway's hands. As an occasional editor and reviewer for a local magazine, he saw them before almost anyone else in Cincinnati. But one volume in this shipment stood above anything else. He read it, and ascended to his pulpit a changed man yet again. That December day in 1859, his parishioners got the shock of their religious lives.

"This formidable man . . ." he said, indicating a modest-looking octavo volume that none of them had heard of yet, "did not intend to give Dogmatic Christianity its deathblow; he meant to utter a simple theory of nature. But henceforth all temples not founded on the rock of natural science are on the sand where the angry tides are setting in." That tide took away much of his congregation, who were appalled by the new book he held in his hand—*The Origin of Species*—and by its notion that everything, including *humanity*, was mutable. Conway's congregation fractured, with the traditionalists moving to a different building altogether.

But Darwin was only the beginning—or, perhaps, the beginning of a clergyman's end. An even more explosive book had already been quietly pressed into the minister's hands by his Jewish friends.

It is a fact that if you want to be left alone on the subway, all you need to do is read a really beat-up old book. A new book won't work—quite the opposite. It must be old, and it needn't even be that wretched-looking. Sure, you can go the full distance and can have a ragged old Bible held together with rubber bands, and hold it in your lap where you stroke it and mutter to it like a pet—I have seen this—and I guarantee you will indeed have that seat on the A train all to yourself. But really, any old book is enough: no theatrics are needed. People don't trust old books, books with browned and yellowed pages, books with scuffed century-old covers . . . or, at least, they don't trust the sort of fellow who would read one on a train.

You think I am joking—but try it sometime.

I root through my backpack and pull out of my bag the shabbiest, oldest-looking book imaginable. Its covers were once a pleasant marbled green, but now worn down to a barklike wooden color; every single page inside is water-stained brown. It appears to have been left in the bottom of a pond, then dragged behind a cart, and finally thrown off a high cliff. There are bore holes in the cover so old that the worms who made them were long ago eaten by other worms. It is, in short, the most disreputable old book you or I have ever seen. I bought it from a man who mused that selling the thing saved him the trouble of throwing it away.

"I can well remember," the critic Augustine Birrell wrote a century ago, "when an asserted intimacy with the writings of Thomas Paine marked a man from his fellows and invested him in children's minds with a horrible fascination. The writings themselves were only seen in bookshops of an evil reputation, and, when hastily turned over with furtive glances, proved to be printed in small type and on villainous paper."

Villainous paper: yes. This paper is so degenerate that even the binding ran away from it years ago, until some man—and it *had* to be a man—had the bright notion of rebinding its spine with duct tape. It's actually a very neat rebinding job, as duct tape projects go. I run my finger along the silver tape, and then open the book carefully:

The Life of Thomas Paine
by G. Vale
New York: Published by the Author
Citizen of the World Office, No. 1 Bowery
1853

The subway begins to move forward, and—well, I have my seat all to myself.

This copy is not much to look at now, but it was Vale's book that fell into Moncure Conway's hands in Cincinnati over 140 years ago. His unlikely benefactor in this was none other than the salacious

Quaker City novelist George Lippard, for Vale had been sitting on this Paine manuscript for years until Lippard's revival of interest in Paine revealed a real need for a new biography. "There are four lives of Mr. Thomas Paine now extant," Vale's book begins, "but none in print in the United States." The first biography had been penned by a hired character assassin on the British government's payroll, and the only American biography had been written over forty years earlier by a man Paine himself had derided as an "idiot" and an "unprincipled bully." To which his biographer responded, *"Likewise,"* for about another hundred pages.

The lecherous brandy-guzzling bomb-throwing God-hating pervert described in hostile biographies was not the man Conway found in the volumes his freethinking friends in Cincinnati were reading, nor in the eyewitness accounts Gilbert Vale had collected. Even Paine's demise had a strangely legendary feel of truth lost to allegory, what with his bones having been dug up by an admirer and then disappearing somewhere in England. Some children were taught that Paine's bones had been turned into shirt buttons, now scattered and doomed to roam the globe with their multitudes of owners. "I discovered that in his legend," Conway mused, "there were traces of the old folktales of the Wandering Jew."

Conway's greatest work now lay in uncovering the man he discovered in these books, and in tracking down his eventual fate. For the Paine he discovered was a one-time lay preacher who had come to distrust religion; a rationalist who demanded proof before tradition; a principled exile who had left behind exasperated friends from both sides of a mighty battle over freedom. Vale's book is not much to look at now, but it is easy to see why Conway was so moved by it. In the story of Paine, the minister had discovered his own.

*   *   *

A long dark rattling: we are crossing over the water, and stare blindly out at the night. These are the same waters that Moncure Conway glided down in 1863, standing on the deck of the *City of Washington* as he left his old country for a new life in London. There was nothing in America, really, for a man who preached emancipation to the South and pacifism to the North. He'd left a White House meeting with Abraham Lincoln exasperated by the president's diffidence toward the fate of blacks, and angered by Lincoln's resort to violence against the South. Conway had seen his family's Virginia manor half ruined and turned into a field hospital; he'd witnessed his old Washington church converted into a Union armory. His own brothers were Confederate officers, and they were fighting Union soldiers led by his best friends and classmates from Harvard.

There was nothing to do but leave.

Conway kept among his belongings a memento of just about the only literary titan he had *not* met before leaving the United States: it was Emerson's copy of *Woman in the Nineteenth Century*. Conway's fondness for Fuller was no surprise to anyone who had seen the minister stalking the streets of Cincinnati to gather information on local wages for clerks and teachers; comparing the men's and women's wages, he complained loudly in print that the two were paid unequally. The more Conway pondered slaves, and violence, and the freedoms written about by Thomas Paine, the more he had found that he could not avert his eyes from the plight of women in American society—and the more he turned to Margaret Fuller.

Inside the book's cover were three initials—*M.F.O.*—Margaret Fuller Ossoli. This was *her* book that he held. And below that, another name in a different hand: "Ralph Waldo Emerson—3 May 1853." It was Fuller's own copy of her masterpiece, sent to her preceptor Emerson—and Emerson, in turn, had given it to his new protégé the first day they met. Held in her own hands, then in Emerson's, and now in his own. It was as close to her as Conway could ever hope to get, for three years before the young Virginian arrived in Concord, Fuller and her husband and newborn child were lost within sight of New York, as the boat *Elizabeth* sank in the frigid waters of Long Island Sound. It had been carrying a cargo of 150 tons of Italian statuary marble; when the vessel struck a sandbar, the blocks shifted and tore out the bottom of the boat. Fuller sang to her baby as water flooded into the holds and over the tombstone marble—they sank with their own fatal monument—and her husband led the other doomed passengers in a final prayer. Thoreau rushed to New York to seek her among the few survivors, and was left an utterly stricken man; he went searching again and again, inconsolably, along the beaches of Fire Island for any trace of her or her last manuscript. It is one of the saddest stories of American literature.

But . . .

I draw out from the back of my copy of Vale's life of Paine a single folded photocopy: an old newspaper article. You find the most curious items in old papers. This one—from the *New York Herald* of May 28, 1893—has a story picked up by a roving reporter from an aged fisherman. The old salt had, in his younger days, been on the nearby beach when the *Elizabeth* foundered. A few days later, as submerged bodies swelled with putrescence, floated, and then washed ashore, the fisherman witnessed Fuller's friends—possibly Thoreau, or even her editors Horace Greeley and Orson Fowler— coming to make their somber visit to view the victims:

> Among these was a woman's corpse, hideously disfigured, wave beaten, fish eaten, a grisly horror to the eye. But it had two very curiously shaped teeth, stopped with gold in a peculiar fashion,

which were known to have characterized Margaret Fuller. And besides she had been the only woman on the bark. When her friends came down to look, as soon as the report of the bodies washed ashore reached New York, and they saw the awful thing vomited up from the jaws of the ocean, they recoiled shuddering, and utterly refused to admit that it could be Margaret Fuller . . . So, dishonoured and rejected of all, the sea-battered remains of what had probably been Margaret Fuller were sent to New York and buried in Potter's Field among paupers, tramps, and outcasts.

I fold the paper and slide it back into my old book. Fuller died an Italian revolutionary, and she may well have been buried with the poor and the forgotten. It's the grave she herself might have picked.

Paine and Fuller alike—these two heroes of Conway's, these idealistic parents of American free thought—both had disappeared in death, so that only their ideas remained. I wonder, as he sailed out of New York Harbor, if the minister thought of Fuller dying within sight of land: whether he pondered his own death someday: whether he clasped that book a little tighter with the very hands that one day would also hold the final remains of Thomas Paine. Whether he knew where *he* would wind up. Whether he could ever have guessed at that terrible last viewing of Fuller. But our effects are preserved— those that are deemed meaningful, at least. The rest is thrown away, it is buried, and it is altered beyond any recognition.

Comfort for the Ruptured

"YEAH?" HE SAYS.

It's bitter cold out on Twenty-eighth Street, and the Chinese truck driver stops and looks warily at his overloaded produce truck, and then at me next to it; I am leaning against the No Parking sign and jotting into my little notebook. He is trying to decide if I'm some sort of plainclothes meter maid.

I smile as blandly as I can and move on. I need a better look into this building anyway. The windows of 120 Lexington Avenue are pretty well obscured by signs—paper and neon alike—shilling for the warren of different businesses wedged into the premises. There is a 110/220 volt appliance store, a dry cleaners, a newly opened restaurant bearing the puzzling name Chinese Mirch, and atop all this an Indian video store. The latter features a dotted damsel's come-hither poster advertising *The Return of the Kaanta Mix*—a title which, at first glance, I mistook for the appetizer of the day at Chinese Mirch.

It was an afternoon in 1879—cold and shivery, much like this one—when a scrawny young man stood here as well, and ventured into the 120 Lexington entranceway. There was only one business for him to call upon back then, one outspoken man whose prosperity had made this address the byword of innumerable books, flyers, and newspaper ads across the country. He was here, the nervous visitor told the doorboy, to see the famed physician and author Dr. Edward B. Foote.

The visitor—he had identified himself as J. Peters, of Newark—was shown into the doctor's office, where a stenographer and a secretary both sat at the ready for dictation from the Great Man. Working from his elegant offices, E. B. Foote ran a business that was a marvel of vertical integration: he was the author and publisher of his medical theories, the doctor who prescribed his own remedies, and the manufacturer and mail-order distributor of those very same medicines. One floor of his headquarters was largely occupied by secretarial staff answering bags of mail from beseeching elderly invalids, young married couples, and book agents in London and Berlin. On another floor his botanical laboratories hummed along, fed by a hydraulic freight elevator that ferried herbs up and elixirs back down; toiling inside rooms fireproofed by six inches of concrete, medical assistants churned out priceless miracle cures to be shipped around the country and around the world.

But where was the doctor himself? The fidgeting visitor had to be kept waiting for a while. Foote was nowhere to be found within his offices: he was upstairs, in his own tastefully appointed quarters. Rather than dictating his newest medical guide for the masses, the fifty-year-old physician was dutifully reading to his aged mother. But at length a hale, mustachioed man came down the stairs, and seeing that there was little privacy in the office with his staff amanuenses hurrying about, he led his new patient into a back office. Foote pulled a sliding door closed on the private consultation room, settled down and motioned his patient to take a seat.

His visitor glared at him.

"Do you recognize me?"

No, the doctor replied. No, he didn't know him at all.

What happened next came in a blur: the patient drew out a .38-caliber revolver from his coat, and leveled it at the doctor's chest. Foote sprang across the room; doctor and patient went crashing to the floor, struggling for the weapon, as the would-be victim jammed a finger in front of the hammer to try to keep it from firing.

"Give me the pistol!" the doctor yelled.

Bang.

The physician staggered away, and the mysterious gunman fled through a back balcony, over a fence, and down Twenty-eighth Street. Doctor Foote collapsed into a nearby sofa. Blood was spattered across the carpet and furniture of the future headquarters of the Thomas Paine National Historical Association—in its consultation rooms, on the file cabinets, and smeared upon the balcony windows.

Now, here's a question that probably forms in the head of any man not long after a gun has been fired at him: how did I get here? To this particular place, I mean. I started as a child running around a backyard and climbing trees, and sifting the dirt and pine needles through my fingers in the summertime: what happened? *What am I doing here with this bullet?*

Who knows just when our youthful predilections and impressions throw out those filaments that will attach the playing child to the working man? What chance event, out of all the millions that occur in half-remembered days, will later cause an adult to look back and say: "Here. *That* is where I started." A historian may guess, but that is all it really is—a guess. We ourselves barely remember our own origins: how can anyone else hope to divine them? So perhaps—I say *perhaps*—it had all begun when the future wealthy doctor of Manhattan was growing up in the 1830s outside Cleveland, and his father hosted three of the famous Beecher clan in his house one Sunday.

Herschel Foote was a prosperous local merchant and town postmaster, and so all curious and learned strangers passing through were liable to meet him: the Foote household was "literally a free hotel for ministers, school teachers, and singing masters." Even as the strict Presbyterian father imbued the young Edward with a sense that reformers like Thomas Paine were little short of an instrument of Satan, it would be hard not to sense the currents of change in respectable visitors like the Beechers, especially now that Henry Ward Beecher and his sister Harriet had both moved nearby. And perhaps the father's exhortations were a lost cause in any case, for Edward was an odd child who nursed some rather strange hobbies. "Pill-making entered conspicuously into the diversions in which I indulged," he later recalled, "and facetious neighbors dignified the contents of my juvenile waistcoat with title of 'Doctor.'"

At the age of twelve a copy of Franklin's *Autobiography* fell into the would-be doctor's hands. Foote was fascinated by it. Paine's old mentor was not just a self-made man, he was *the* self-made man of all time: a runaway boy turned Founding Father. His autobiography was like an epistle from the past to boys stranded in pious and sleepy American towns, transporting them to the far shores of Humanism as surely as Franklin's letter tucked into Paine's pocket had once transported that bankrupt grocer to the shores of the New World. And young Edward took Franklin's message to heart. As he grew to be a teenager and was charged with finding himself a profession, he decided to become a printer's devil in Cleveland. He might as well have announced that he had become the *Devil's* devil. But his parents' disapproval could only make the job more appealing to his independent turn of mind.

It was there at the print shop, amid the presses and worn trays of type, that he came across a book by the very man his father had warned him against: *Common Sense*, its cover proclaimed. As he read, he saw Paine sweep away tradition and precedence with a wave of the hand: new politics for a new world, Paine said. The young man who had filled his pockets with homemade pills sat in Cleveland and pondered this inquisitive mind that would not defer to any self-proclaimed authority. New politics for the new world . . . why not new medicine? And so Edward did what one always expects in any incipient American writer and radical—yes—it *is* inevitable, isn't it? He moved to New York.

But then, so had his assassin.

The man who called himself J. Peters, of Newark, stood in a newly rented room of his Fourth Avenue walk-up. His name was not Peters; he was not from Newark. And he had not come to *live* in this boardinghouse. He was deciding whether to kill himself. He'd meant to do it yesterday, or the day before, but he kept putting it off.

It had taken two days to even get out of bed after the attack. His hand kept bleeding and bleeding. It was not fair that his hand should keep bleeding like this: he had come to commit the straightforward act of emptying every chamber of his brand-new .38, which he just had paid good money for, into Dr. E. B. Foote. But the revolver fired off only once; it was his own blood that had been smeared all over Foote's office.

New York papers that breathlessly recounted the strange attack simply mentioned the victim as the "eclectic physician." Foote needed no introduction to the newspaper's readers: his story had already been immortalized in innumerable pamphlets, popular encyclopedias, and *Who's Who* entries. They always noted how his road to medicine had passed through the print shop first— and how, after becoming the precocious twenty-year-old editor of the *Brooklyn Morning Journal*, Foote fatefully undertook the study of medicine. In those years, if you saw a bearded and bohemian

Brooklyn newspaper editor walking down Ryerton Street, absorbed in reading a volume of Fowler's *Practical Phrenology*, you'd have been forgiven for calling out the wrong name in greeting. It could have been one of two men—Walt Whitman, or E. B. Foote.

Just as literature was having its American Renaissance, the medical profession was experiencing explosive growth in the 1850s. A relatively uncommon and orthodox profession was invaded by middle-class students, becoming a warren of competing self-styled medical colleges, from those of conventional anatomists to the anti-intellectual rumblings of homeopathy. Arcane sects of Indian bonesetting and "chrono-thermalism" sprang up like mushrooms. One of the greatest iconoclasts was the botanical therapist Samuel Thomson, whose almost cultlike followers ceaselessly attacked conventional medicine as an elitist monopoly hiding behind obscure Latin terminology. *Their* medicine used plain English . . . and the enthusiastic therapeutic use of cayenne pepper.

Foote was fascinated, never dedicating himself entirely to any one movement, but brilliantly retrieving their most provocative aspects like a medical magpie. Moving to Saratoga Springs, a spa town beloved by hypochondriacs everywhere, Foote studied more and more deeply into the works of Orson Fowler—the very same man who, like his would-be author Paine, sought to remake the world anew. Fired up by the works of both, Foote set about writing down a manifesto, his own philosophy of health. And so it was that in 1858 his curious medical tract began to show up on bookseller shelves across the country.

Which brings us to our suicidal boarder on Fourth Avenue, Mr. J. Peters of Newark. Before he became a gunman, the hapless assassin was once a timid Hartford barber named August Woehler. In Foote's work this young man had eagerly read what he thought was his salvation. Nor had he been the only one to be struck by

Foote's new book. For those who knew their history, the book's title had a strangely familiar ring.

Medical Common Sense.

Think of how many lives were altered at this address—lives whose unchanged course meant that you or I might not be here, or that someone else, nonexistent today, might be sitting in our place. Think of ailing men and women dragging themselves in, desperate for one last hope of a cure. Think of Manchurian Prawns, seasoned in crushed garlic.

"Hot and sour soup," I tell the waiter at Chinese Mirch.

Millions of books, pamphlets, and letters issued forth from this building. How many, I wonder, have ever made the trip back? I reach into my backpack, and pull out the ancient, faded chocolate brown volume. *Murray Hill Publishing, 120 Lexington Avenue,* it informs me. Perhaps this is the first to make the journey home. One thinks of a salmon swimming back upstream to spawn and die: but books spawn out in the world, among readers unseen and unknown to the publisher, and one never really knows when they are dead, or even how many progeny they left.

I set the prodigal book upon the table and start paging through it. "Rebels of the Year 1900 Against Old King Custom," reads one caption below a crude engraving of three smiling liberated ladies of the future. Yes, they are liberated!—and not just from King George. No, they have been liberated from King Tom, King Dick, and King Harry—from their husbands—and thus from bad marriages, from unwanted pregnancies, and from unequal pay. *Medical Common Sense* was an extraordinarily ambitious book, covering every ailment from yeast infections to stomach cancer, but Foote's 1858 book also went on to take a stand no less unthinkable to many Americans than Paine's own *Common Sense* had been:

BUSINESS AVOCATIONS SHOULD BE OPEN TO
FEMALES.

One prolific cause of unhappy marriages, is the limited sphere
allowed females in which to exercise their ingenuity and talents
for self-maintenance . . . Much has already been written con-
cerning the poor pay females receive in the limited branches of
industry which social despotism allows them to pursue, and I
shall not here dwell on the subject. I will only advise, nay, urge
ladies to crowd themselves into all business pursuits for which
they are physically qualified . . . that they may become less
dependent upon their legal protectors, and be enabled to live
lives of "single blessedness" rather than unite themselves to
disagreeable masses of masculine blood and bones . . .

But what if you had already married one of these disagreeable
masses of man-flesh? Not to worry: men had their uses. In a section
on "The Philosophy of Intercourse," Foote explains that, thanks to
animal magnetism, the opposite sexes quite literally kept each other
charged up.

This wasn't the first time that the healthy presence of the
opposite sex had such a vogue in a medical treatise. A strange little
octavo volume titled *Hermippus Redivivus* appeared in London in
1743: it related how two patients had achieved the ages of 115 and
155, respectively. Their secret? Gasping in the breath of young boys
and girls—especially the girls. Vital fluid permeated their lungs, it
claimed, and the author had himself procured it from "servant girls,
and liquefied in glass instruments curved like trumpets . . . Life may
be easily prolonged over a hundred years, for this vapour of breath
collected from maidens in trumpets, when distilled, becomes an
elixir of life." Unfortunately for the many doctors who got giddy
with excitement over his book—one physician even moved into a

girl's boarding school, to stay close to the best air in town—
Hermippus Redivivus was an immense and splendid hoax.

E. B. Foote's notion, at least, sounded like it had a little more
science to it. After all, hadn't galvanism shown that our bodies ran
on electrical impulses? Intercourse was a veritable spinning dynamo,
Foote announced, generating "frictional energy" between men and
women. This was why lonely singles resorted to masturbation: it was
precisely the same action, he noted, as rubbing a piece of flannel
back and forth across a piece of amber to get a little static shock.
Sadly, Foote never explains why masturbation wouldn't therefore
shoot bolts of lightning from between your legs and make your hair
stand on end.

Some genteel Victorian readers might be forgiven for having *their*
hair standing on end after reading Foote. Yet others would find it
familiar reading indeed, for he admiringly quoted for pages at a time
from none other than Orson Fowler. Phrenology was a key element
to Foote's medical advice. He firmly believed that needless marriages—and all the unhappiness, and death in childbirth that
attended them—were a plague upon womankind. So if a woman
was going to have a man, she needed the *right* man. But how could
you determine a proper match? Foote knew: "Does the reader ask
how? I reply, by doing away with the present rotten system for
legalizing marriage, and substituting therefore *a Board of Phrenologists and Physiologists in every county seat.*" Under Foote's plan,
divorce would be made easy but marriage difficult, for the screening
tests would result in such perfectly matched mates that divorces
wouldn't happen much anyway. Assuming your mate had the right
sort of skull—a bump to complement your every lump—then all
that remained for marital happiness was one last step that was
downright unheard of in Foote's time. "Every married man should
confide to his wife the real condition of his finances," Foote

lectured. "It is high time that men began to appear to the wives exactly what they are, pecunarily, morally, and socially."

Common financial sense, perhaps. But was it *Medical Common Sense?* To Foote, it was indeed. Unhappy unemployed women meant nervous prostration and sedentary illness. And if the family finances were open, men couldn't sneak off to squander money on prostitutes: ergo, less syphilis. Their wives, apprised of the true tightness of funds, might not approve of debilitating cigars and steaks. You start to see at this point why Foote seemed to have a greater following among women readers than men. But change a fellow's insides, Foote thought, and you will change their outside conduct as well. "Gross minds beget gross ideas," he warned, "—[they] demand gross food and gross remedies." Fill them with healthy food and healthy remedies, and healthy thoughts might well follow.

What exactly was healthy proved to be debatable. Amid sensible pronouncements on drinking plenty of water, getting lots of exercise and plenty of fresh air, there were thundering condemnations against condiments and the role they played in sex. Their spiciness incited immorality and thus contributed toward prostitution, you understand.

Well, *I'm* certainly not feeling very randy. I do, however, feel the need to patronize a Kidde fire extinguisher, or maybe some of that foaming gel that they spray onto burning airplanes.

"Water," I cough. "Thank you."

I regard my hot and sour soup as it is taken away almost uneaten. Perhaps I should have bothered reading the italicized description in the Chinese Mirch menu: *A fiery creation.* It is at moments like this that memories of my old elementary school report cards come back to haunt me. "Does Not Pay Attention." And: "Does Not Follow Instructions."

I slump back into the squeaky bamboo chair, humiliated. Spices? My God, Foote's old headquarters are now a veritable den of Szechuan iniquity. He'd be scandalized. But then, a lot scandalized him. In addition to spicy food, the doctor did not approve of other habits as seemingly innocuous as children sleeping in the same bed as their parents. The reason—as with nearly everything in Foote— involved animal magnetism. The effect of putting a child and an adult in the same bed was like putting a new battery and a dead battery together. "Children, compared with adults, are electrically in a positive condition," he explained. Completing a circuit with an adult would literally drain them. "See to it," Foote warned parents, "that his nervous vitality is not absorbed by some diseased or aged relative." Or, for that matter, by a crazy doctor trying to catch his breath in a glass trumpet.

Foote also rather cryptically forbids children from standing on their heads.

Yet some of Foote's *Common Sense* was so far ahead of the world of 1858 that its work remains unfinished even today. Like Thoreau and Fowler, he shook his head over Americans killing themselves with overwork, all for luxuries that they didn't actually need in the first place. He berated readers for artificial lighting that was creating a generation of night owls living in sleep-deprived "nervous irrita-tion," and for the tight lacing and impractical fashions that were hindering women's health and welfare. Tobacco was poisoning the nation, he warned, and "Fast eating, a universal habit with Anglo-Americans," was wreaking havoc on the public's diet.

Indeed, meals were of a special concern to the doctor. He boasted of his three-year-old son Edward Jr.'s vegetarian diet, one that sounds pretty appealing after you read Daddy's stories of filthy abattoirs where worm-ridden livestock have tumors "that when laid open by the knife, purulent matter gushes out." Foote was also strongly against artificial colors and flavorings in food, and no wonder: in his era coal tar gas was used to create pineapple flavoring, and unregulated dyes flourished. When used externally in striped stockings, some dyes even created banded skin eruptions running up the legs. One can only imagine the ornamental patterns they wrought upon the guts of young children as they ate pretty green arsenite-of-copper lollipops and dazzling blue ferrocyanide hard candies. Foote's uncommon notions, it seemed, were pretty sensible after all.

Consider this diligent doctor eagerly rereading Paine's works. Here was a man pondering a reformist Founding Father who took on nothing less than the greatest issues of the day: gods and kings. How could a Manhattan doctor possibly follow in footsteps like those?

Consider this question as you sit on the toilet.

Really. In fact, consider it as you sit on the hopper at Chinese Mirch, or at any number of other Manhattan restrooms. Should you have brought reading matter into the Chinese Mirch restroom with you, you'll have noticed that in today's paper there is an insert by Home Depot advertising American Standard toilets in the Champion line. We are informed:

29 Golf Balls in One Flush!

Now, while this is not a new ploy—rival manufacturer Koehler has rather pointedly flushed two pounds of cocktail sausages down their model—there *is* something appealing in the notion that, should the fancy grab you, you could pour a bucket of Titleists down a magic portal that whisks them out to the East River.

But in the 1870s, this was deadly serious stuff. For a mid-century Victorian reformer, there were two obvious impediments to human happiness, two forces creating more misery, illness, and death than any other. The first was pregnancy. The second was the natural result of that fecundity: sewage. Fish inspectors surveying Britain in 1867 found, in that soot-blackened country, that as many rivers were poisoned by human sewage as by coal waste. America's cities were quickly finding themselves in an equally dire situation. Cities were becoming a stinking and fetid morass of their own wastes, breeding typhus, yellow fever, and dysentery. Victorians became justly fearful of the "miasma" around ponds, gutters, and cesspools, and ineffectually sprayed carbolic acid and swigged useless alcoholic patent medicines to no avail.

So readers of *Harper's* magazine would have been delighted to find an ad like this one in 1871:

The Wakefield
EARTH CLOSET,
IS by all means the *best* yet patented.
Send to WAKEFIELD EARTH CLOSET CO., 36 Dey St., NY,
for Descriptive pamphlet,
or call and examine.

And the principal of this company? Why, Dr. E. B. Foote.

It is one of those happily juvenile accidents of history that while the greatest seller of water closets in Britain was one Thomas Crapper, the earth closet salesman at 36 Dey Street was named Asa Butts. Ah, where would the world be without its Butts and Crappers? Graced with far fewer restrooms, to be sure. Yet Butts had more to bring to the job than a melodious name: he was also known as the publisher of the progressive magazine *Truth Seeker*. To put this in modern terms: imagine finding the publisher of the *Nation* working the floor of an American Standard showroom.

What would draw wild-eyed reformers to such a prosaic thing as selling commodes? For one thing, sewage was still—I use this phrase advisedly—up for grabs. Today we naturally equate toilets with running water; Victorians did not. Impractical early water closets had been tried out in Britain, including a "slop system" with a tipper tank collecting sink and rainwater until it filled up enough to tip down and flush out the entire house with a powerful cleansing roar. This seemed like a keen idea until you had rainy weather—not unknown in Britain—whereupon the tank filled up and clanged empty constantly, scaring the bejesus out of children as all the house's toilets roared in monstrous unison in the dead of night.

Eventually water closets evolved into the familiar tank-and-chain model. But water is an imperfect medium for waste. For one thing, what water was to be found in cities was not very palatable to begin with. Some wells located near graveyards even had what was delicately termed "a churchyard taste" to their water, and discharging massive amounts of fecal matter into the groundwater and into rivers hardly helped. And the underwater decomposition of sewage is inefficient; it's an anaerobic process that works much more slowly than aerobic decomposition.

So if water was the problem, why not remove the water? Earth closets were, not to put too fine a point upon things, a wooden box you squatted over. Equipped with a little beach shovel and a bucket of ashes and dirt to scatter over your pile—a primitive charcoal system—it both covered up the smell and speeded your waste's conversion into usable farm manure. But earth closets, in the early days, sometimes had the look of . . . well, a *contraption*.

Foote's insight was that it was no good to sermonize people into doing the right thing: that only works briefly with most people, and permanently with the conscientious few. Most have to see why something is in their own interest, and it needs to be made convenient and attractive. And so the burnished mahogany Wakefield earth closets hawked by Dr. Foote were handsome, refined—

rather like relieving oneself into a really nice piano. It featured an array of levers and spring-loaded slats to automatically cover everything up for you. And as they improved in design over the years, earth closets did indeed have their converts. In Britain, the Lancaster Grammar School found them splendid for schoolboys, as their old water closets had kept getting clogged up "by reason of marbles, Latin grammar covers, and other properties being thrown down them."

I suppose earth closets had other healthful advantages too. Any number of Victorian sexual neuroses become understandable when you learn that one water commode mass-produced in Lancashire was named the Clencher.

But August Woehler was a dissatisfied customer. A *very* dissatisfied customer. He wanted his *life*—his health, his love, his manhood— back from the doctor who had stolen it from him. Yet when Foote insisted to detectives that he hadn't recognized his assailant, the doctor was telling the truth. Foote had to be, because once his assailant was well enough, the fellow had gone back to the corner of Twenty-eighth and Lexington every night since, and nearly every day. And there he lurked, holding his injured hand, watching the house. The doctor had gone about his business again, unaware that just yards away stood August Woehler: watching, waiting, deciding on the best moment to kill him.

"I have been trying to throw it off mind, and not die a murderer, but when night comes on I can't help myself," agonized one unsent letter in Woehler's pocket. "The nearer I come to this house, the more I feel like committing the deed."

He had come close—so close—that afternoon in Foote's examination room. "I was thinking how, in a few minutes, he would be shot in the bowels, and he would lie there, with his brains blown out.

But things did not turn out that way," he admitted in another letter. "I might have shot him in the back," he mused, "but I did not want to do that, for it would have looked kind of mean."

And so there, on a cold November night, this thoughtful would-be murderer and his careless would-be victim went about their separate business. The world would find out about the gunman's life soon enough; Foote's was already well-known. For while Paine's boldest assertion—that we had no need of kings—was laid forth from the outset of *Common Sense*, its medical namesake was more circumspect but no less stunning. Hidden in the back of *Medical Common Sense* is a short section marked "The Prevention of Conception." It contains perhaps the single most important sentence written by any American author of his time:

"I shall be willing to direct married people in this important matter, who apply in writing."

Traveling through the West when it was still at its wildest, the writer George Macdonald kept finding that one man had apparently preceded him everywhere he went—and it didn't matter just how far into the wilderness he ventured. "I went into a shack where a wood chopper lived alone," he marveled. "There was one room, one shelf, and two books on the shelf." One was an almanac; the other was by Edward Bliss Foote.

It is hard to realize today how profound—or how profoundly forgotten—the impact of Dr. Foote's little book was. *Medical Common Sense* sold 250,000 copies, and an expanded 1870 version retitled *Plain Home Talk* went on to sell 500,000—blockbuster numbers even today, and an absolutely immense run back then. The contraception advice alone would have saved many from death in childbirth, and changed the economic prospects of innumerable others. Publishers in New York, London, and Berlin sold editions in

English and German, featuring endless permutations of size and content—excerpted pamphlets, weighty family editions covering all facets of health, and little easy-to-hide editions focused on sex.

When Foote inserted that fateful line "I shall be willing to direct married people in this important matter," he was opening a cultural floodgate. Trickles had been seeping in for years already, beginning with the first smuggled copies of Richard Carlile's *Every Woman's Book*. By 1830, New Yorkers could prevent the "social brutality of illegitimate pregnancy" with the vaginal sponges described in Robert Dale Owen's *Moral Physiology*, while Dr. Charles Knowlton's similar *Fruits of Philosophy* (1832) proved so popular that, even after Knowlton was convicted of obscenity in Massachusetts, a juror came up to him afterward and asked if he could buy a copy.

But these guides were often published or pirated under the murkiest of circumstances, with pseudonyms and a "correspondence system" of different publishers in each city, and then distributed at railway stations and other locales fit for quick and anonymous transactions. In what must be the beginning of targeted spam, marital aid manufacturers and publishers would cleverly slip pamphlets for their goods under the doors of couples whose marriages had been announced in local newspapers. Books directed to married couples, at least, were less liable to be prosecuted; one, Frederick Hollick's *Marriage Guide*, went through an astonishing two hundred printings between 1850 and 1860.

What made E. B. Foote different from his predecessors was his shamelessness. Foote was perhaps the first American sexual reformer to hide in plain sight. He gave you his addresses, his prices, and his products. And sex—though admittedly "his favorite subject"— was only part of the continuum of his health services for everything from indigestion to consumption. He was not a dirty old man at the railway platform; he had nothing to hide; he was a *physician*.

Business at the doctor's new Manhattan office boomed. Foote patent medicines like Magnetic Ointment and Dr. Foote's Eye Sharpener turned handsome profits. Meanwhile, Magnetic Anti-Bilious Pills were also hawked for impotency and—for your inevitable return visit after that first cure—for syphilitic sores and gonorrhea. Foote pamphlets claimed that his offices at 120 Lexington Avenue were flooded with letters from grateful patients: "They are convincing. They are overwhelming! . . . There are cords of letters—actually cords—which the doctor has no time to look over." The *New York Times* carried Foote ads trumpeting OLD EYES MADE NEW WITHOUT SPECTACLES and COMFORT FOR THE RUPTURED, and the enticing CONFIDENTIAL INFORMATION FOR THE MARRIED.

His letters probably also included a fair number of attorney bills. As befitted a leading birth control publisher, Foote was also the inventor and manufacturer of his own line of condoms—made from the membranes of specially selected Rhine fish, and "flexible, and silky in texture, and a perfect conductor of electricity and magnetism"—and he also sold his own patented rubber diaphragms. For his inventive troubles, Foote found himself squarely in the sights of postal inspector Anthony Comstock. As Comstock's moral grandstanding and influence grew, so did Foote's problems. After Congress passed the so-called Comstock Law in 1873, which outlawed contraceptive advertising, Special Agent Comstock's very first act was to indict the man he considered the worst sexual menace in the country: Dr. Edward Bliss Foote.

And yet it proved peculiarly difficult to peg Foote as some sort of nasty little pervert. Like a medical Walt Whitman, E. B. Foote saw nothing impure in human bodies. He sang the body electric. He also sang the "electro-magnetic preventive machine," a worthless birth control gizmo hawked for $15 by his mail-order business. But for a man denounced in early credit reports as "a splendid specimen of the genus humbug," Foote was an extraordinarily successful and respected entrepreneur. He even ran for Congress, albeit unsuccessfully—for, as one friend mused, Foote was in "every party that never carried an election." But the money kept flowing in, and when Comstock came after him, Foote could afford good lawyers: not only did he get off from his charges with a fine, he then went on to finance the legal defense of Susan B. Anthony and other persecuted colleagues. Foote was also helping finance, of all people, *Comstock's own father.* Apparently the old miscreant had been thrown out of the house, nearly penniless, by his morally zealous son.

By the time E. B. Foote revised *Medical Common Sense* in 1870, his book had become a veritable Sears catalogue of the latest radical idealism for the 1870 season: everything from animal rights ("The dawn of the millennium cannot light up human hands and arms red with blood of slaughtered animals . . . The ingenious Yankee will invent a substitute for leather, and we already have enough substitutes for ivory and bone.") to dancing lessons being included in Christian masses. Eat lots of fruits and vegetables, Foote recommends heartily: try shiatsu and botanical remedies! These are now all the stuff of Style section and *Mother Jones* ads; the only surprise is finding them in Victorian garb. Other predictions by Foote are familiar in a more haunting way, though:

> It is urged by many that capital punishment restrains people from committing crimes for which that penalty is inflicted; but statistics show that more murders are committed in Massachusetts where the death penalty is rigidly administered, than in Wisconsin where it has been for several years abolished. People

laboring under violent passion seldom pause to consider con-
sequences . . . Remove this barbaric example from high places
and the example will be Christianizing to the whole human
family.

Foote felt confident that people would eventually adopt the rational
approach: "The death penalty, happily, is becoming unpopular."

Well, it has indeed remained deeply unpopular among the many
people now slated to *receive* it. Over a century later, Foote's hopes
would still seem to many some distant and even hopeless utopia. Yet
he had *seen* a utopia: he had shaken hands with its inhabitants.
Foote had some years earlier paid a visit at one of the branches of the
Oneida Community—an extraordinary Christian sect of self-
proclaimed "Perfectionists." As laid out in their 1847 pamphlet
Biblical Communism, this sect recognized neither private property
nor private relations: they were polyamorous communists.

It's hard to imagine a combination of beliefs more likely to whip
up small-town residents into a scandalized froth: Perfectionists were
run out of towns and endured decades of pulpit attacks and bigamy
prosecutions. They shrugged these off and diligently built up
businesses in lumber and blacksmithing; meanwhile, their children
were raised by the community, instead of by parents; they had both
open marriages and open parenting. These children, visiting doctors
marveled, grew up remarkably robust and healthy. The Perfectionists had, in short, created precisely the sort of society that Paine's old
friend John "Walking" Stewart had envisioned decades before. If
there was ever a community not for everyone, Oneida was surely it.
And yet, Foote mused, those who were there did seem happy. Since
he'd first read *Common Sense*, Foote had come to see the wisdom of
the exact inverse of Paine's great proverb: he realized that a long
habit of not thinking a thing *right* gives it a superficial appearance of

being *wrong*. Upon careful thought, he could not find anything actually wrong with Oneida.

And so Foote came to this startling conclusion: "Freedom of affection, *and even sexual promiscuity*, do not necessarily degrade or demoralize women or generate diseases." He had seen no degradation at Oneida. No, he decided: it was legal codes and bans on condoms that were the source of that. It was the Anthony Comstocks of the world who were degrading women. If women were granted control of their bodies, Foote announced, there would be no need of Mr. Comstock and chivalrous efforts on behalf of their honor:

> The conservative man exclaims, "We worship them as angels" . . . Gallantry is mistaken for justice, and soft soap for equity. Even these exist only on the surface. They compose the cream that rises to the top of polite society, and this is fed only to the handsome, rich, and otherwise fortunate; all below that is skim milk, and this is dealt out sparingly and grudgingly to toiling women, unhappy wives, and to all, indeed, who most need sympathy and help. But let no man who suddenly awakes to this injustice, suppose in his arrogance that he can give woman her rights. The very fact that men talk of *allowing* women this or that liberty is evidence that authority itself has been usurped. As well might a pickpocket talk of giving a port-monnaie to someone from whom he had clandestinely filched it. I tell you, reader, we men have no rights to *give* women; she possesses naturally the same rights as we do.

Fine words. But how exactly might a woman secure these natural rights?

A modern reader of old medical guides and women's magazines might wonder why there are so many ads for syringes . . . but not for *needles.* Victorian women knew why. Their most popular form of contraception was douching after sex—and though crude and potentially even dangerous, the commonly used weak solutions of vinegar or borax could indeed have prevented pregnancy. You'll gain an appreciation for modern central heating upon learning that spirits were sometimes added so that the solution would not freeze sitting on the nightstand. But even to use that solution, you still needed a way to deliver it.

Enter, so to speak, the syringe. Medical suppliers came to offer a dizzying array of brass and glass squirters that had no clear purpose other than some vaguely advertised "cleanliness." Moral crusaders like Comstock were quick to catch on, raiding and fining retailers of these syringes, who were thereby driven to some pretty strange subterfuges in their advertising. Turn to the back of Foote's books and you will find ads for an "Impregnating Syringe," a magnificent piece of doublespeak if there ever was one. Not to be outdone, the George C. Goodwin & Company catalogue for 1885 took its Female Syringe, reversed the engraving so that it faced left instead of right, and relabeled it as a House-Plant Syringe. Yes, so now you could water your . . . petunia.

The ruses didn't always work. After one sexual reformer and publisher, Ezra Heywood, was tossed into jail for advertising syringes, his wife Angela proclaimed in the press: "This womb-syringe question is to the North what the Negro question was to the South." It is a jarring comparison. Slavery: pregnancy. *Really?*

No: not really. And yet a curiously large number of sex reformers had indeed cut their teeth in abolitionist movements. That one societal question had led a generation of activists down a tangled path into innumerable others, not the least of which was the plight of women who were dying in childbirth from unwanted pregnancies, or finding themselves locked into loveless marriages and miserable social illegitimacy. It wasn't slavery, but it did share one key element: *these were people forbidden from control over their own bodies.*

Race and sex were the two great unspeakables of American society. And to speak of *both* in the same breath—why, that was just asking for trouble.

Trouble came—as trouble so often does—with a monkey.

It is truth universally acknowledged that Everything Is Funnier With Monkeys. I defy you to name a human endeavor that is *not* enriched by the addition of a screaming, leg-humping, ass-biting primate. Which brings us to what must be the strangest book of the nineteenth century—E. B. Foote's wildly bizarre *Sammy Tubbs, the Boy Doctor, and Sponsie, the Troublesome Monkey* (1874). It is the five-volume Manhattan saga of the twelve-year-old son of freed slaves. It does indeed also feature a sidekick monkey named Sponsie—and yes, as promised, he is troublesome.

Sammy is the doorboy for kindly local doctor Samuel Hubbs, who apparently is a splendid fellow in every way. In case you were wondering whether Hubbs might be meant to resemble anyone, I should mention that Hubbs and E. B. Foote share this same 120 Lexington Avenue address. And they have authored books with *the same titles.*

Sammy Tubbs becomes the young protégé of Foote—sorry, *Hubbs*—and in a sort of med-school *Pygmalion*, the older white Hubbs molds the young black Tubbs into a doctor. In each respective volume, amid servant hijinks and literal monkeyshines, Tubbs gets lectured on Muscles, Circulation, Digestion, and the Nervous System. But the fifth and final volume bears a curious inscription on its cover: "A Book for Private Reading." Leaf through

it, and you'll see why: it has line drawings of genitals, and of Rand
McNally road-map accuracy.

It's a Victorian sex-ed manual. For children. Starring a monkey.

The *Sammy Tubbs* series mixes nearly every progressive and fringe
element of nineteenth-century physiology and politics into a sort of
patent-medicine speedball. There are lectures against tight-fitting
clothes, tobacco and alcohol, and for phrenology and animal
magnetism; there are thrilling showdowns between bigotry and
the rights of women and minorities. And every few pages there is a
moralizing medical lecture from good old Dr. Hubbs. In his hands,
the human body becomes the embodiment of reform, a vessel of
progressivism that is constantly reinventing itself:

> "Particles of matter are all the time dying in your body, and fresh
> ones are as constantly taking their places, when you are in a
> condition of health. Some physiologists say that we change our
> bodies completely as often as once in seven years" . . .
>
> "Then," said Sammy, with a look of surprise, "the body I was
> born with has been buried, and in smaller pieces and more places
> than if it had been cut up by the physicians!"

"We can begin the world anew," Foote's own mentor once wrote of
America, and the doctor agreed. The past was quite literally dead
and dying. There was no point to conservatism, *because there was
nothing to conserve.*

Anchoring these extraordinary sentiments are, courtesy of illus-
trator H. L. Stephens, hundreds of drawings of everything from
shrublike capillary diagrams to flying monkeys and animated kitchen
appliances. Rather more down-to-earth—if not downright earthy—
illustrations include those of genitalia. One set of these occur on pages
$180\frac{1}{2}$ and $180\frac{3}{4}$. The idea was that mortified parents could razor out

the drawings without Junior noticing a break in pagination. But even razored copies still contained a drawing of a vagina with a tiny musical note tooting out of it—a sly touch by Stephens removed from later printings. Hank seems to be a bit of a late-night joker in the print shop: in one edition of *Plain Home Talk*, the caption "A Delicious Looking Medicine" leers beneath his illustration of grapes bunched in a dangling manner that will either put you very much off or very much onto your Smuckers for the rest of the week.

Sammy Tubbs himself is no slouch in such bodily matters. Beginning as a "poor little ignorant colored boy" living in the attic of Hubbs's genteel Manhattan home, he rises to become a self-appointed neighborhood practitioner and health lecturer, addressing halls packed with rapturous black and white women—where his reproduction lecture is introduced by a certain "Miss Goodlove"—and treating not only black patients in his family's neighborhood, but poor whites as well. He gets particularly familiar with white bodies in the form of his girlfriend, Julia Barkenstir. She is—pause for irony—the daughter of a cotton broker.

Foote advocated interracial relationships on eugenic grounds of avoiding racial inbreeding, resulting in an extraordinary *Sammy Tubbs* illustration of Sammy and Julia kissing. Bear in mind that this was not only in an era when most states had laws against such relations, but where more than a few enforced them by means of ropes and trees. Yet Sammy is unapologetic about it, yelling over the protests of Julia's father: "White men are constantly decrying miscegenation, miscegenation!—while they are the only ones that want to miscegenate . . ."

Indeed. You might even say they invented it.

The word *miscegenation* was scarcely a decade old when Foote wrote of Sammy and Julia's kiss: it was a made-up word, a neologism, coined in a mysterious pamphlet. *Miscegenation: The Theory of the Blending of the Races, Applied to the American White Man and the Negro* had appeared on Manhattan newsstands on Christmas Day, 1863. Foote himself might have bought a copy as he strolled up Lexington Avenue. Though published by the local firm of Dexter Hamilton & Co., the seventy-two page pamphlet gave no hint of its authorship. Peruse the chapter titles, and you'll discover why:

Superiority of Mixed Races
The Love of the Blond for the Black
The Miscegenetic Ideal of Beauty in Women
The Future—No White, No Black

The author helpfully coined a new word for this happy state of affairs, clapping together the Latin *miscere* (to mix) with *genus* (race). "White man should marry the black woman," he vowed, "and the white woman the black man."

Racists went *berserk*. This was absolutely explosive stuff in 1863, coming on the heels of a not entirely popular Emancipation Proclamation. Democrats tried pinning the whole thing on Lincoln, who was coming up for reelection, and to whom the pamphlet addressed itself directly by heartily recommending that he add a miscegenation plank in the Republican platform. Senators waved *Miscegenation* around as damning evidence that, thanks to Lincoln, a coming colored tide would swamp white purity.

And so fancy this: the pamphlet itself was written by a racist.

Miscegenation was, like Swift's *A Modest Proposal*, a hoax meant to be so absurd that it would backfire on its erstwhile proponents. When writer David Croly, a journalist at the staunchly Democratic *New York World*, tried to think of the most appalling, unthinkable outrage imaginable in America, this is what he imagined: a white woman having sex with a black man. To many readers, he was right. And his faux "Republican" pamphlet might have worked, except for one problem: it seems some people rather *liked* the idea of mixing races. But then, that is the problem with such arguments. When the pastor or politician inveighing against *x* sneers, "What next, will they be wanting *y*?"—it just might be that we realize that, why yes, dear sir, we *do* want *y* next. And so what began as a racist smear turned, in the course of a decade, into a liberal doctor's prescription for saving humanity.

But I doubt the children were paying any attention.

"*What about the monkey?*" Foote sighs. "*We want to know how he is,* I imagine some of my uninterested young readers are clamorously inquiring." It's true. There are actually *two* monkeys in these children's books: nobody can much tell them apart. Sponsie 1 and Sponsie 2 are berserk stand-ins for the uncontrollable animality of the human body; observed by the coolly rational Sammy, their mishaps provide the forensic grist for Foote's medical theories.

How? Well, Sponsie 2 gets accidentally sealed alive under some floorboards—his starvation being a handy segue into a lecture on Digestion. He gets his rectum shot off after playing with a gun, all the better to explain incontinence. Ultimately, the unfortunate fellow is accidentally disemboweled by the belt drive of an industrial knife sharpener—"torn all to strings," a witness sadly notes. We are informed that Sponsie 1 "contracted a taste for malt liquors while living in Hoboken"—who wouldn't?—and the instructive result of that is the alcoholic simian tries hanging himself in the attic. After being revived, he turns into a pickpocket, a kidnapper, and a Central Park carriage thief; his life of prehensile crime only ends when he gets shot in the head in a duel with the other Sponsie.

But even death is turned to good purpose: Sammy Tubbs yanks out the dead Sponsie's brain and spine to use as props for a lecture on the nervous system, all the better to prepare him for the full medical school scholarship that he has been awarded at the series' end.

So all's well that ends well . . . unless, of course, you're the monkey.

"Banana."

The waiter sets my dessert down in front of me: Banana Toffee, a caramelized confection with vanilla ice cream. It's very good, a dish fit for a troublesome monkey. Sad to say, there's no record that Foote ever actually *kept* monkeys in this building, but one can always hope. I pay my bill, and walk back out in the cold afternoon air, down to Twenty-Fourth Street. A clutch of taxis race past: a man and woman walk past me holding hands, black and white. Maybe Foote would be pleased with his old neighborhood.

I stop: *here*.

Nobody had seen "Mr. Peters" leave his room at Putnam House near Twenty-Fourth Street; he certainly was a most mysterious boarder. Evening and then morning passed without a sign of him, and by afternoon it was time for room cleaning. A chambermaid knocked on his door. Nothing. She knocked again, and then tried his door: locked. The key had not been left downstairs, so the gentleman must still be in. Why wasn't he answering?

The maid grabbed a chair and stood atop it to peek in through a transom. And here is what she saw: probably a little of her own reflection in the glass. Perhaps her breath misting its surface slightly. And then: a painfully thin man, alone, lying very still. He still did not return her greeting. He would not be returning anyone's greetings. His face was bulging and ashen and blue: the kerchief under his jaw was red, the fabric running tautly from around his neck up to a coat rack on the wall, where it was securely tied. It had strangled his breathing hours before.

In his pockets police found some old receipts, a penknife, and $1.40. There was also a letter marked "To Be Opened After I Am Dead." In it, August Woehler poured out his life story for one final time to the world. He had, he said, struggled for years with the perilous state of his own body and soul.

"I wanted to be somebody in the world," the deceased wrote, "so I made up my mind to control my passion and be above low living." As a young man in 1866, he'd moved to California for a while to seek his fortune, to shake his old self away. He found his salvation at this task in the writings of E. B. Foote: "I thought he was the greatest doctor there was." But there were, you see, some things that even Doctor Foote could not cure—some passions that could not be controlled, some diseases that could not be remedied because *they were not diseases at all*. Three hundred dollars' worth of mail-order treatments later, Woehler was no better than before. Infuriated and depressed, he went back to living miserably with his mother in Hartford.

His life was ruined: it had been from the start, it seemed, and now its ruination was confirmed:

> When I think of my whole life from my childhood up, I cannot see much in this life that I need regret leaving it for. How I was abused by my own father worse than any man ever used his bull-pup, and always standing in constant fear of doing something that might offend my mother. I have had to lead a life that is altogether unnatural for me. I might have had one of the best of lives, but I tell you it is pretty hard to make water run uphill, and that is the way my folk has wanted me to live.

And so this was how August Woehler spent his final days and hours of November 15, 1879: in a cheap boardinghouse by the corner of

Twenty-third and Fourth, hiding under an assumed name, bereft of hope, a man wanted by the police. Here he lay staring at the ceiling, at the walls, and out the windows at the city around him as the minutes trickled away, lost in the most powerful city of the world's freest country—but lacking the one freedom that he cared about. He wrote bitterly:

> Compelled since I was 7 years of age to live against my whole nature. And then leave home and for nearly two years live as moral a life as any man ever lived and then come home again and live as straight as string so as not to offend the old lady.
>
> They all said, Why don't you get married?

"Marriage," I hear on the street.

I saw it in the newspaper kiosks coming on my way over: MA COURT UPHOLDS SAME SEX MARRIAGE. Murmur civil murmur union murmur. It's all anyone at the next table could talk about in Chinese Mirch, or in the shop I stopped in for peppermints down the street, and on the AM radio station crackling across the taxi that I hail. Will it be legal? Will we have tolerance for it? Will it . . .

Tolerance is an ugly word. When Foote wrote of men granting women rights that already rightfully belonged to them, he was mindful of what his preceptor had written a lifetime before in 1787: "Toleration is not the opposite of intoleration, but the counterfeit of it," Paine wrote. "Both are despotisms. The one assumes the right of withholding liberty of conscience, and the other of granting it." Casting a baleful eye over the citizenry's concern over what they should or should not tolerate, Paine had a simple directive: "*Mind thine own concerns.*"

In public discourse it would be instructive, I suspect, to always replace the word *tolerance* with *liberty*.

"JFK," I tell the driver. "British Airways."

We slice downtown through avenues that Foote once trotted through in his fine carriage, the streets that the disconsolate Woehler wandered with a .38 in his pocket. Having survived both assassins and attorneys, Foote turned to the man that inspired him decades before. Using the house on Lexington as its headquarters, the Thomas Paine National Historical Association began to form around a nucleus of the leading troublemakers in New York City. Foote was its treasurer, and its shared address with his house meant there was scarcely a day when the association's business did not cross his path. A clever fellow named Thomas Edison even began turning up at their informal meetings, recalling wistfully how picking up a volume of Paine from his father's bookshelf, at the age of thirteen, had been "a revelation." Edison himself eventually wrote a book on Paine and became a Vice President of the Association. But in those earliest days, the choice of the man to serve alongside Foote, leading the freethinker's charge—to be the Thomas Paine National Historical Association's first president—was very clear.

I shuffle through the old documents in my backseat. Here, staring out from me in a photograph, is their Association's leader: a Southern gentleman in a top hat and with a cane, gravely dignified with his graying beard and an expression of perpetual inquisitiveness. In his decades abroad in London and in Paris, he'd spent years preparing *The Writings of Thomas Paine*, the first comprehensive edition ever published. He'd also written the first serious biography of Paine—a weighty two-volume set that remains a definitive work. There is a caption underneath the photograph: "Moncure Conway."

"The law," wafts from the taxi's AM radio. ". . . the right . . ."

Conway possessed an advantage that no modern scholar can: when he first wandered out to Paine's old homes and haunts, they were still *there*. And what's more, so were the last remnants of

Paine's old neighbors and cronies. Paine was not a distant Founding Father to Conway or his interviewees, but a man who still existed in living memory. He had a *physical presence*. He was tangible: he ate *here*, he walked *there*, he drank a brandy *in this very spot*.

And so, among the living recollections that gave some hint into the man's soul, there was one last thing Conway could bring to Foote. Something that the doctor and other association members had long been quietly wondering about. For years Conway had been pursuing an elusive quarry that had led him across an ocean and through country lanes and city alleyways.

Paine's body.

EVERYWHERE

The Mornington Crescent Game

IT WAS JUST above freezing outside when they had shoveled the soil out for the grave—a shivering December day in 1874—and now Moncure stood officiating by the graveside as the coffin was laid into the ground and the first handfuls of dirt thrown upon the lid. Through the gathered mourners, a glimpse could be caught of a square block of polished red granite at the head of the grave:

IN MEMORY OF
JAMES WATSON
PUBLISHER
Born Sept. 21, 1799—Died Nov. 29, 1874

Conway paused to consider the crowd of grizzled old radicals. His Unitarian church in London was now the most famous liberal outpost in the country; he often invited leading progressives to speak at it, and from his pulpit in Finsbury Square he produced pamphlets urging not only the end of racism and militarism, but supporting racial intermarriage as the true route to social stability. NEGRO THE SAVIOR OF AMERICA, one newspaper had headlined his views. Little wonder that Richard Carlile's old apprentice in radicalism, John Stuart Mill, had befriended him—or that the fellow

Carlile veteran James Watson had become a member of Conway's congregation. The old Quaker publisher was, Conway mused, a "serene man of such calm mind that I could hardly realize his age." Yet he bore the living memory of Cobbett and Carlile; indeed, the most ancient members of Conway's congregation had known Thomas Paine himself in their earliest youth.

It had been over a decade since Conway bitterly left the United States; here in England he'd found his friendship with Emerson was enough to make him welcomed by any author; the young man soon found himself regaled well into the night at Alfred Lord Tennyson's house, and when the two got lost trying to find the inn Conway was staying in, they fell down a muddy embankment roaring with boozy laughter. "Do not mention this to the temperance folk," the disheveled poet laureate mock-pleaded of him. And so it was that the amiable minister was initiated into the fraternity of authors. Before the year was out, he was walking away from the funeral of William Thackeray side by side with Robert Browning and Charles Dickens; later he'd preside over the burial of their beloved humorist Artemus Ward. But this latest funeral was . . . *different*, somehow.

Watson had spent his final few years living simply in quiet retirement: after his many run-ins with censors and years of jail time in the service of a free press, he spent his old age peacefully living near the immense exhibition halls of the Crystal Palace. He delighted in strolling its grounds each day, taking in the science displays, and attending the free recitals played upon the hall's immense pipe organ. There he could linger for hours, serenely listening to Handel and Beethoven. Old friends could rely on finding him there each day until, at last, he showed up no more: he had passed away in his sleep.

As the crowd slowly dispersed from the freshly covered grave and Conway comforted James's steadfast wife Eleanor, one question still hung over the proceedings, one that the calm old man had taken into the silence of his own grave. *What had he done with the bones?*

Here is what I can tell you about the town of Guildford: if you are taking a child there, bring a helmet. Maybe it's the steep slope of their High Street, or the uneven cobbles of the market-town streets, but I've never seen so many little tykes turning involuntary somersaults in my life. In the last fifteen minutes I've seen four of them go crashing down onto the pavement. There is the moment of stung realization, and then they burst out crying. For such a pleasant little city, Guildford is a good place to get your baby teeth knocked out.

I sit down on a bench by Trinity Church, watch the youth of Britain go sprawling by, and thumb through a book I picked up on High Street. *Surrey Privies* starts with what is surely one of the better opening lines in literature—"Privy hunting is a curious occupation"—before going into the fine points of Moule earth closets, "four-holer" group models, and a local brand of toilet paper that repeated across its sheets the printed injunction NOW WASH YOUR HANDS. Better still is this outhouse advice from one elderly Surrey resident: "It was always advisable to kick the door before going in to get rid of any rats."

Elderly couples keep passing me, wandering around the Guildhall, the Guildford castle grounds, and up and down the High Street, all clutching sheets of paper and looking rather lost. They're not looking for privies, at least: the modern restrooms are well marked here. One husband and wife pair stop in front of my bench, eyes squinting at their sheet.

"Um . . ." Suddenly it dawns on me. "Scavenger hunt?"

"Why, yes." He smiles delightedly. "An historical one."

Me too.

Back in the 1850s, when Cobbett's old secretary Ben Tilly had gone broke, his possessions wound up going to the Richards auction house, where the box of Paine's bones was purchased by none other than James Watson. He'd already published a biography of Paine the year before, not to mention a pamphlet on the bones; clearly Watson's concerns that Paine receive a decent burial had never left him. Soon he was quietly inquiring how he might go about making a burial in Kensal Green cemetery. And here is where the darkness of history closes upon us: where a curtain comes down upon the scene before it is quite ended. For we do not know what Watson then did—he took that secret to his grave. He may have given the bones back to Ben Tilly; or, the remains of Thomas Paine may be buried in some nameless consecrated plot in London. Only James Watson knows. But even so . . . he did not quite know *everything*.

I walk down the street, gaping at the ancient architecture and the glassy modern storefronts, scanning for the occasional building that bothers to list its street number outside. I come up to Tunsgate Arch, as lost as any of the scavenger hunt retirees, and wander into the next store I see. Inside are bare wooden floorboards and coolly minimalist displays of tiny translucent colored bottles of essence of jasmine, vanilla, lemongrass, coconut. The shopgirl watches me with the sharpened stare of one who has been practicing for runway modeling.

"Can I help you?"

I am strangely transfixed upon a sales display that glows with backlighting, the tinctured green, pink, and yellow bottles like a hypnotic array of hard candies. It's oddly appropriate, for the Tunsgate was a massive Tuscan arch built to shelter the town's corn market. Once they sold the fruits of the soil in these buildings: now only the scents remain.

"I'm looking"—I pull my gaze away—"for 130 High Street."

"They're the other side of the arch."

I cross over to find a building with a shop simply called Games. They sell games, you understand. Inside it is crammed with video game sets and titles leering out at shoppers: Vietnam Battlefield, Grand Theft Auto, the usual. WE WANT YOUR GAMES: TRADE IN exhorts a sign. But I come up to the counter empty-handed.

"Excuse me," I ask an employee about to hit Level 5 in his game. "Is this number 130?"

" 'Tis." *Blap.* "130." *Kablooey.* "Bugger!"

I look around at the displays, imagining a time when burlap sacks and iron-hooped barrels stood where track-lit wire racks of CDs and game carts are now. It makes sense that a corn merchant would have lived and worked in the building closest to the town's corn market. It was in the summer of 1849 that a next-door neighbor visiting this store, and lingering aimlessly much as I am right now, got to talking with the shopkeeper John Chennell about the missing bones of Thomas Paine.

The corn merchant couldn't have been much fazed by the subject. The clan of Chennells, long a pillar of brewing and farming around Guildford, had their own spectacularly grisly family affair back when Cobbett was still swiping bones in New York. In 1817 local shoemaker George Chennell and his housekeeper were both found murdered, their throats slashed, and the shop till emptied out. Suspicion quickly fell upon the victim's dissolute son, George Jr., and a deliveryman named William Chalcroft. Pound notes found in George Jr.'s pocket were speckled with blood.

I turn and look out the front window. It was through these streets that Chalcroft and Chennell, shackled in heavy irons, were borne by carriage out to a meadow. There they were hung on the gallows, and their still-warm bodies immediately conveyed to the house where the murders occurred. The corpses were carried into the kitchen—Chalcroft's was laid on the precise spot where the housekeeper's body had been found—and two local surgeons fell upon them with scalpels, dissecting the men at the very scene of their crimes. Then, with their innards exposed, they were left splayed out for the rest of the day, viewed by thousands of locals who queued up outside and shuffled through the shoemaker's shop to see the dissected criminals.

So the bones of a man who'd died of natural causes? Hardly worth raising an eyebrow over. But it was good local gossip between neighbors, after all; John Chennell's neighbor had heard about Pigott the auctioneer, some years back, refusing to sell a box of Paine's bones a few villages over, in the hamlet of Normandy. That's what *he'd* heard, anyway.

Oh, Chennell said, *it's true.*

"Come with me," the corn merchant added. The two men descended into the shop's cellar; and there, in the dank underground room, Chennell produced a container. It was a porcelain jar, sealed at the top with a piece of parchment. In the darkness the words inscribed upon it could just be made out: *The great Paine's bones.*

The bassoon lies comically—for every posture assumed by a bassoon is a comical one—by the side of a grand piano; and a breeze passes through the French doors that lead out into Charles Darwin's garden. Four chairs are sociably arranged into a circle within his drawing room, awaiting a family concert that will never happen again. I stroll out onto the croquet pitch-perfect lawn, and upon crunching gravel back toward Darwin's greenhouse and his laboratory. I'm still a little rumpled from hours of travel on three different trains and one bus to get here from Guildford. But I feel the footsteps beneath me that I follow: for it was here, one fine spring morning, that Moncure Conway awoke in a guest room and pondered the great man he had not yet met.

Well, at least this time he'd find a hero of his who was alive and still in one place. The other great influence on his life had proven rather more elusive. Conway had heard the stories about Tom Paine's bones mysteriously showing up at Chennell's shop over twenty years earlier. It seems people had been pocketing bits of Tom Paine at each step of the old patriot's journey. Before sending the bones back up from London to Normandy in 1833, Ben Tilly had quietly lifted the hard black lump that was once a brain, and wrapped his prize in a labeled piece of oilcloth. The bones, sent back to Surrey in a corn merchant's wagon, appear to have been plundered yet again by Chennell, who may have taken a few bones to store in a jar. And even with the bones returned to him years later by George West, Tilly kept Paine's brain separate from the box: when he lost the box to a debtor's auction in the 1850s, Tilly cheated the auctioneer out of his one cloth-wrapped souvenir.

Well, that was fair enough: it might be that the auctioneer was cheating too. The box sold at Richards the Auctioneer was an incomplete set, because the skull and a hand were secretly pieced out for separate sale. So the box that James Watson won that day was rather *lighter* than the one William Cobbett carried from the Liverpool Customs Yard. Even if Watson had tried to bury Paine in Kensal Green, he couldn't have buried *all* of Paine. The body was becoming impossibly scattered.

It was enough to give Moncure a headache. But the air here, in the countryside outside Bromley, was a good cordial to raise his spirits. Rising from his bed, he looked out his window to see Darwin already up and inspecting the flowers out in this garden. Conway could hardly help remarking to himself on the man's very form, as he bent down with his gray beard as if to talk with his flowers.

"All that phrenologists had written," he mused, "was feeble compared with a look at that big head with its wonderful dome."

The dissenting minister's laudatory sermons on evolution had earned him an invitation to Darwin's house, but he'd arrived here after Darwin's early bedtime. Now, crossing the garden, the two men finally met for the first time. A hermit thrush was singing loudly in a tree, and Conway paused to gaze at it. "He is justifying his hermit profession," he ventured, "by a Vedic hymn to the rising sun."

No, Darwin countered good-naturedly—*he is singing a canticle to his beloved.*

Their talk turned more serious as they strolled about the garden. Inspired by reading *The Origin of Species* weeks after it first came out, Conway had plunged himself into years of scientific study in London, mingling easily in the company of Lyell, Galton, and Huxley. Darwin had heard of Conway's resulting sermons, which lofted evolution as the great hope and wonder of the world, as the very essence of progress itself—and still entirely divine as well. As one paleontologist mused to Conway, "If you tell me of a mechanic who made a remarkable steam engine I may admire his skill; but if you tell me of a man who has made an engine which can of itself produce another engine, and then another, an engine from which is evolved an endless series of steadily self-improving engines, I might say that inventor was a god." But Darwin wouldn't quite say whether he agreed with Conway's friendly theological interpretation of his work, though he appreciated its intent. While denying that his theory attacked religion, in private he was less sure of just how viable religion had been left in the wake of his work, and—unknown to Conway or nearly anyone else—his former piety had long drifted into a realm of agnostic doubts.

I stop in front of Darwin's laboratory. It's a formality, really: nature was his laboratory, and his laboratory was nature. You can step over the stone threshold from one to the other, but there was no real boundary at all.

Over breakfast they read the letters for the day. There were always letters, and his daughters had to sort the ones from friends from the great mass sent by strangers. It still amused Darwin's family that he never quite grasped just how famous he'd become. His sister confided to Moncure that, after the Prime Minister came by to visit one day, Darwin was left astounded. "To think of such a great man coming to see me!" he'd kept exclaiming afterward. But the letters he received were often of a humbler sort: rural gardeners writing about a new variety of bean they thought they'd developed. A man writing in with what he clearly believed to be important observations on pigeons. An unlettered farmer excited over his dog, who—evolving into a more intelligent being, clearly—seemed to know *exactly* when his master was about to take him outside for a walk. Darwin's family laughed over the well-meaning but crude letters, but the old scientist turned thoughtful as he dispatched the remains of his breakfast.

"Let them all be pleasantly answered," he said. "It is something to have people observing the things in their gardens and backyards."

As I walk out of Darwin's backyard, nobody seems to be observing *me* very much: the road back down to the village bus stop has almost no verge, so that Rovers and Renaults keep whistling past just inches away, sending me diving into the hedges. Overhead, every few minutes, a plane distantly rumbles up a steep angle of ascent as it leaves London. But then—improbably—one side of the road opens up into a glorious vision of old England. A manor, a blue sky, a line of trees. A woman on horseback clops by behind me, and suddenly there are no cars visible anywhere, no planes overhead: for a moment, the past is visible not in the mute sepia of antiquity, but in the color and living silence of actual being.

Trowmer Lodge is an ancient dwelling, so much so that it has acquired at least three different spellings—Troumer, Trowmer, and Tromer. It is set behind struck-off flint walls and a drained fishpond now filled in with lush green grass and the shade of a weeping willow. An actual Troumer family lived here from at least the 1300s, and held on to their home for centuries until the reign of Henry VIII. By 1868 Darwin's daughter Elizabeth owned the house, and as Moncure Conway walked past Trowmer Lodge, he didn't notice the tenant to whom Elizabeth had rented the house. Within was a fellow man of the cloth—one that he in fact already knew.

The Reverend Robert Ainslie was a respectable fellow, as orthodox in his belief as Conway was liberal; the two men had met years before, soon after Conway arrived in England. By then Ainslie had led a series of London lectures against "Infidel Socialism," and written pamphlets bearing titles like *Is There a God?* (In case you were wondering, apparently the answer is: yes.) But amid his old Hebrew and Latin books, his volumes of theology and history, something rather more curious sat in Ainslie's study—and had been sitting there for twenty years when Conway walked right past his house completely unaware.

I walk onward, my gaze following the stolid house in an arc as it moves out of sight. A chance comment by Elizabeth or Charles on the tenant, and Conway would have sat up and taken note: he always stopped off to visit other clergymen. Indeed, he generally found that even the most conservative ministers gave him the politest reception of all the people he met when traveling. Yes: he *could* have been invited inside, had a cup of tea in that very study where . . .

Ah, but chance did not work that way.

The road comes to a T in front of an old chapel. St. Mary's is the end of the line: the bus into Bromley terminates at this end, making its turnaround in front of a churchyard that forms the very final stop indeed for town residents. The church, like everything else around here, is built of handsome chunks of flint, and surrounding it are the wind-blasted and lichen-covered stubs of old tombstones. I lean down to read one. It is for James Fontaine, a minister who died at the age of twenty soon after preaching a sermon titled "In the Midst of Life We Are in Death." Very astute of him, if rather more astute than he might have hoped. *Thursday saw him cheerful and grateful for health*, the stone's inscription notes. *August 6th, 1825, a pale corpse.*

Charles Darwin's wife Emma is buried here, as is his brother Erasmus. So are Charles's faithful house servants of thirty-six years, Joseph and Eliza Parslow. But . . . *Charles* is not here. This is the churchyard where Darwin himself wished to be buried, and in as modest a casket and simple a ceremony as possible. It didn't happen. The government, pleading national pride with Darwin's family, buried him in Westminster Abbey in a blazingly sumptuous coffin. And so now instead of voyaging through eternity with his wife by his side, his closest company, within whispering distance of him below the ground, is Sir Isaac Newton. Somehow it seems unsurprising by now: for once dead, we no longer belong to ourselves. It is the final loss of control.

I'm the only person to board the bus, and it roars me back toward my London-bound train, its silence punctuated only by an occasional immense sneeze from the burly driver. We pass the vast fields of nature that Darwin loved so well: shady trees, grazing cows, and the ripe smell of manure in the air. As I settle in to peruse through some old maps and directories I picked up back in Guildford, back where I was searching for Chennell's house, a notation on one catches my eye: "The High Street was renumbered in 1959," it says, and . . . *Dammit.* I pore over a 1739 merchant directory and map, and—for chrissake—the numbers *are* all different. I trace my thumb over the old numbering of the municipal lots to a notation of 132, the location of a fruiterer. So 130, where Chennell lived? That used to be on the *other* side of Tunsgate.

The perfume shop.

As the cows look up with bored eyes at our passing bus, with nobody but me to hear, I laugh incredulously. It's perfect. I'd done exactly what everyone else has ever done. I walked right through a resting place of Paine's bones without realizing it at all.

Since you already know the rules of Mornington Crescent game, I won't bore you with them here. But, needless to say, I have studied them deeply: I have examined the routes of Victorian hansom drivers, read the Welsh-language texts on the Double-Reverse Stratagem, and in the Public Records Office I found the first known description of Trumpington's Gambit scrawled into the margins of a torn-out page of *Beeton's Christmas Annual* for 1889. The curious thing about the latter text is that . . .

Sorry? You haven't heard the rules?

"Mind the gap," the tunnel scolds.

The elevator begins the long ascent to the surface. Mornington Crescent is one of the deeper tube stations in London; you wouldn't want to install escalators here. In fact, once the elevators broke down in the early 1990s, they closed the place for five years and almost shut it down for good. For decades beforehand, many trains wouldn't even stop here: nobody ever much uses this station. True, it's got a rather lovely glazed terra-cotta building atop it, the inspiration for the 1920s comic song "The Night I Appeared As Macbeth":

> *The audience yelled "You're sublime!"*
> *They made me a present of Mornington Crescent*
> *They threw it one brick at a time.*

The bricks are all back in place, the station very nicely restored—and still nobody much uses it. I emerge into daylight and almost immediately trip up: pavers are scattered everywhere, along with sawhorses and taped-off areas, all haphazardly arranged as if a local drunk stumbling out of the Mornington Arms had been put in charge of the sidewalk repairs.

And out here is where Conway stood, wondering—where? *Where is he?*

Days after burying James Watson in 1874, Conway placed a notice in the *National Reformer* asking for any information from readers about Paine's remains. Watson *had* them, true, but the question of whether he'd buried Paine, and that jar of bones sighted in Guildford in 1849 . . . well, it was all very confusing. The mystery only deepened when a minister in Manchester wrote to Conway and not only claimed to have seen the revolutionary's skeleton, but also spoke of burying it.

This was hardly an idle claim, for it came from Alexander Gordon, who along with Conway was one of the most prominent Unitarian ministers in the country. It's not hard to see how Paine held an interest for him. Gordon was a well-regarded historian of religious dissent, and not long before writing Conway, he'd already come to notice for his sensational discovery of the continuing existence of the Muggletonians. A religious sect as whimsical sounding in its theology as in its name, the Muggletonians were founded by two London tailors in the 1640s, John Reeve and Lodowick Muggleton. They believed they were living in end times, but of an exceedingly curious sort: namely that they, when not busy taking up people's trousers, were endowed with God-like powers— not least because God himself no longer cared about the Earth and wouldn't interfere. Their God lived six miles above the ground, in a realm of planets and stars that were actually exceedingly small: in fact, what we perceived in the sky was their *actual size.*

One can only imagine Gordon's amazement when he stumbled upon a Muggletonian meeting in 1860. It was a veritable religious version of *The Lost World:* the sect was not even thought to exist anymore. And yet, sure enough, there they were: in fact, the members had been creating some very lovely Muggletonian celestial maps over the last few decades. Their utter obscurity makes sense when you realize that, almost alone among every religious sect ever known, the Muggletonians had no interest in proselytizing. They were the world's laziest cult, and assumed that anyone meant to join them would eventually find them somehow. Not that they'd have been easy to find. The Muggletonians did not believe in churches: they liked to hold their meetings in taverns.

After getting his head around a Muggletonian meeting, encountering a boxful of Tom Paine must have seemed downright normal to Gordon. And if it took him a few years to get around to burying them, well, he was certainly already busy with other projects as it was. Gordon was one of the most prolific contributors to that monument of Victorian historical reference, the *Dictionary of National Biography*, writing a staggering 699 entries for it. But the voluble minister turned very quiet when pressed for any further details about Paine, even when asked by a colleague like Conway. Perhaps, Conway theorized, Gordon had buried the remains near those of Paine's parents at Thetford. But perhaps not. It *sounded* like Gordon had buried Paine, but as Conway noted, "that gentleman gave no further particulars."

And with this final mystery, that should have been that: the end of Paine's travels.

But after giving a London lecture on Paine in 1876, Conway received a curious note in the mail from a London bookseller. "I remember a gentleman who had Paine's skull," it claimed. Once, in '53 or '54 and scarcely after the auction of Tilly's goods, a customer saw Paine's *Works* on display in his London shop and blurted out—maybe he couldn't help but gloat—"I have Paine's skull and right hand." When the shopkeeper pressed him for details, he clammed up. But clearly the customer felt safely anonymous in the first place, and figured the clerk didn't know who he was. Only—the clerk *did*. And years later, when the same man stopped by the store once again, the same shopkeeper recognized him again and pestered him anew for details. *Where's the skull? What did you do with it? Where's the. . . ?*

And the customer . . . ? It was none other than the Reverend Robert Ainslie.

When visiting Darwin a few years earlier Conway had walked *right past* the skull at Trowmer Lodge. It was absolutely maddening to realize, and he was determined not to miss it this time. The reverend now lived just steps from here, at 71 Mornington Road, and so Conway fired off a letter to him asking for details—but what he got back in reply was crushing. The reply was addressed in a feminine hand, and not in the writing of the reverend at all. Ainslie, it seemed, had died immediately before Conway's letter arrived. "Mr. Thomas Paine's bones were in our possession," a grieving daughter wrote back to Conway. "I remember them as a child, but I believe they were lost in various movings which my father had some years ago. I can find no trace of them . . ."

First Watson, now Ainslie: authors kept taking Paine's secret to their graves. And this latest lead made no sense at all. Why would this strictly conventional minister want the skull of the great infidel himself? Conway pondered the possibilities: was, he wondered, the Reverend Ainslie studying Paine's phrenology?

A trio of teens come up the sidewalk, bouncing a soccer ball on their way home from practice.

". . . and so it's shit then, innit?" one explains.

"S'not."

This dialectic is interrupted when the ball bounces wildly off one of the loose pavers and into the street; it's about as random a shot as any round of the Mornington Crescent game would be.

Ah—the Game. If you're an American, then I will have to explain. There is an ancient and honorable Mornington Crescent *game*, one which you will occasionally hear Brits speaking of: but when pressed for details of how the game is played, they not only wriggle out of an explanation, but will leave you more confused about it than when you started. *Oh*, they will say, *surely you already know*. Or: *The rules are easy to find. I won't trouble you with recounting them*. It is a game that seems to involve a strategic recitation of tube stops, the goal being the first to be able to utter "Mornington Crescent." The game's roots go back centuries, enthusiasts will tell you—perhaps even to the era of Roman occupation. And it has wildly proliferated over that time into innumerable stratagems and alternate rules: there's Crockford's Official Gambling Version, Lord Grosvenor's Original Metropolitan Rules, Tobermory's Stratagem, and of course Thornton's Controversial Third Amendment. There are books on Mornington Crescent, even an almanac, and yet somehow they get one no closer to understanding it. But when pressed, a veteran player did outline some of the rules once for the BBC:

* Boxing out the F, J, O and W placings draws the partner into an elliptical progression north to south.
* In a weak positional play, it is vital to consolidate an already strong outer square, eg Pentonville Road.
* The lateral shift decisively breaks opponents' horizontal and vertical approaches.

There. Now do you understand the game?

The glory of the Mornington Crescent game is that it is *complete and utter nonsense.* It's an immense put-on: the product of a radio show where contestants sit stroking their beards and oracularly muttering tube station names, all while the host gives impenetrable play-by-play analyses befitting chess grandmasters. It ends when one player, at no particular prompting, shouts out "Mornington Crescent!"—and the audience goes wild. Any rube visiting Britain who asks what it all means, or what the rules are, is then methodically flummoxed with absurdly fake histories of the game and utter evasion as to its actual workings.

Want to know where Tom Paine is? You might as well consult the *Mornington Crescent Game Almanac.* Tom Paine is lost: Tom Paine is found: Tom Paine is destroyed: Tom Paine is preserved: he is here: he is there. Tom Paine is everywhere and Tom Paine is nowhere. Where is Tom Paine? *You didn't know?* Where . . . *I have buried his skeleton but can't tell you about it.* Where is he? *Well, we had his bones but lost them.* Where is . . . *Well, we won't trouble you with an explanation of where he is, since surely you already know . . .*

Of course Tom Paine's bones got off at Mornington Crescent. Ha bloody ha.

That year Conway made one of his occasional forays back to the United States, where the Centennial was now in full swing. The minister felt ambivalent about the celebrations, and the halo that martyrdom had placed upon Lincoln's head did not impress him much either. He had met Lincoln: the man was not a mythical figure to Conway, nor could he be. "Lincoln decided that the fate of the country should be determined by powder and shot," he wrote bitterly. "In the canonization of Lincoln there lurks the canonization of the sword . . . By the same method Booth placed in the presidential chair a tipsy tailor from Tennessee, who founded in the South a reign of terror over the negro race."

But Conway rallied in the genial company of Mark Twain. The two had met in London years earlier, and now, staying in Twain's house in Hartford, Conway found the author in fine mischievous form.

"Here's a fellow"—Twain quietly stole into Conway's guest room, flourishing a letter—"who has for some time been trying to get my autograph under the pretense of business. I have to answer his notes, but have been playing a game. *Mrs.* Clemens has been writing my replies, but just for a change we want *you* to write one." Conway had already been writing, and so with his pen at the ready he scratched out a reply to the correspondent, signed: *S. L. Clemens . . . per M.D.C.*

"Mark," he wrote afterward, "went out with a triumphant smile."

The two enjoyed simple pranks and entertainments, and the billiards room got plenty of use any time Moncure visited. Once, when a friend brought Twain a mechanical hopping frog she'd found in Paris, Conway watched Twain "more amused than I had ever seen him. He got down on his hands and knees and followed the leaping automaton all about the room." On the pretext of introducing Moncure, they visited next door, where Mark's neighbor Harriet Beecher Stowe was piously writing her book *Biblical Heroines*; the men pretended to be surprised when their sober conversation was interrupted by an invasion of costumed neighborhood children. Twain had conspired with them to stage a "Mrs. Jarvis's Wax Works"—a living tableau of famous historical scenes and paintings that was one of the great parlor games of the time. Twain proceeded to narrate each scene illustrated to Stowe and Conway, drolly instructing, "Bring on that tin-shop!" to introduce one boy in clanking knight's armor.

But Twain and Conway were both writing prolifically that summer too—indeed, Twain trusted the minister's moral and literary judgment so implicitly that he now appointed him as his British literary agent. It was an auspicious time to do so. Twain had just composed a tale based upon his own childhood, much of it written in an octagonal study. If Twain found the Fowler brothers and their phrenology suspect—he'd once visited a Fowler office months apart, under an assumed name and then as his own famous self, and amused himself with the utterly contradictory head-readings they gave him—he certainly seemed to find their architecture productive for writing. He gave Conway a handwritten manuscript to take back to London with him, in the hope that publishing the book there first would help secure copyright for its American publication.

Conway was to be one of the book's very first readers. And as his steamboat made its way back across the Atlantic, he read the manuscript and realized with awe that his friend was now something much more than a humorist. "Twain," he wrote, "had entered upon a larger literary field." But fellow passengers who spied the unfamiliar title scrawled across the sheaf's first page would hardly have any notion of what they were seeing: *The Adventures of Tom Sawyer.*

The ball goes back and forth, from one side of the court to the other. *Pock,* bounce, *pock.* Bounce. *Pock.* I can never quite get used to the sight of a tennis court in Lincoln's Inn Field: central London is an area of such density that it seems almost fanciful. But I finally turn my back on the players and face a brutal modern building that elbows aside the line of brick Georgians. Ah, now *that's* more like the dog's breakfast of a city that I expect.

Is *that* where Conway went looking? It's hard to tell sometimes. Walking around London after Conway had returned bearing *Tom Sawyer,* Twain's editor Laurence Hutton would occasionally interrupt his own obsessive hunt for famous death masks—of Wordsworth, Paine, Cromwell, and the like—to marvel at how utterly changeable the city's addresses were. "It is easier to-day to discover the house of a man who died two hundred years ago, before the streets were numbered at all, than to identify the houses of men who have died within a few years, and since the mania for changing the names and numbers of streets began," he complained.

Lincoln's Inn Fields is quite the reverse: the addresses have stayed the same while the use of the place has changed over time. They used to hang people here, back before it was remade into a lush green space. And even then, as one of the largest open spaces in the neighborhood, this field became a favorite spot for staging duels. But now—*pock*, swish, *pock*—it has become rather less violent. Office workers eat their cheese-and-pickle sandwiches out here, loll on the grass, and watch the little tennis ball bouncing. A great many of them are from that monstrous newer building—the Cancer Trust—and more are from the old building next to it, the Royal College of Surgeons.

The Reverend Ainslie's daughter, it seems, hadn't been quite right when she wrote back to Conway. The skull of Paine wasn't lost at all—it *was* still with Reverend Ainslie when he died. As he went through his late father's belongings, the Reverend Ainslie's son Oliver innocently took the bones back to his own house here at 48 Lincoln's Inn Fields. Given that he was next door to the Royal College of Surgeons, it seemed rather a shame not to have someone look at these curios—and so, bones in hand, that's just what Oliver did.

They raised an uncommon interest in the building next door. Their examiner, John Marshall, was rightly regarded as one of the best surgeons and anatomists in the country. He was particularly noted for his interest in the shape of people's limbs and bodies, and had published theories on bodily proportion and the "perfect human form." When presented with the bony hand of Tom Paine, though, Marshall did not quite consider their form those of an ideal man. *This looks like the hand of a woman.*

Closer examination of the hand and skull showed that it was indeed a man, albeit a rather delicate one. "The head was also small for a man," Oliver reported of Marshall's findings, "and of the Celtic type I might say, and somewhat conical in shape, and with more cerebellum than frontal development." But beyond that, Marshall could not say much—after all, the rest of the body was missing.

Where *was* Paine's body?

"Haaauuuck."

The two young schoolgirls in hijabs duck in and out of the doorway of a chip shop, engaged in the tender feminine art of hawking loogies at each other. THE CONFIDENTIAL ANTI-TERRORISM HOTLINE, exhorts the header of a defaced poster behind them; nobody cares, and the spittle of ten-year-old girls screaming with comically horrified laughter at each other is flying everywhere. This goes on until the shopkeeper, noticing them—or noticing me noticing them—yells with exasperation at his girls to knock it off. Mouths frowning closed, they disappear.

I walk onward, facing in the distance the immense gray torpedo-shaped building known universally as the Gherkin—though I have heard substantially ruder names for it. But there is no such modern flash in this neighborhood. Stepney Green has been a London home for immigrants for as long as anyone can remember, its old Jewish population now giving way to a thriving Muslim one. Victorian tenements still bear faint painted advertisements on their brick sides—DAREN BREAD, BEST FOR HEALTH, announces one—and in front of them, the bricks of Stepney Green Road sometimes shine an almost iridescent blue, the telltale sheen of a neighborhood built partly of mining slag.

There is indeed a tiny green along this stretch of street—not *the* Stepney Green, which is farther down the road—but a rather sorry block-long patch featuring a bench missing every single one of its slats. So you can't sit here: but if you stand, you can look right into 23 Stepney Green, a respectable old brick house on a charitable block of good works and good intentions. When Conway first moved to London, number 23 housed a neighborhood Shoeblack Society, which found homeless urchins a place to live and fitted them with uniforms, brushes, rags, and blacking—this was a noxious brew of vinegar, treacle, and charred ivory—and sent them swarming into streets teeming with dirtily shod Londoners. A few houses down lodged Dr. Thomas Barnardo, the best known and most controversial of London crusaders for poor children—he was not above faking dramatic photos of squalor, and his "Dr." title proved to be equally fanciful.

But by 1879 number 23 was home to George Reynolds, a Baptist minister who was famous, as it happened, for his attacks on Barnardo's fakeries. Away from the glare of public debate, something altogether more curious had come into his life. A woman in his congregation let slip that her mother owned some rather *strange* relics and papers. They'd been sitting around since 1860, when an old tenant had died in their house at Bethnal Green. Intrigued, Reynolds paid a visit and examined a box filled with papers. *The Life of Cobbett*, read one; another was titled *The Poor Man's Bible*, and its style of writing had a curiously familiar ring to anyone who still remembered the political newspapers of half a century earlier. With these papers was a small black lump wrapped in an oilcloth, along with some snips of hair.

Who, he asked, had been her tenant?

An old tailor, she explained. Fellow by the name of Tilly.

As he read through the dead man's papers, it became obvious that there was something else that was supposed to be in this wooden box. Did you find more in here? he asked. A skeleton, perhaps?

The bones? I threw them out. They went out with the rag and bone man.

Reynolds paid the elderly landlady for the box and carried it back to Stepney Green. Something about her story did not sound quite right, and Reynolds was an experienced debunker. He and Conway, corresponding together, came to the conclusion that Tilly's landlords had sold the horrid skeleton left in the vacated apartment—possibly to the mysterious Alexander Gordon, who would now not tell either minister, Reynolds or Conway, any further details. Well, that was understandable: given Paine's peripatetic afterlife, perhaps Gordon wanted to insure that the much-abused revolutionary was never disturbed again.

But why would the landlady lie about the body? Perhaps, Conway reasoned, she wanted to appear less greedy and more pious by having destroyed the last earthly remains of the infamous Tom Paine. But the intriguing thing was not her lies about where the skeleton *was*, but an inadvertent revelation of where it *wasn't*. For a curious detail came out when she recalled to Reynolds how she and her husband first peered inside the contents of Tilly's deathly silent room.

The box, she said, was missing a skull and a limb.

By the time I get back to Lincoln's Inn, the sun is just beginning to set and the tennis court has emptied out. It's curious, really—after so many travels, Paine's skull had returned to a place scarcely a five-minute walk from its old home in the *Lancet* office at Bolt Court. But it soon became quite as neglected here as it had been in

Cobbett's hands. It seems Ainslie's daughter did not remember to tell her brother Oliver of Conway's inquiries—either that, or she did not even know that her brother had found the bones among their father's personal effects. By the time Conway had caught word of the skull's discovery and arrived here at Lincoln's Inn, it was far too late—Oliver Ainslie had carelessly left the bones along with other items in a room that was being cleared out for a tenant. The Reverend's son vaguely remembered that the man involved in carting out the rubbish was named Mr. Penny, but did not know his first name or address.

"He fears," Conway commented grimly, "that Penny may have disposed of the skull to one of the wastepaper dealers nearby." Conway held on to the hope that Penny might have been enterprising enough to separate the skull out from the other rubbish and sell it. "Every physician must possess a skull . . ." he reasoned hopefully. "It is probable that Paine's skull is now in some doctor's office or craniological collection."

Indeed, all Mr. Penny had to do to find a buyer was to go next door to the Royal College's Hunterian Museum. It is the greatest collection of anatomical oddities in the world, assembled obsessively by John Hunter, the ghastly founding father of modern surgery. When not, say, sending out an assistant to unnervingly follow one famed giant around, ready to pounce for his immense skeleton the moment the fellow dropped dead, Hunter amused himself by keeping leopards and tigers in his backyard at Earl's Court, or by apparently injecting himself with venereal pus *just to see what would happen*. His museum was a temple of human frailty and strangeness: the feet of smallpox victims floated in jars; elephantine skulls gazed out painfully; gouty skeletons encrusted with uric deposits remained frozen in agony. Body parts of the famous were always welcomed, too: and given that it boasted the Bishop of Durham's rectum among its holdings, surely the Hunterian would have found a spot on its shelves for Tom Paine's head.

But if Penny did the sensible thing and brought Paine's skull here, the public was never told. And if it *was* here . . . it is not now. You see, there is a reason that great ugly Cancer Trust building inhabits the space where Oliver Ainslie's house once stood next door. It is the same reason most ugly modern buildings in London inhabit the lots once occupied by quaint old ones: a German bomb. In May 1941 a succession of incendiary bombs rained down upon this block; ceilings and floors collapsed, pillars toppled, and fire roared through the Hunterian Museum. Giants and dwarves, fetuses and ancient skeletons, tongues and tails, entire families of native bodies collected from around the world were cremated in the searing heat; the jars of formaldehyde boiled about them and burst, and the remains were dashed to pieces as the walls collapsed upon them. Among the ruins were copious bone fragments, melted glass, and remains burned to charcoal. Some sixty thousand specimens, comprising most of the collection, were utterly lost. The museum has been closed for years now as the College finally renovates it fully back to life—or living death, rather—once again.

But that was all still to come. Back in the 1870s, the chance of a doctor claiming the skull was still a hopeful one, and perhaps Conway was simply trying to put his best face on the situation. But all Conway had was a hope, and the silence that greeted his subsequent efforts to find any bones did not bode well. A landlady claimed she'd rubbished Paine's bones; now Oliver Ainslie feared the same. But what, exactly, would throwing them out mean? Where *would* Paine have then gone?

As early as 1822, the *Times* mockingly advised Cobbett to dispose of Paine's skull with bone-dealers and phosphorus manufacturers in Whitechapel. Their joke might be closer to the truth than they imagined. Rag and bone men were a vital part of London's urban ecology: roaming the streets in horse-drawn carts bellowing "Rag-a Bo-oone!," they collected worn-out and unwanted goods that were too bulky or useful to simply be thrown out. Factories awaited them at the end of their scavenging routes. Cotton rags were ground up and turned into paper and thread, while entire towns of "Mungo and Shoddy" manufacturers in West Yorkshire made an industry of dissolving and grinding woolen garments with sulfuric acid, and recycling the extracted fibers ("shoddy") as wallpaper flocking, mattress stuffing, and yarn. And bones? They were most visibly reused in knife and fork handles, and also burned at high temperature into bone black, an animal charcoal which turned up everywhere from sugar refining to varnish and pigment. Others were ground up in immense quantities for fertilizer.

There was a certain cannibalistic quality to all this. One visitor to a chemical manure manufacturer in Bristol in the 1880s noted the very large quantity of what were clearly human bones getting thrown into the steam-powered grinders. According to the proprietor, this was not at all unusual. But then, entire human bodies were liable to be reused in Victorian Britain in a most nonchalant manner. There was a roaring trade in Egyptian mummies—the cheaper sort, the masses of men and women who had simply been buried in the sand with nothing but their windings and perhaps a scarab—because, dried out for a couple of thousand years until they were as light and crumbly as bark, these mummies made a splendid powder for paint pigment. In times like these, how much notice would a single skull in the ragman's cart attract?

The tennis players have come back again, back to play one last time today on the grounds where gallows once stood. And so I leave as Conway once left: empty-handed. There is nothing more to be found here. My feet tread across the lush grass of Lincoln's Inn

Fields—*fertilizer? Really?*—and I guess maybe the skull of Thomas
Paine really did go where he'd intended all along. It went back into
the soil.

Whhoooo-OOOOOOO-oooo.

Tambourines rattled from out of nowhere as the spectral presence
entered.

Whoooo-OOOOO-ooooo. (Twang twang twang.)

Banjos tinkled; a cold hand of fear passed over the shabby London
séance room, and then from the depths of the underworld a voice
spoke:

"I . . . am . . . the spirit . . . *of Thomas Paine.*"

Whhoooo-OOOOO-oooo.

The music—the banjo music of the damned—started up again,
and another tiny voice came out of the darkness.

"I . . . am . . . *a little Indian girl.*"

Whhhoooo-OOOO-oo . . . *Oof!*

The spiritualist went sprawling as the audience tackled him in the
darkness: banjos crashed to the floor and lights were raised to reveal
the con in all its fraudulent glory. It was a sting, and he was to be
arrested yet again for faking séances. A hidden confederate provid-
ing the spectral music and voices was now pinned down by undercover audience members: and the spirit world, it seemed, wasn't
going to pitch in to help them make bail.

And Paine? Well, he was nowhere to be found.

Despite the disappearance of Paine's bones, his spirit still made
the rounds of fashionable séance rooms in London. The old rebel
was well rested, presumably, from all those spectral memoirs that
he'd been writing back in New York for several decades. Conway
was not particularly impressed by the prospect of meeting his hero
under such circumstances; after compiling his 1879 study *Demons*

and Demonology, Conway was all too aware of the very earthly motives that appeals to demons and spirits relied upon. Séances struck him as almost laughably childish sleights of hand, and he humiliated medium after medium in London with the simplest tests. After listening to the usual table-rapping, voice-channeling, and ghostly banjo-playing at one meeting comprised entirely of mediums, the skeptical minister tossed his coin pouch on the table.

"Let anyone here tell me how much money I have in my purse," Conway demanded.

"I am surprised," one medium reproached him, "that your faith should rest on a thing like that."

"Well, it happens to occur to me: I do not know how much there is in it."

After much hushed muttering and imprecations to the vasty deep, one woman gave her answer. *Eighteen coins.* The pouch was opened, and—lo! behold!—it . . . it . . . it did not have eighteen coins.

At another séance, the participants in a darkened room asked spirits to materialize objects for them—a sausage, a slipper, an onion, and so forth. From within the darkness, a gracious Southern voice ventured that *he'd* like something too large to fit under anyone's coat. A large bandbox, say. When the lights came up, the table had its magical slipper, its phantasmal onion, an ectoplasmic sausage . . . but no bandbox. At still another séance, Conway suspected that the medium "held hands" with participants in the dark by having them eventually hold only one of his hands—one participant unwittingly holding the pinkie, the other a thumb—thus leaving the medium's other hand free to produce music and ghostly raps from underneath the table. When the medium asked to shift his hand a moment in the dark, as it was getting tired, Conway and an associate refused to let go. The medium leaped from his seat and fled the house without even picking up his banjo.

Still, Conway could not hold any real contempt for those involved. Had he not once been a traveling hellfire minister himself, preaching the presence of devils upon the earth? He knew what it was like to believe in the unseen. Looking over one séance, Conway mused: "The scene was not ridiculous but pathetic; its grotesque features vanished under the thought that if I should believe—really, and without any trace of doubt—that a deceased person had spoken to me, I also would be frantic, and my life revolutionized."

But no: Thomas Paine was gone. If he lived on, it was through the rationalist crusading of followers like Conway, and not through sepulchral voices in a roomful of badly tuned banjos. Paine himself would never again give voice to his thoughts with that too-small head of his. But as for the brain that had formed those thoughts— that was another matter altogether.

The windows are papered over from the inside with yellowing posters, rendered ever more ghastly as the sodium street lamps switch on:

The World Famous Moscow State Circus of 2003
The Sensational 6 Flying Akhtyamous!
Wed 22 Oct at Wanstead Flats

I give the door a halfhearted tug: it doesn't budge. 407 High Street is a boarded-up Lloyd's Bank that is grimly rotting at the end of the Jubilee tube line; you can only tell that it was a Lloyd's because of the letter-shaped scars left behind in the concrete from where they tore down the sign, and the skeletal remains of 4 0 7 are spelled out by a pattern of steel pegs that once held the actual numbers up.

An Asian family passes by, on their way to a restaurant for dinner, the boys chasing each other around their bemused parents. There are now a number of Asian medicine shops in the neighborhood; but a century ago, if you wanted your alternative medicine, the site of this boarded-up bank is where you went to. Louis Breeze and his family ran an herb shop here in the 1880s, along with vapour baths where Londoners suffering from colds could sit in chairs and cabinets and breathe in wintergreen-scented steam as it rose from pans heated by alcohol lamps. Breeze was a widower, and he ran the herb and bath shop with his teenaged daughter Florence; sometimes their housekeeper Sarah and servant girl Clara could be seen tidying the premises and preparing the store for the day's weary and sickly customers. They scrubbed down the baths and arranged the precious bottles of wild parsnip seeds and juniper extract under the gaze of Louis Breeze . . . and, of course, Thomas Paine.

Breeze had an oil portrait of his fellow rebel proudly displayed, along with pieces of wood taken from Paine's old house in Thetford when it had been demolished. Perhaps it helped buck him up a bit to look upon them and think of Paine's troubles whenever he en-countered his own. Aside from the sorrows of being a widower, his medical notions occasionally ran him afoul of compulsory vaccina-tion laws—for when not petitioning Parliament against these laws, he flouted them by refusing to vaccinate Florence. And among his bottles of wintergreen, his antivaccine pamphlets, and his jars of rose hips, Louis Breeze had another unusual item in his shop: a small black lump shrunken to about two inches by one inch in size, wrapped in an oiled piece of paper that bore the familiar writing of a long-dead tailor: *B. Tilly.*

It is always death or debt that shakes the remains of Tom Paine loose from their owners' hands: both would prove true for Louis Breeze. The stubborn herbalist bought the brain of Thomas Paine from his old friend George Reynolds—the Baptist minister was now short of money after ruinous legal battles with his neighborhood rival Dr. Barnardo. But Reynolds knew that at least Louis Breeze would be an appreciative guardian of Paine's brain. Taking time off from administering steam baths, the brain's new owner was happy to show the hardened chunk to Moncure Conway, and even lent it for a two-day exhibition of Paine memorabilia that Conway held over at the South Place Institute. The institute, after all, hosted everything from socialist and anarchist meetings to a convention of vegetarian Esperanto speakers; these were the kind of idealists well acquainted with the words that this now inert lump had once so stirringly produced. So there now was, at long last, the public viewing of Paine—albeit with a body now reduced through theft and secret burial to a piece the size of an india-rubber eraser.

And as for the rest—who knew? In 1887, there came yet another report of Paine's bones. Some years before, perhaps in 1880, one George Potter rode on the train from Winchester to Waterloo Station and ran into a London bookseller of vague acquaintance; while chatting the fellow mentioned that he'd bought a trunk of some papers belonging to a Cobbett descendant—and that, at the bottom, he found a single sheet of paper reading "The Bones of Thomas Paine." It sounded like the cover parchment of John Chennell's jar of bones, which nobody seemed to know the fate of anymore. And it would be easy enough to check, except . . . ah, wouldn't you know it? Potter couldn't remember the name of the bookseller now.

Of course.

Surely you know the rules to the Mornington Cresc . . .

I walk away from Louis Breeze's shop—from the lifeless space that once held it. My legs feel tired, like watch springs wound up too tight, and I could probably use one of Breeze's steam baths myself. But that's long gone: even as he showed the remains of Paine, the old herbalist was being borne down into the grave. The brain and a snippet of hair disappeared in an estate auction in 1897, first reappearing in the hands of George Reynolds, and then with Charles Higham, who ran a theological bookshop on Farrington Street. And there, for £5, a polite and aging Southern minister bought it from him.

Years and miles passed. Within a rented room on the Boulevard de Strasbourg, the steel nib of the minister's pen traced out the words on a carefully wrapped mail parcel: *New York*.

Forgetting

WHEN YOU THINK of the thousands of days you have lived by now, it is strange to realize that there are probably only a few that you can specifically remember. Most are forgotten: they only exist as a date in the indistinct past, one of an unmemorable many. But for the McNeil family, July 17, 1976, was a memorable day indeed.

Jack McNeil had been living in Tivoli for fourteen years with his wife and kids, out among the open fields of rural New York on a stretch of Kerley Corners Road, and he could be pretty sure that he knew the surrounding land and everyone on it: after all, they'd bought their property back in '62 from the neighbor who still lived across the road. Enough years had passed now that the place was needing some work, and they had to lay in a leach line out to the septic field. They had better things to do that day: indoors, ABC was televising the opening ceremonies of the Olympics up in Montreal, while other channels had talking heads nattering away about yesterday's announcement by Jimmy Carter that Walter Mondale would be his running mate. And outside? It was a glorious day—warm, sunny, a hint of a breeze. Digging a sewage ditch wasn't what anybody would pick as an ideal way to spend a perfect weekend in July—but then, septic system work isn't the sort of thing one puts off for too long.

The backhoe operator from Pease & Sons had shown up and was

getting ready to dig a furrow through the lawn. Jack McNeil probably could have run the backhoe himself—he was a highway worker, after all, a heavy-equipment operator, and he looked the part. He was a muscular guy with the sort of blond mustache that might have suited him just as well on Ted Nugent's road crew as on his DOT road crew. But today was his day off, a Saturday, and in any case this wasn't his equipment. So Jack stood aside and, mindful of the nature of the digging business, offered up a piece of advice before the operator started.

"Look out for bones," he joked.

The backhoe chugged to life and began pawing away at the old farmland, gouging out chunks of dirt and severed roots from the ground. As it tore a ditch into the earth, just a few yards from the property's old hemlock tree, the shovel hit a rock: *Crack.*

It was not the ordinary sound of pebbles and stones: this was something altogether more solid. The men stopped their work and peered into the ditch. *What was it?*

Sticking up from the earth, buried about three feet down, jutted the top of a curious piece of stone—a buried obelisk, the tip of which had been smashed away by the backhoe. As they dug down around its sides, and scraped and brushed the dirt off its marble sides, an inscription appeared beneath their fingertips:

In memory of . . .
Thomas . . .

Josephine had been out running errands—picking up shopping, that sort of thing. It was just a regular day. But when she pulled up the driveway, the kids were jumping around, running to her excitedly.

"There's a grave! A grave!" they yelled gleefully. "We found a grave!"

Oh *christ.*

Jack had been assiduously digging and scraping the dirt away, and now they worked with brushes to get the dirt off that clung to the obelisk's side. More and more words appeared on the side, and . . . And there were numbers written on it too: years.

"Let's get the encyclopedia," someone brightly suggested.

And so they went into the house and grabbed the volume covering the letter *P*, found their entry and looked at the dates in it. "Born 1737, and died 1809."

Jack started to get excited. It was the Bicentennial, after all. The names and faces of the Founding Fathers had been everywhere: Washington and Franklin reproduced endlessly on Bob's Big Boy place mats, Jefferson on Qwisp cereal boxes, Patrick Henry on Jim Beam decanter bottles. So this . . . well, this was a name they knew. This was in their *front yard*. The family looked at the obelisk that lay broken in two amid the roots of their old hemlock tree, and they examined it in disbelief. Its inscription read:

In memory of
Thomas
PAINE
who was born at
Thetford, England
Jan. 29, 1737
Died
at New York
June 8, 1809
Aged 72 years, 4 months
And 9 days

They looked in their encyclopedia. Thomas Paine: from Thetford, England. Born 1737, died 1809. The encyclopedia entry said that

Paine's body had been stolen two centuries before by an enemy turned admirer, and had been lost and never found. It could be anywhere, anywhere at all now.

They viewed their yard with widening eyes: it was him. *It was him.*

The father of our country! Or, at least, our eccentric uncle. The man who wrote *Common Sense*! The patriot who flipped off King George! Here he was!

So they laid in the sewer pipe and covered him up.

Well, come on. People needed to use the toilet. What were the kids supposed to do: wait around, hopping on one foot and then the other? And Josie, being a practical sort, had an even more pressing concern. "What if it *is* him?" she asked. "I don't want the state taking over our land."

Jack wasn't sure. But if they were reimbursed, well . . . anyway, he was at least ready to let someone dig up the grave plot. "If," he added, "they are willing to pay for it." He wasn't going to be paying Pease & Sons to dig the same ditch twice, Founding Father or not. Still, he had to admit, it was an interesting situation. Jack *had* heard something about graves out in the front yard, right by the hemlock tree—a tree, he remembered, that was traditionally planted by gravesites. So that made sense. There was some story about a previous owner here getting rid of some graves. A guy named Jesse Rockefeller—no, no relation to *those*—he'd bought the place knowing full well that Mrs. Rockefeller would never move in if she knew there was a burial plot on the lawn. And so, before she ever saw the new house, he made sure the graves . . . vanished. He did this by hitting upon the expedient of kicking over the gravestones and then shoveling dirt over them.

You could hardly blame Jesse. Paine's original grave in New

Rochelle had itself been a neglected farm plot. Everybody did it back then. Graves out on farms were only hallowed ground as long as the family owned the land: once someone else moved in, country graves had a tendency to . . . go away, shall we say. It was no different in the city, really. In the old days graves and stones were moved all the time to make way for developing midtowns and suburbs, and the plots rearranged helter-skelter, if they even bothered moving them at all. So Jesse probably didn't lose much sleep over it. What difference did it make? Who would know?

Everyone would—now.

Word was getting out in the village of Tivoli and over the phones about Jack McNeil's find. And the next day, there came the roar of vans, trucks, and cars down Kerley Corners Road. TV crews were coming. Newspapermen. Radio reporters. Historians. Politicians . . . It was the Bicentennial, and by God, *they had found Thomas Paine.*

"Are we lost?"

"No . . . maybe." I examine the useless map I've printed out from Yahoo. "Yes. No. I don't know. I thought you were *from* here?"

"Well, Kingston. Not Tivoli," Olivia explains, and laughs. "You wouldn't *choose* to come here. We used to make fun of the Tivoli kids in school. It was the total redneck place to live back then."

Back then. And those news crews didn't even have a crappy map printout to follow in '76. I watch a line of picket-fenced old houses flash by at the side of the road. Quaint shops. Nice cars. The rednecks have been quietly cashing out to Manhattan exiles for a while now.

"Roller coaster!" Elena yells from the backseat when we approach a hill. "Wheeeeeeeee!"

She throws up her arms, Coney Island Comet style, as we descend a minute grade in the road. Well, she's six: she's entitled. She's grinning happily.

"Funny way to spend a Saturday, isn't it?"

"We're going to see *Home on the Range*," she asserts.

"Soon," Olivia corrects her. "We'll go to the movie soon, okay? Paul's visiting up here and we're going to this house first."

It is a strange visit: on any remotely normal day they would be halfway to the cineplex by now. But I've known Olivia since college—since before we had real jobs, before she had a daughter and before I had a son—since before I can even remember anymore, having become a forgetful grownup—and the idea of taking a jaunt to what should be an utterly random address in Tivoli was too good to miss.

"Wheeeeee!"

Somehow, after zipping back and forth along a stretch of rural routes, we find West Kerley Corners Road.

"147 . . . 147 . . ." I read from my notes, and then point accusingly at a mailbox. "There."

The house still looks the same, I imagine: an early sixties ranch home, clad in wood and stone siding that is, unfortunately, every bit as durable as its manufacturer promised. Off to one side is a low garage, sprouting some ad-hoc plywood additions. A few rolling acres of fields spread out from each side of the house, and when we step out of Olivia's car and onto the long dirt and gravel driveway, we can hear what sounds like dogs from three surrounding farms barking at us all at once.

I ascend the concrete stoop up to the house gingerly, and as I lift up my hand to knock, the front door flies open. She has been waiting for us.

"Hi," Josie McNeil greets me. "So you're here about the grave?"

*   *   *

Well, it's all dead people now, pretty much. It's only Josephine who still lives here. There are more dead than living on this property. "That's me." Picture. "That's Jack." Another picture. "He passed away ten years ago." Shuffle. "That's me and Jack with, um, this politician—a representative from Red Hook who came out here. He's probably dead now too." Another sheet. "Here's the news reports. They're from all over. Here's one from Colorado, even. We had the *Times* here, TV people. Everybody."

The *Times* article shows Jack McNeil, shirtless, standing next to the upright obelisk, the smashed-off top lying in the grass at his feet. PAINE TOMBSTONE UNCOVERED UPSTATE REVIVES MYSTERY ABOUT PAMPHLETEER the headline reads.

"M-o-m-me-eee." Elena skips around the yard, occasionally pausing to listen to the dogs behind the house.

"Hang on." Olivia leans in and looks over our shoulders at the *Times* clipping. *"The political theorist whose writing had a profound effect on the Declaration of Independence was originally buried in New Rochelle,"* it explains, *"but his body was disinterred for reburial in his native England a few years later."*

"Nobody knows where he went," Josie adds.

I nod.

"He was never reburied in New Rochelle," the article ends, *"or, as far as is known, buried in England."*

"It made news all over the country," she says, as I gently leaf through the few other clippings in her folder. I realize I'm not seeing the one that brought me here.

"You know, it went further than that."

She looks at me quizzically.

"Have you seen . . . ? You haven't. Wait a moment."

I jog back to Olivia's car, retrieve a photocopy from my bag, and return to Josie with it.

"Here. Have it if you like."

She looks at the date: July 19, 1976.

"It's from the other *Times*," I explain. "London."

Her eyebrows nearly rise up into her knit cap at this, and she sits back down on her stoop to read it.

"Burial was refused in England, and it is not known what happened to the remains after that . . . 'Why else would the tombstone show up here?' McNeil asked today. He believed that the remains were 'right here'."

"I didn't know about this one." She takes a moment to absorb the idea of worldwide fame, and then neatly sets the clipping in her folder with the others. "I had no idea. Hmmph. Want to see it?"

"The grave? Sure."

"You don't have to go anywhere for *that*. It's right there." She indicates a spot in the grass a few feet away. "That's where we found the obelisk."

"Right here," Jack once said. Now he is gone, and probably in a well-marked grave. But Thomas Paine is not. And there is nothing marking this spot now save for the mute hemlock tree.

"So they didn't exhume . . ."

"No, no. The grave is still there."

"And this is it? This is the same tree?"

"Yeah. Though a big piece of it came off in a storm last year." She waves us to follow her. "Tombstone's in my garage now. This way."

The three of us follow her across the driveway, Elena skipping alongside Olivia. As we get closer to the back garage, the dogs get louder. Much louder.

"I raise German shepherds," Josie explains. "Just had two litters of pups. They're in the house, oh, they're taking over the place. The others I have out here. You know—did I tell you?—there's a kid down the road who had a project to do at school. Had to write about something. So he chose the tombstone in our yard. And his teacher didn't believe him. Didn't believe him! So he wrote about it and brought all the clippings in. Oh, did *she* apologize."

You can imagine the teacher's droll dubiousness; but what you can't imagine, I suspect, is how she felt when she saw what he had brought. There was headline after headline, all from 1976, all datelined Tivoli, New York. It just didn't make *sense*. I mean, how would you not know about that? How could the whole town, the whole country, not know about that? How could something that big be forgotten?

"He got an A," Josie absently concludes her story, and wrenches open the shed door.

Arrr-rrrr-rrrr-arrrrhhHHH. I jerk back; a dog lunges forward, and bangs into his cage. The smell of dog urine wallops me.

"It's okay," Josie says, taking special notice of Elena, whose eyes are widening. "They're okay. They're in their cages."

And there it is, just inside the door of a rural garage. The obelisk is surrounded on every side by caged German shepherds, inches away, like the idol of some canine religion. They are all facing it— facing us—and whining and barking and howling and banging at the cages all at once. The din is unbelievable. But there it is: on a concrete floor of a rural shed, in the filtered light of some dirty glass and fiberglass roofing, there it stands. PAINE, the stone announces.

"What," I start, "is, uh—"

There is a saddle atop the obelisk.

"—does someone *ride* this?" I finish my thought, as a howling dog bangs his muzzle several inches from my head. Josie begins to answer, but I have to strain to hear her over the baying. So her answer goes something like:

Dog 1: *Arr-arrr-arrr-arrrr*
    "Oh, that saddle . . ."
Dog 2: *ooohhwooo*
      "I keep that there . . ."
Dog 3: *RRRRRRrrrrRRRRR*
        "just to store it"
Dog 4: *Uff! Uff! Uff! Uh-uh-uFF!*
          "but I've been meaning to move it."

The dogs' sentiments, as best I can tell, may be translated loosely into English as: "Come closer, that I may separate you from your extremities."

"So, umm . . ."

"Look at both sides of that stone," Josie orders me. "Both sides. There's inscriptions on both sides. See them?"

Yes, there are *two* sets of inscriptions on this tombstone, for two different men altogether, and they are on opposite sides of the obelisk shaft. I kneel down, resting my hand lightly against the stone. The Paine inscription is still as clear as ever. Then I look at the other side. (*Rrrrr-Grrrrrr.*) Then I move back several inches from that cage. Then I look again.

John G. Lasher
born Mar. 5, 1797
died Mar. 9, 1877
aged 80 years 4 days

Why, the man barely had time to digest his birthday cake.

"Now," Josie says, "what do you think? You look too, um . . ."

"Olivia."

"Olivia. You look too. Doesn't the writing look different? The Paine looks a lot older, doesn't it?"

We look back and forth, from side to side, comparing, and . . . I can't *tell*. It's an old inscription on a tombstone, one that was buried and hit with a backhoe. The difference is a very, well . . . I mean, really, if Adobe doesn't provide it on a pull-down menu, then I don't *know* those fonts.

"So," I start. Josie is clearly waiting for my answer. "Uh. Yeah, I guess that could be different."

"Yeah," Olivia adds vaguely. "It could be."

"That's what *I* said." Josie nods. "Now why would they do that? Why would there be two kinds of writing, unless the Paine was a lot older?"

Ahhh. And there is the problem.

On July 19, 1976, the Thomas Paine story ran everywhere. Readers of both the New York and London *Times* could see Jack McNeil, shirtless and burly, gazing at his newfound tombstone. So could readers of the *Times Recorder* of Zanesville, Ohio, and subscribers to the *Walla Walla Union Bulletin*, Nebraskans who picked up a rolled-up *Lincoln Star* from their front step, and innumerable other newspaper readers and TV watchers across America. But on July 20, 1976—the day after that exciting Thomas Paine story hit the AP and UPI wires—a very different story ran back in New York.

THOMAS PAINE MYSTERY AT TIVOLI, N.Y., SOLVED, the paper announced. "The tombstone," the *Times* reported, "was a token of admiration ordered by a local resident." Looking through records, even as media were descending upon the McNeil residence, a local historian found a newspaper article, this one dated September 9, 1874, about the mysterious Mr. John Lasher. He was a former owner of the McNeil property—"an eccentric individual," as the old paper put it—and "a staunch follower of Thomas Paine." He had, apparently, simply ordered the obelisk as a monument to his hero. When Lasher himself died a few years later, the wonderfully nickel-grubbing shortcut was taken of putting his own inscription into the other side of the monument already sitting in his front yard. John Lasher was the man buried underneath that stone. His descendants still lived nearby, even. But nobody remembered him now, or where he had been buried.

But that's what happens, isn't it? Even the remains of Thomas Paine are half remembered and half forgotten at odd intervals over the centuries. There are true stories of his travels and just as many untrue ones. Some claimed that he had never been moved at all; others that Cobbett had lost him overboard on the way to Britain. That there were a number of witnesses to what Cobbett had done, not to mention a depression left in the ground on Paine's farm, didn't stop such idle speculation. The evidence gathered by Paine's biographers didn't keep ministers from entertaining children with fables of how Paine had recanted on his deathbed, or that he'd been turned into buttons and doomed to roam the world scattered into little pieces on men's shirts. And so it's little surprise that one woman in Brighton who claimed to own Paine's jaw never actually produced it: she didn't need to for such stories to become part of his hazy legend. Perhaps inevitably, another murmur arose a few years ago, along with talk of DNA testing, that Paine's skull had been found in an antiques store in London. But the buyers seem to have lapsed into silence. The hopeful shouts get heard: the disappointing facts are always strangely muted.

The Tivoli discovery—but *not* its retraction—was the greatest media exposure the story of Tom Paine's missing body has had in nearly two centuries. Most papers didn't bother with the second wire story, which inconveniently refuted the first. And so to the millions who thought of it, if they'd even bothered to think of it at all, as they flipped past the weather, past the sports, and past the CARLTON IS LOWEST ads, they all went along with their lives believing that Thomas Paine had been found after all. And so they forgot him once again.

Why do we forget?

I don't remember much of 1976. But here's the funny thing: I *do* remember the particular day they found that tombstone. I was seven years old, hundreds of miles away, and never heard the news, but I do remember the *day*. In fact, I remember every day during and surrounding that weekend. The day Jack McNeil dug up his tombstone, police in California were digging a bus out of a California quarry with twenty-six abducted schoolchildren in it. The next day, as TV crews arrived in Tivoli, everyone else in America was glued to the TVs in their living rooms: there, to the swelling of a weepy piano and string accompaniment, a young Romanian gymnast received the first perfect Olympic score. And then, the day after, as the Paine story became yesterday's news, the *Times* had a huge photo and headline across its front page: VIKING ROBOT SETS DOWN SAFELY ON MARS AND SENDS BACK PICTURES OF ROCKY PLAIN.

I can even remember, I think, the cereal I was eating back then— it was called Grins & Smiles & Giggles & Laughs. ("The first cereal that smiles back at you.") It was comprised entirely of iconic yellow smiley faces; it was like eating the seventies in a cereal bowl. I can remember by proxy, through movies that I was not yet allowed to go see, and would not be able to see for many years. But if you read the movie listings for that weekend, here's what was playing: *All the President's Men. The Man Who Fell to Earth. The Omen. Mother, Jugs & Speed. Midway. Murder by Death. Logan's Run* . . . you might as well stick a red pushpin into it, and announce: there. *That* is where our culture was at this precise moment. And yet, for periods of months, years, before and after that weekend—nothing. I can't remember a thing.

We forget *all the time*. We forget very nearly every single impression that passes through our minds. What we ate for lunch: who our roommate was ten years ago: what we paid for a soda in 1982: what we just came from the living room to the kitchen for. It is constant and vital, and we only notice it if everyday useful things go missing. Every moment gets thrown out like so much garbage— which, in a sense, is what the past is. Memory is a toxin, and its overretention—the constant replaying of the past—is the hallmark of stress disorders and clinical depression. The elimination of memory is a bodily function, like the elimination of urine. Stop urinating and you have renal failure: stop forgetting and you go mad. And so it is that the details of nearly every single day that we have lived, nearly every single moment of each day, nearly every person that we have met and spoken to, *the exact wording of the paragraph that you have just read* . . .

Gone.

(*RrrrrRRR-rrrrr.*)

"Okay!" Josie reassures the dog nearest me. "Calm down."

My ears are ringing from the guard-dog chorus gnashing within inches of us, and I notice Elena clinging tightly to the hem of her mother's shirt. We'd better get out.

"By the way," I ask Josie as we back gingerly out of the shed, and the door slaps shut on the infernal din. "Where did the top of the obelisk go?"

"Oh, the broken-off bit? It's behind the garage. It's just sitting in the grass. Sometimes I think of putting it together and putting the whole thing back up. I think that would look nice, don't you? See that little hill over there? Actually, right there—" She points at a neighboring house a few hundred yards away, with an unhitched big rig parked out front. "That's my brother's place. Anyway, I've thought of putting it on that hill. Wouldn't that be a good place for it? It'd be like the . . . oh, what is that, the guys with the flag . . . like the Iwo Jima monument."

"Oh." I nod.

Josie goes back into the garage a moment to quiet her dogs.

"Mommy?" Elena retrieves an animal quiz book from the car. "Mommy, I have a question."

"Yes?"

" 'What-do-horses-eat,' " she reads from the book in a single breath.   " 'Steaks-ice-cream-apples-pickles-oats-pineapples-hot-dogs-or-pizza?' "

"Apples," Olivia says. "And oats."

This satisfies Elena for the moment. I look at her, and then back at the garage.

"You ever have a childhood memory that you simply *cannot* place?" I finally ask Olivia. "Some random thing or place that makes no sense, that you can't figure why you'd possess in that place?"

"I do have memories like that."

"I wonder if Elena will remember this. Because it will make no sense."

" '*I went to this farm,*' " Olivia muses, " '*with this strange man, and we went to a shed full of barking dogs, and there was a lady with a funny white hat, and a tombstone with Thomas Paine's name on it—*' "

"And it had a saddle on it."

"Right," she laughs. "Right."

"Well, who knows what she'll remember."

Mrs. McNeil comes back out and explains that she has to get back to her puppies, who will now be merrily shredding the inside of her ranch home.

"They get into so much trouble at this age," she says, and adds abruptly: "Think about what I said about the writing on that stone."

"I will," I promise.

I get into the car and look over my papers while Olivia checks Elena's child seat in the back.

"Are we okay on time to make your train?"

"Sure."

"So"—Olivia snaps the buckle again—"*do* you know where Paine is?"

"Maybe." I drum a newspaper article under my fingers. "I've got one clue left."

I'm still tapping my finger against the date *1905* when Josephine dashes out of her house, struck by a final thought about the tombstone.

"You find anyone who's interested," she calls down the driveway as Olivia's car starts, "*tell them I'll sell it.*"

Eternity in a Box

THEY WERE AN unlucky bunch. Well, they *should* have been unlucky: thirteen men apiece at thirteen tables, all seated themselves for a dinner at Mills Hotel on February 13, at 7:13 sharp in the evening. A flag with the original thirteen states hung above them, and as they dined upon a thirteen-course meal that cost them thirteen cents each—Irish stew, boiled potatoes, and rice pudding all being wolfed down with gusto—the master of ceremonies addressed the doomed crowd.

"Thirteen!" he bellowed. "This banquet is held at Mills Hotel No. 1, because there are thirteen letters in the name. This will be the most prosperous year in history. Reason: 1898 is divisible by thirteen."

"Hurrah!" yelled the crowd, puffing vigorously on thirteen-cent stogies. "Bravo!"

He was followed by the landlord of the hotel.

"We furnish you tonight," he said, "with a dinner for thirteen cents which you could not get at the Waldorf-Astoria, the New Netherlands, or the Holland House for thirteen dollars."

"Hurrah! Hurrah!" they yelled, and walked under ladders and spilled some salt for good measure. But just to keep things from getting *too* uproarious, there was also a policeman at hand—

Captain O'Reilly, badge number 13 from Brooklyn's Thirteenth Precinct.

Presiding grandly over this latest meeting of the Thirteen Club, dedicated one and all to laughing at superstition, was the eccentric and appropriately named train promoter George Francis Train. After running disastrously for President, he'd famously set a record by traveling around the world in eighty days. He still hadn't forgiven Jules Verne for immediately swiping his story—"*I'm* Phileas Fogg!" he'd say, banging the table—but at least here Train was in good company. Joining him at the head table were Manhattan's greatest rationalists, all dedicated to banishing superstitious fears and traditions. Most prominent among them was an elderly man that any liberal in Manhattan would immediately recognize: the good doctor himself, Edward Bliss Foote.

Times were changing as the century came to a close, and Foote had changed along with them. His books were still selling as well as ever, but a careful reader would notice that his love of phrenology was much diminished—it didn't seem very *rational* anymore, and surely not a fit subject for a member of the Thirteen Club.

Well, maybe it was all Tom Paine's fault: in his posthumous "memoir" *Light From the Spirit World*, as popular as it was, one could glimpse the downfall of the House of Fowler. Even as phrenology overran a credulous public, it fought a rearguard action with increasingly doubtful medical professionals. "Its professors do not pursue a course calculated to elevate it to the public esteem," the *Brooklyn Daily Eagle* had warned as the Thomas Paine memoirs first emerged. "Unless Phrenology is speedily rescued from its present position, it soon will take its place beside spirit rapping, mesmerism and the other follies of the day." And that is indeed what had happened. Its idealism soon curdled; it turned from prescriptive medicine to descriptive ethnology, from a progressive vision of brain improvement to a conservative assumption of racial and genetic predestination. Phrenology became the province of carnies and charlatans, of eugenicists and racists, and by the 1890s Foote was warning that phrenology needed to shed its "crude teachings."

The host of the dinner stood up again.

"We have with us tonight," Train noted grandly, "Mr. Charles A. Montgomery, president of the Vegetarian Club."

There were approving nods. Not only were there vegetarians in attendance, but the dinner itself was a teetotaling one. These were men dedicated to rationality and *progress*.

Ah, Orson should have been here! But he never would be, nor could be. If Foote's old friends at Fowler & Wells seemed to have wandered far from their moral bearings, it was in no small part because Orson Fowler himself was no longer around. Aging, perpetually broke, and hopelessly idealistic, Foote's hero had enthusiastically taken up what he believed was the next stage in bodily reform and healthy families: sex education. But where Foote succeeded, Fowler failed. The phrenologist's *Private Lectures* sold well, but his controversial lecture tours on the subject were an embarrassment to the Fowler clan: portraits of Fowler circulated with the caption "The Foulest Man on Earth." Orson was nudged out of the running of Fowler & Wells, left to wander the U.S. on his lonely crusade: at one point, he was spotted mournfully clambering around the abandoned ruins of his Octagon House. When he died in 1887, the relieved family buried him in an unmarked Brooklyn grave. The man who had spent a lifetime studying human bodies now had his own buried and lost, never to be found again.

Well, that was the past. But as he dined on the thirteenth course of stewed prunes, Foote could sit back and look over the room with some satisfaction at a new generation of liberals. He'd been cajoling them into raising a couple thousand dollars to place a commemorative bronze bust at Paine's long-emptied gravesite up in New Rochelle. It was a project he was reminded of nearly every day, for though he still kept his offices on Lexington Avenue, his son Edward Jr. was doing much of the work now; the old man liked to relax at the mansion they'd built right next to Paine's old farm. When guests came up to visit, he and Junior would immediately take them on a jaunt around the property, showing off Paine's old cottage and the long-emptied grave.

There. They'd point. *Someday we'll get him back.*

North Avenue begins as a dreary succession of hair salons, KFCs, and broken pay phones. It was along here that General Gage and British troops once marched; and after the war, it's where a seventy-year-old man used to make the long and painful walk into town from his farm. But I don't think Paine would recognize a single block of the New Rochelle of today.

The avenue curves and the houses slowly begin to fall away; eventually bare trees and a lake appear, and the air itself starts becoming a little cleaner as I watch my breath whiten the cold air before me.

Blam!

What?

A cloud of blue smoke disperses as a couple of kids whoop and laugh hysterically; their beagle is jumping and barking wildly at a Minuteman in full uniform as he reloads. Ah, I see. They're firing off muskets by Tom Paine's cottage again. The rifleman nods and smiles at me as I walk past.

"Loud, isn't it?" He beams.

"Yeah! *Yeah!*" the boys yell. "Louder!"

Aside from the occasional musket blast, and the cars shushing by on North Avenue, it's actually pretty quiet around here. There are no other tourists in sight; in fact, you could drive right past this tidy shingle-sided home with its bright blue shutters without realizing it. Many people do. The old cottage has always been a little bit overlooked; until about a hundred years ago it wasn't even in this spot, but much farther back from the road, and so neglected that at one point the property's owner was going to demolish it for firewood. He was just barely stopped by the local Huguenot society— not because it was Tom Paine's house, but because when it was built in 1720 it was one of the earliest Huguenot refugee homes in the area. If it had been a little less unique, and built a few years later, Paine's old home would have gone up the chimneys of New Rochelle, reduced to Colonial soot.

Out at the roadside is a rather ungainly obelisk to Paine. It started out in 1839 as a column erected by Paine's followers, and was duly defaced by locals; and then, in 1899, the bronze bust that Foote lobbied for finally got cast, and stuck atop the obelisk like an architectural afterthought. But the monument is as close as you can get to a grave site, I suppose, since you can't see Thomas Paine's original plot anymore. It's now under this bit of sidewalk, right by where steps descended toward Paine's cottage—which, of course, is itself no longer where it used to be. Come to think of it, even the memorial has moved around a bit: soon after the bust went up, another road-building project meant that the whole thing had to be dragged away, stuck in storage for years, and then put out here by the road.

Just up a small rise from the cottage is a 1920s colonial with oversized columns absurdly dominating its entrance. It doesn't quite look like a home, and yet . . . it sort of is. I can't even tell, walking up to it, whether it's inhabited at all until I see that a young boy, maybe nine years old, is in the vestibule. He is industriously yanking his boots off. He's missing the musket demonstration next door, but somehow I have the feeling he's seen quite a few of those by now.

I tap at the door, and he looks up calmly, not in the least bit startled.

"Hi," I say hesitantly. "Ahh . . . I'm looking for the Thomas Paine National Historical Association."

He nods nonchalantly, as if this was a question that every growing American boy gets asked by strangers at their doorstep.

"Okay." He starts up a staircase. "I'll go get my dad."

The spade sits in a corner of the room, still waiting its next use—for another building, perhaps, or for digging a sewage ditch out in Tivoli.

"That's Edison's shovel," explains Brian McCartin, gesturing around the exhibit hall that we stand in. "When they broke ground for this building in 1925, they had Edison break ground for it. He was the vice president of the association by then."

I nod as he keeps talking; there's an old black-and-white photo of the inventor leaning on the shovel, probably standing just a few feet from where we are now.

"Anyway, what I was saying before is, Paine was the connection between the Enlightenment and the nineteenth-century Progressives . . ." McCartin continues.

Brian's got the build of a linebacker, and speaks with a Bronx accent. He actually *lives* in this museum, in quarters with his wife and son up on the second floor. The house has always been something of a refuge for New Yorkers, I guess; for a long time the tenant was Robert Emmet Owen, an American Impressionist painter who back in 1941 simply up and sold his Madison Avenue gallery and moved in here to guard Paine's legacy. Every decade or two, another keeper of the Paine relics takes a turn living and growing old here, waiting to pass it on to the next guardian.

Here is the inkwell Paine used to write *Common Sense*; over there are his spectacles, stylishly thin and back in fashion after two centuries; here is his tattered wallet and some change. It's stuff you might expect to have found on the nightstand as he died, or perhaps left atop clothes folded for the morning.

". . . And he remained probably the most important reformer of the time, at least until Marx . . ." Brian keeps talking.

I occasionally take a step backward as he talks, and McCartin takes a step forward; and in this manner we complete nearly an entire orbit around the exhibit hall, past an exhibit of Paine's design for smokeless wax candles—bought many years later by Moncure Conway—near the pieces of Paine's tombstone found in Mrs. Badeau's tavern wall, and past the time-blackened death mask that Jarvis once molded with his fingers across Paine's unseeing face. The nose is crooked, like a boxer's: the weight of the plaster, they say. But the effect is to make him look every bit as pugnacious in his person as he was in his writing.

"Now, the common rap against Paine is that he was atheist. He was in fact a Theist . . ." Brian monologues. I keep nodding. We pass a display of Conder tokens, coins minted by British businesses in the late 1700s, because their government was too broke and stingy to issue its own metal currency; citizens could design them however they liked, and amused themselves by issuing currency showing Paine dangling from a gallows over the legend "The End of Pain." Imagine traveling back to Britain and finding the very coins in your pocket calling for your death.

". . . and so . . . ," Brian is finishing his speech, and then pauses to cough and sneeze. "Sorry. Ugh. Ahh . . . What, what was your question again?"

I think back, and realize my question had been: *"Hi, my name is Paul."*

He breathes in to start another disquisition on eighteenth-century economics, and I blurt out: "I'm here about E. B. Foote."

His eyebrows go up.

"Dr. Foote?"

"Yes." I nod vigorously, suddenly excited. There is *another living person* who knows about this man. "Dr. Foote. And Moncure Conway. See . . . I'm actually here about the early history of the Association itself."

"Really?"

"Very much so."

His volubility is suddenly gone. He is looking at me as if realizing that he has no idea who on earth has walked into his museum.

"Maybe . . . maybe we should have a seat." He motions me to a table at the back of the exhibition hall. "What can I tell you?"

I look at the table a moment. It might well have come from Foote's old mansion. I wonder if this is where Foote and Conway themselves once sat? Where Foote unwrapped the package that . . .

"Well, I've been researching Conway and Foote." I pull some of their books and notes out of my bag, and riffle through them. "Following them around. I went to Foote's old mansion on Lexington Avenue, which I gather is where the Association's first meetings were held . . ."

Brian nods silently.

"And I've followed Conway's path through New York and London, read his archives, traced him all the way to Farringdon Road, where he bought Paine's brain off of Higham . . . and then followed him to the Hotel Strasbourg, where he mailed the parcel. And, then—see, I came across this . . . uh . . ."

I dig through my notes.

"This old newspaper story. About a burial cerem—"

Blam!

I start and drop my news clipping. "**October 15, 1905,**" it reads across the top.

"*Whoo-hooo!*" comes the distant cry of children outside.

"Um . . ." I hold my old article out, not sure what to say next. "About a . . . burial . . . ceremony?"

And then, for a moment, it is dead quiet in the museum. Him, me, and a hundred-year-old article: I can hear the ticking of my own watch.

"Here's what I was told." He pauses. Then he leans forward. "The monument they dedicated outside? You know that it's *two* pieces?"

I nod. Of course: there's an obelisk that some admirers erected in 1839, and there's the bronze bust that Foote commissioned at the turn of the century. In fact, he commissioned it right about the time Conway bought . . . *wait* . . .

"Well," McCartin says, "there's a *reason* they stuck the bust on top of the column. Conway had a cavity carved out of the top of the obelisk." His hand makes a scooping-out motion. "Right between the capstone and the bronze bust of Paine's head."

He lets this sink in.

"So that cavity," I mutter. "Is where . . . Dr. Foote . . . ?"

"That's right. That's where he cemented in the box."

I look out a window in the direction of the roadside monument— that awkward combination of a bust atop an obelisk—and then I look back at Brian, not sure whether to grin or let my jaw drop.

"You mean . . . it's . . . it's . . ."

"Yes."

I stare back out in disbelief, and then a smile spreads across my face. Of course. Of course. Of course that's what they did.

They put his brain in his head.

*　　*　　*

The mayor had asked the townspeople of New Rochelle to hang out flags on their porches for that fine autumn day, but not many of them did.

"New Rochelle," a *Times* reporter dryly noted, "is a city of churchgoers."

Well, that reaction was to be expected when the honoree was old Tom Paine. But the townspeople began pouring out into the streets that afternoon anyway to follow the parade as it headed up North Avenue: headed by four rather stout mustachioed men in tight-fitting Minutemen uniforms, the Fort Slocum army band struck up a march on their tubas and trombones as children on bicycles darted in and out and ran alongside.

A line of American flags was hastily strung up between two trees on either side of the avenue so that as the procession of town worthies, schoolchildren, members of the Fort Slocum band, and local military representatives made their way up North Avenue, they found a stage erected with a suitable festooning of red, white, and blue. Behind it all stood the newly moved Paine monument, awaiting its rededication to the care and protection of the citizens of New Rochelle. Soon the avenue became a small sea of hundreds of curious townspeople and visiting big-city reformers alike; children in newsboy caps, men in vests and derbies, women in long skirts. The band launched into a rousing overture, and then paused for the schoolchildren to begin singing:

> *In a chariot of light, from the regions of the day,*
> *The Goddess of Liberty came,*
> *Ten thousand celestials directed her way . . .*

The brass band struggled to keep time with the children, whose singing of Tom Paine's song lyrics got increasingly wobbly. The children appeared a little frightened. "Somebody must have been telling them dreadful stories about Tom Paine," one man in the crowd theorized aloud as the band stumbled over the final bars of "The Liberty Tree."

The last off-key notes died out. A minister pronounced a benediction upon the proceedings, and stood aside as a thin, dapper man surmounted the stage: it was Dr. E. B. Foote Jr., proudly stepping in for his ailing father. An autumn wind passed through the orange and yellow leaves of trees about the procession as his first words rang out over the crowd.

"Ladies and gentlemen," he called out. "Others will tell you today of the life and works of Thomas Paine. I am here to give you the *last* chapter in his story."

The men in the band set their trombones at rest, and the children stopped running about; the crowd strained to hear the doctor's voice.

"Paine died," he continued, "at number fifty-nine Grove Street, in New York City, on the morning of June eighth, 1809, and the funeral was held a few days later. His body was brought up from New York and buried somewhere within fifty feet of this monument . . . William Cobbett, an Englishman, raised the bones of Paine and took them back to England with him. At that time Cobbett thought he could effect a revolution in the government of England with the bones of Paine, and that men would get together and erect a great monument to Paine, but from Mr. Cobbett's large idea only small results came.

"The fact is"—the doctor looked out over the crowd—"that nothing was accomplished by the project, and the bones knocked about England for many years until now. No one, Mr. Conway says, knows where they are. In 1833 a man named Tilly . . . secured a small portion of his hair and brain. That piece of brain was handed down until Mr. Conway got hold of it in London. This relic of Paine is here . . ."

Foote paused and drew from his pocket a copper box, patinaed green with age.

"*Here.*" He held it aloft. "In *this* small box."

The crowd jostled and gawked upward at the object.

"Now," the doctor continued, "this portion of the remains is all that we have left, and it will be placed within this monument. Then we can say the remains of Paine, all that we have, are to be found *here.*"

Here.

Here's the strange thing about the bust of Thomas Paine: he's looking away. And I don't mean up into the lofty heavens or straight out into the middle distance. I mean his eyes are averted to one side. I follow his gaze and see that he is looking directly into a house far across the street; in its living room window there is a telltale flicker. And so this is how Paine's big brass head, with his brain clapped firmly inside, is spending eternity: staring into a suburban den and watching *The Price Is Right.*

Actually, the way the monument is built, I suppose his brain might be right where his heart would be. But it's the cold green metal of his face that I gaze up at, trying to imagine that day a hundred years ago—and trying to imagine the strange moment when that little box was first opened. They say the brain resembled a small piece of hardened black putty. Well, that's what they *said*: nobody knows now. You see, pretty much everyone who handled Paine's brain died, from one cause or another, not many years after the ceremony. Moncure Conway, now a lonely old widower still struggling for the cause of peace, passed away in Paris in 1909. The junior Dr. Foote followed just a few years later. Despite his father's lifelong vegetarian and electromagnetic regimens for him, Junior had always been a curiously morose and sickly boy. He had not much outlived his father; though holding the senior Dr. Foote's cold fingers one last time, he was able to reach into the coffin and wrap his father's folded fingers around a copy of *Dr. Foote's Home Cyclopedia of Medical, Social and Sexual Science.* With his words clutched to his breast, the old doctor carried his works into the hereafter.

As do we all, I suppose.

I turn and look down the road back into town—the road Paine once walked, the road that Cobbett raced away on, and that Foote rode eighty years later to gently return him. When I first began to trace the route of his bones, I was struck by the extraordinary coincidence of how they fell into the hands of activists for everything from abolition and women's rights to vegetarianism and pacifism. But that such people would place themselves in his path was no coincidence at all. Like saint's relics, Tom Paine has passed from one idealistic reformer to another over the years: his travels are those of democracy itself. Who else could have brought together a Manhattan physician, a Virginia minister, a Surrey farmer, and a London publisher? They always came back to that call to common sense—to our sense of rationality, of hope, of kindness—against tradition and fearful irrationality, against the dead authority of the past. And now they are the past themselves: we are the unseen future that they progressed toward, the inheritors of all the struggles they began.

Where is Tom Paine?

Reader, where is he not?

(E L S E W H E R E)

Further Reading

A Note on the Epigraph

But who knows the fate of his bones, or how often he is to be buried?

Indeed.

The famed writer of *Religio Medici* spoke truer than he knew. In August 1840, workmen at the St. Peter Mancroft Church in Norwich were digging a grave in the chapel's chancel when a blow of the pickax rebounded from the earth with a mighty *crack*. The gravediggers leaned in to look at what they'd struck: it proved to be an ancient leaden coffin, its lid now badly fractured by the pickax. Atop that lid, and also split in half, was the brass plate that had been affixed to it:

Amplissimus Vir. Dns. Thomas Browne,
Miles, Medicinae, Dr. Annos Natus 77
Denatus 19 Die mensis Octobris, Anno. Dni. 1682,
hoc Loculo indormiens.
Corpis Spagyrici pulvere plumbum in aurum Convertit.

In the dim light of the chapel, they could see a skeleton through the fracture in the lid. It was the body of an aged but respectable gentleman, with but one tooth left in its head, and a fussy auburn wig was still draped about its skull. The remains of a beard was peppered atop the jaws and neck. The inscription was indeed for Sir Thomas Browne—fallen on his seventy-seventh birthday, according to one account of the time, having "dyed after eating too plentifully of a Venison Feast." The bones were to be properly reburied; now that they knew who it was, it was sacrilege to keep them above-ground any longer.

That's not quite what happened.

George Potter, the sexton and apparently a rather enterprising fellow, decided that the skull wouldn't be missed much by its former owner. Skulls were much in demand these days, after all, as medical men tried to keep up with advances in phrenology; and what better model of the shape of human genius than in the skull of Sir Browne? So, before reburying the final works of Thomas Browne, he, shall we say, *edited* them.

George first approached Dr. G.W.W. Frith at the Norwich Hospital, and offered him the grisly relic for sale; being the sort of respectable fellow with three initials in his name, the good doctor refused. But his colleague Dr. Edward Lubbock had rather fewer initials and fewer qualms, and thus became the proud possessor of Browne's skull. After a few years of fond gazing upon his find, in 1845 the doctor deposited it in the hospital's Pathological Museum—literary genius, presumably, constituting a dread pathology. And there the story ended for a while: both the sticky-fingered sexton and the doctor died in 1847, taking to their graves any particular concern over Browne's skull.

It wasn't until 1893 that the church sat up and noticed that its most prized skull had been missing for some fifty-three years. It demanded it back from the hospital, whereupon the hospital's board met, gravely considered the matter, and answered: no. The skull was not, the board argued, a "mere curiosity"—why, it helped inspire visitors to the hospital *to read Sir Thomas Browne*. One imagines this is why Browne's skull was loaned out to be posed and photographed sitting atop a stack of his own books—a rather perverse twist on the notion of an author having a *body of work*. You can view this unnerving photo as the frontispiece in volume II of Charles Sayle's edition of *The Works of Sir Thomas Browne* (1904): in it, the skull and jaw have been wired together in such a way as to keep the toothless jaw open at a rather jolly angle, as if old Sir Thomas was having a good laugh over the whole situation.

The skull was finally reinterred in 1922, along with an entry in the church register that drolly notes the deceased's age as "317 Years." The story lives on, though, in articles in the journal *Notes and Queries* (the issues dated 28 July 1894 and 22 September 1894) and in the continuing research of James Eason at the University of Chicago, where he maintains a splendid Sir Thomas Browne's Skull Web page.

The End

In piecing together Paine's final days I was confronted by accounts of greatly varying trustworthiness. The standard account of Paine's life remains Moncure Conway's *Life of Thomas Paine* (1892) and *Writings of Thomas Paine* (1894). Conway was able to meet some of Paine's friends and neighbors while they were still living, and brought a level of sheer dogged scholarship and fairness to the task that no previous biographer ever remotely approached. But there are sympathetic accounts by W. T. Sherwin (*Memoirs of the Life of Thomas Paine*, 1819) and Thomas Clio Rickman (*The Life of Thomas Paine*, 1819). Peter Eckler's later *Life of Thomas Paine* (1892) is useful for its accounts of Paine's contemporaries. It was from the fearless British radical publisher George Holyoake—the last man in Britain to be prosecuted for atheism—and his 1840 book *The Life of Thomas Paine* that we find a detailed debunking of some hostile accounts of Paine's dying days. He also helpfully quotes the research of Gilbert Vale, as Vale's own corrective *Life of Thomas Paine* would not appear until 1853. Vale's account includes a number of testimonies by those quoted in hostile accounts of Paine, and shows them either disowning their earlier statements or placing them in a less misleading context.

But even these debunkers can slip. Holyoake mentions "Amasa Woodsworth," and identifies him as an engineer who lived next door to Paine in his last days. But an examination of the 1810 New York Census Index finds an Amasa *Woodworth* (no *s*) living there. This reveals a rather less random pattern of friendships during Paine's final days than one might have previously thought, as *Woodworth* was involved in the development of Daniel French's oscillating steam engine, which French patented in 1809.

So much for friends: now for enemies. The first Paine biography, Francis Oldys's *Life of Thomas Pain, the Author of The Rights of Man, With a Defense of His Writings* (London, 1791), was nothing of the sort: it was written by the scholar George Chalmers under a pseudonym, and very ingeniously mixed diligent research and newly discovered facts (it is to Chalmers that we owe most of our understanding of Paine's early life in Britain) with outright slander. A similar approach was adopted just weeks after Paine's death by James Cheetham for his 1809 biography *The Life of Thomas Paine.* Cheetham and Paine were former colleagues who had turned bitter enemies; Paine was about to sue Cheetham for libel when he died, and Cheetham lost a separate libel suit over this book. But Cheetham did indeed contact many of Paine's friends and neighbors, and—though his quotations from them are utterly misleading—his *identification* of the people and places frequented by Paine remain invaluable. Hostile biographies since then—Cobbett's edition of Oldys, for example, or John Harford's *Some Account of the Life, Death, and Principles of Thomas Paine* (1819)—are almost all rehashings of Oldys and Cheetham.

I suppose you want to know about the drinking.

Sure, they all do. Whether Tom Paine was a drunk is a perennial concern of biographers. Cheetham made much of this in his hostile biography. Leaving aside whether it matters—since it doesn't—I would guess that Paine was a social drinker most of his life, but that he did indeed drink heavily in his final years. Considering that he was dying in an age before painkillers, it's hard to see why he *shouldn't* have drunk heavily. The clearest evidence comes in a letter by Thomas Haynes, dated October 30, 1807, and now in the Robert Hunter Correspondence file at the New York Public Library. (Elihu and Mary Palmer's letters about Paine are also in this file.) Haynes makes clear his anger over Cheetham's attacks and his regard for

Paine while *also* noting Paine's drinking. The wording seems to indicate that this was a new development. Unlike Paine's print biographers, all of whom had an ax to grind for or against him, Haynes's letter is both private and by a friend of Paine's and thus far more believable.

It is also Haynes's letter that notes Walking Stewart's visit to New York City, and the fear that he had drowned in a shipwreck. In fact, Stewart survived and indeed prospered. After a period of poverty— Thomas De Quincey hesitated to visit him at his quarters, because he didn't want the gracious Stewart to feel obliged to offer scarce tea or bread—Stewart won a spectacular legal claim against the Nabob of Arcot in 1813. He recovered a £14,000 award that enabled him to live out his remaining years on Northumberland Street surrounded by a salon of literary and musical friends, and enjoying a massive organ he had installed in his apartment, which was the only instrument capable of blasting through his deafness. Stewart left an extraordinary collection of books and pamphlets in the British Library; my references were largely drawn from the entertainingly odd *Revelation of Nature* (1794). Stewart's life cries out for a scholar to write his biography, but until then the primary accounts come from *The Life and Adventures of the Celebrated Walking Stewart* (1822) and particularly the profile in volume III of *The Collected Writings of Thomas De Quincey* (1890).

For Paine's other great colorful friend of these years, see Harold E. Dickson's *John Wesley Jarvis, American Painter 1780–1840: With a Checklist of His Works* (1949). Jarvis was prolific, and a great many of his paintings turn up with dealers and museums; in fact, the same year Dickson published his book, the long-lost 1806/7 Jarvis portrait of Paine was discovered.

But Jarvis's cartoon of a Quaker abandoning Paine scarcely hinted at the tensions that Paine's awkward burial request played upon. H. Larry Ingle's *Quakers in Conflict: The Hicksite Reformation* (1998), Henry Wilbur's *The Life and Labors of Elias Hicks* (1910), give a sense of how Paine's death came just as modern liberal Quakerism was coalescing, and Walt Whitman's "Notes (Such as They Are) Founded On Elias Hicks" appears in his 1888 newspaper column collection *November Boughs*. Ironically, Elias Hicks also went to an unquiet grave: the *Niles Weekly Register* of April 10, 1830, reveals that an artist, unsuccessful in asking the Friends to take a death mask of Hicks, secretly exhumed him and made one. The Friends, suspicious when they saw the ground disturbed, dug Hicks up and found bits of plaster still stuck to his hair.

In describing the past dwellings of Paine in his final days, I was greatly helped by the *New York Times* archive. There are a number of hints about 309 Bleecker Street; ads for the Lee & Co. window screen company ran throughout the 1850s, a January 29, 1876, article on "The Birthday of Thomas Paine" identifies it as "a beer and billiard saloon," and the February 28, 1930, article "Old Home of Thomas Paine Faces Demolition" features a large AP photo of the old building in its final days. A mortgage notice from June 22, 1933, shows the building as still standing, but I believe it was demolished soon afterward. Of the old newspapers mentioned relating to Paine's death, the *United States Gazette for the Country* (June 12, 1809) can barely be bothered to mention him; while the Tontine House auction ad can be found on page 4 of the *New-York Herald* for May 5, 1810.

Details of the life of Benjamin Lay can be found in Robert Vaux's *Memoirs of Benjamin Lay and Ralph Sandiford* (1815), and Lydia Marie Child's *Memoir of Benjamin Lay: Compiled from Various Sources*, published by the American Anti-Slavery Society in 1842. There's also a colorful account of Lay's "fake blood" antics in John

Greenleaf Whittier's introduction to the 1871 edition of *The Journal of John Woolman*. Lay is a neglected figure these days, and the man surely warrants a modern biography.

And finally, for Paine's American beginnings, you can get some of the flavor of the Philadelphia of yore from George Barton's 1925 *Little Journeys Around Old Philadelphia* and Christopher Morley's 1920 *Travels in Philadelphia*. Do buy yourself some old prewar editions of Morley: they're charming, and always staggeringly cheap—often priced in the single digits.

Committed to the Ground

Cobbett embodied so many contradictory opinions that it's hard to summarize him. Sometimes he wrote for Paine, sometimes against; he fought against child labor and for worker's rights, but was indifferent to slaves and hostile to Jews. There is no lack of venom and ignorance to be found in his work, and yet occasionally he soars far above his peers, as in this speech decrying claims that outlawing child labor would damage the economy:

> Hitherto, we have been told that our navy was the glory of the country, and that our maritime commerce and extensive man-ufactures were the mainstays of the realm. We have also been told that the land has its share in our greatness, and should be justly considered as the pride and glory of England. The Bank, also, has put in its claim to share in this praise, and has stated that public credit is due to it; but now, a most surprising discovery has been made, namely, that our superiority over other nations is owing to 300,000 little girls in Lancashire.

Perhaps the best way to understand him is the way so many of his countrymen did, by reading Cobbett's *Political Register*. The British Library has a bound set, and those interested in the tale of Paine's bones will particularly want to read volume 35, which covers the period of 1819 to 1820. It's easy to find paperback reprints of his amiable *Rural Rides* (1830) and *The American Gardener* (1821); but perhaps the best sense of the man can come from editor William Reitzel's *The Autobiography of William Cobbett* (1947), which cle-verly assembles fragments from Cobbett's voluminous writings into a very readable and entertaining "in his own words" autobiography.

It goes along quite nicely with Laurence Vulliany's *William Cobbett's Rural Rides Revisited* (1977), a photo essay which traces Cobbett's footsteps and finds power stations and modern bungalows where farmland once stood, but also finds a surprising number of old vistas still largely unchanged or gently decaying. I'm particularly fond of the photo of a haplessly bashed-up old cast-iron sign on one trailside, sternly warning:

PERSONS

THR   NG

ST   S

AT TH

TELEGRAPHS

ILL BE

PROSEC TED

It would appear that the sign made for excellent target practice.

References to Cobbett and the bones, though hostile and not to be overly trusted, can be found in the *Times* of London for November 18 and December 22, 1819, and July 13, 1820. For a sense of the graveyard chaos of the era, see Philip Neve's 1790 pamphlet *A Narrative of the Disinterment of Milton's Coffin in the Parish Church of St. Giles, Cripplegate* (the New York Public Library has a copy); a letter to the April 17, 1852, issue of the journal *Notes and Queries* claims "I have handled one of Milton's ribs . . . One fell to the lot of an old and esteemed friend, and between forty and forty-five years ago, at his house, not many miles from London, I have often examined the said rib-bone." But for a particularly useful annotated firsthand account of medical grave-robbing, read James Blake Bailey's *The Diary of a Resurrectionist* (1896).

It would be an almost hopeless task to compile all the newspaper and pamphlet attacks made on Cobbett during his lifetime, but one of the prime examples, using the side-by-side format to damn Cobbett with his own conflicting opinions, is *Cobbett's Gridiron* (1822). Of the numerous pamphlets mocking Cobbett and the bones—bear in mind that Cobbett arrived in Liverpool on November 21, so these illustrated satirical pamphlets flooded out within a matter of weeks—two typical examples are *Sketches of the Life of Billy Cobb and Tommy Pain* (1819) and *The Real or Constitutional House that Jack Built* (1819). The latter is itself one of many ripoffs of a very successful pamphlet published earlier that year by Cobbett's fellow radical William Hone, *The Political House That Jack Built*, which cleverly used the structure of the children's rhyme to build up an argument against the suspension of habeas corpus and other injustices resulting from Peterloo.

To get a broad sense of the economic and social pressures building up in Britain prior to Cobbett's arrival with Paine's bones, it's still hard to beat R. J. White's classic study *Waterloo to Peterloo* (1957), as well as J. H. Plumb's *England in the Eighteenth Century* (1950); there have been many useful studies before and since, but these remain models of clarity. Paine's essays are available in numerous editions, but M. Beer's 1920 anthology *The Pioneers of Land Reform* is a particularly useful compilation, as it places *Agrarian Justice* (1796) in the context of William Ogilvie's *Essay on the Right of Property* (1781) and William Spence's *The Real Rights of Man* (1775 / 1793). These make it clear that Paine's thinking, while certainly striking, was part of a wider radical property-theory tradition. Spence, though not mentioned in this book, is a striking protosocialist figure from the era. He and Paine were commonly paired together in the discussions of reform; Conder tokens often show them together, and indeed sometimes hanging together at the gallows.

For a charming old essay on the very deepest roots of British property laws, see Augustus Jessopp's *Studies by a Recluse* (1893). Jessopp was one of those eccentric country parsons that Britain once seems to have cornered the market on; a friend of Gothic writer M. R. James and the novelist Angela Thirkell, he wrote about antiquities like a ghost story writer, and ghost stories like an antiquities writer. Those looking for his fiction might want to try *Frivola* (1896); sadly, and rather like one of his own plots, he became a bit of a ghost in his old age, slowly descending into lonely madness.

Finally, mention of the notice against writing on skulls can be found in the fourth volume (i.e., Fourth Series) of Frank Buckland's wonderful *Curiosities of Natural History* (1879), in his essay "Ancestral Skulls." In this same essay he makes an extraordinary suggestion that seems prophetic of modern forensic reconstruction: "I feel convinced that sculptors would do well to practice restoring the features by means of modelling clay to skulls. The student might take a modern African skull, and on it mould the features of a negro; the same with a European or Mongolian specimen, & c."

The Bone Grubbers

There are three primary contemporary accounts of the travels of Thomas Paine's bones. Two are by active participants and possessors of Paine's remains. The first is *A Brief History of the Remains of the late Thomas Paine, From the Time of Their Disinterment in 1819 by the Late William Cobbett M.P., Down to the Year 1846*, which was published in 1847 by James Watson and almost certainly written by him as well—it includes, suitably enough, a substantial list in the back of Paine books published by Watson. Watson's pamphlet ends with the bones still in Tilly's possession; Watson had no inkling of the possible lifting of bones by John Chennell, or indeed of his own eventual ownership of the bones.

The second account is Moncure Conway's *The Adventures of Thomas Paine's Bones*, a handwritten manuscript in the archives of the Thomas Paine Historical Association. Conway published two excerpts from this article in *The Truth Seeker* in June 1902; these fell into obscurity and their existence is not even known to many Paine scholars. Rarer still is the original, more detailed manuscript, which was never seen in its entirety until Kenneth Burchell transcribed it for members of the Thomas Paine Historical Association in their *Journal* of March 2002. Conway also has a brief commentary on Paine's remains in volume 2 of his *Life of Thomas Paine* (1892), but this is largely superseded by *The Adventures of Thomas Paine's Bones*.

Rather more mysteriously, in 1908 the anonymous booklet *Thomas Paine's Bones and Their Owners* appeared; in addition to recounting the facts of the previous pamphlets (and in some cases, reconfirming them by contacting participants who were still alive), it introduces a number of new details about Benjamin Tilly's final days, and reveals Watson's purchase of Paine's bones at Tilly's auction around 1853. The New York Public Library's copy of the booklet is of particular interest, as it apparently reveals the writer's real name (Jabez Hunns, of Wood Green, London) and includes annotations in the author's own hand. Though they are largely in agreement anyway, when in doubt I have tended to favor the explanations in Conway and Watson over those by Hunns, since they are known and credible witnesses; nonetheless, Hunns does appear to have been in some position to know the people involved in tracking down Paine. This copy was given to the library by William Van Der Wyde in 1912, who at the time was the president of the Thomas Paine Historical Association. He knew Conway and probably knew Hunns too, since he came into possession of this personally annotated copy.

In addition to the articles noted for the previous chapter, references to Cobbett and Paine's bones can be found in the *Times* of London for 29 January 1821, 15 February 1822, 24 July 1822, 31 January 1823, 11 October 1823, 13 February 1826, 28 March 1826, 9 May 1826, 4 May 1827, 25 October 1828, 26 January 1836, 14 June 1836, and 16 November 1836. The publishing activities on Bolt Court can also be glimpsed in the many publishers listed there during the nineteenth century, including the firms W. Tyler, Bensley & Son, Mills Jowett & Mills, and in Rupert Cannon's *The Bolt Court Connection: A History of the LCC School of Photoengraving and Lithography: 1893–1949* (1985). The long publishing history of Paternoster Row and Queen's Head Passage can be seen in Samuel Leigh's *Leigh's New Picture of London* (1819) and *The London Book Trades 1775–1800: A Topographical Guide to the Streets* (Exeter Working Papers in British Book Trade History, 1980), which is now available online at the Devon County Library's Web site.

The main account of Carlile for most scholars remains Joel Wiener's *Radicalism and Freethought in Nineteenth Century Britain:*

The Life of Richard Carlile (1983); there's also a very useful account in Theophilia Carlile Campbell's *The Battle of the Press, as Told in a Story of the Life of Richard Carlile, by His Daughter* (1899)—this can be hard to find, but the New York Public Library has one. See also the chapter on the War of the Shopmen in David Nash's *Blasphemy in Modern Britain: 1789 to Present* (1999), and in T. A. Jackson's *Trials of British Freedom* (1968). For an interesting if scattershot account of Carlile, see Guy Aldred's *Richard Carlile, Agitator: His Life and Times* (1941); *Richard Carlile: His Battle . . .* (1917), and Aldred's edition of Carlile's *Jail Journal: Prison Thoughts and Other Writings* (1942); it's a wartime book, and by a socialist publisher at that, so it's all rather slapped together and chaotic. Nonetheless, it's worth picking up.

The trials of Carlile and his assistant made up quite a body of literature in the 1820s, much of it published by Carlile himself. Some representative examples can be seen in the *Report of the Trial of Mrs. Susannah Wright* (1822), and many others are compiled in *The Trials with the Defences at Large of Mrs. Jane Carlile, Mary-Anne Carlile, William Holmes, John Barkley, Humphrey Boyle, Joseph Rhodes, Mrs. Wright, William Tunbridge, James Watson, William Campion, Thomas Jefferies, Richard Hassell, William Haley, John Clarke, William Cochrane, and Thomas Riley Perry, being the Persons who were Prosecuted for selling the publication of Richard Carlile in various Shops* (1825). The tale of the ingenious "puss and mew" gin-vending machine can be found in Jessica Warner's *Craze: Gin and Debauchery in an Age of Reason* (2002). John Stuart Mill's account in the July 1824 issue of the *Westminster Review* was reprinted in 1883—this time, in the wake of the prosecution of freethinker G. W. Foote— under the title *J. S. Mill On Blasphemy.*

Carlile's medical crusades are best understood through the pages of his own newspaper *The Republican,* but there's also an interesting (if slightly incoherent) assemblage of his and Thomas Wakley's battles in Charles Wortham Brooks's *Carlile and the Surgeons* (1943). It is quite difficult to find old copies of Richard Carlile's *Every Woman's Book* (1826)—not surprisingly, since they were kept well hidden, and were probably read to pieces—but fortunately M. L. Bush's fascinating *What Is Love?: Richard Carlile's Philosophy of Sex* (1998) includes both the full text of *Every Woman's Book* and extensive commentary on its history.

S. Squire Sprigge's *The Life and Times of Thomas Wakley* (1899) provides not only a history of the early *Lancet* editorial meetings, but also some fascinating accounts of Wakley's work as a consumer advocate tangling in the 1850s with London food vendors. When the magazine investigated cocoa powders, "of fifty-six samples examined, many of which were warranted pure and possessing all sorts and kinds of charming qualities, eight only were found to be genuine." And while imported American nutmeg was found entirely genuine, "of twenty-one curry powders nineteen contained ground-rice, flour, salt, and colouring matter—red lead, for example—in varying proportions."

W. J. Linton's brief biography *James Watson: A Memoir* (1880) gives a rare glimpse into his friend's home life, and into his spartan life behind the counter. For information on the movements of Cobbett and George West, many thanks are due to the Normandy Historians group and their transcription of that town's parish tax records. Some curious legal history of posthumous debt collection can be found in a series of letters in *Notes and Queries* on "Arresting A Dead Body For Debt" for March 28, May 2, and July 18, 1896, as well as in John Timbs's *Popular Errors Illustrated and Explained* (1856)—which also helpfully notes among other errors that hedgehogs do not suck cows dry, and that cats do not suck the breath out of sleeping infants.

The Talking Heads

The life and works of George Lippard have been slowly making their way back into the canon of nineteenth-century literature, thanks in no small part to the efforts of my old professor David Reynolds. *The Quaker City* (also known as *The Monks of Monk Hall*) is now easy to find in reprints. It really is too bad that Lippard didn't get to put on his stage extravaganza of *The Quaker City*, for it would have been some fine viewing to see how he pulled off the culminating vision of the book: archvillain Devil-Bug's dream of the destruction of Philadelphia in the far-off year of 1950. Led by a mournful ghost through the ruins of Independence Hall—for the republic has fallen and monarchy reestablished—Devil-Bug gleefully finds only one telltale institution of the old America still thriving:

> "It is the gallows!" said the Ghost. "And thanks to the exertions of some of the Holy Ministers of God, it is never idle! Day after day its rope is distended by the wriggling body of some murderer . . ."
>
> "Hurrah!" shouted Devil-Bug. "The gallows is livin' yet! Hurrah!"
>
> "For some years it was utterly abolished," said the Ghost.— "Murders became few in number, convicts were restored to society, redeemed from their sins, and gaols began to echo to the solitary footsteps of the gaoler. But these good Preachers arose in the Senate and the Pulpit and plead beseechingly for blood!"
>
> "Hurrah for the Preachers! Them's the jockies!"
>
> " 'Give us but the gibbet,' they shrieked. 'Only give us the gibbet and we'll reform the world!' "
>
> "They said this? The jolly fellers!"

Devil-Bug merrily watches the vengeful dead rise up from their graves and slaughter each other all over again in a massive conflagration on the Schuylkill River, where fleets of thousands of floating coffins, piloted by corpses, row to doleful drumbeats sounded upon burning skulls affixed at the prow of each casket.

Ah, Philly in the old days!

Lippard's *Thomas Paine: Author-Soldier of the American Revolution, delivered in Philadelphia on January 25, 1852,* is altogether more rare; a reprint can be found in the Gimbell Collection of the American Philosophical Library in Philadelphia. An editor's note by Jason Elliott notes the effect that Lippard's speech had in reviving Paine's popularity among publishers.

Charles Hammond's *Light from the Spirit World* was published by different publishers in various cities across the country, but most copies turn up from the New York publishing house of Partridge & Brittan, which did a roaring business in the popular spiritualist writings of A. J. Davis, along with hawking their magazine *The Spiritual Telegraph*—a title that, for the 1850s, must have carried the edgy cachet of the latest technology. Hammond's Boston publisher was Bela Marsh, who was also a primary publisher of Paine's "sequel," *The Philosophy of Creation* (1854) by Gordon Wood. Curiously, the Library of Congress's copy of Wood's *Philosophy of Creation* comes from the personal collection of Harry Houdini, who was no doubt much amused by Paine's ethereal shenanigans. Inevitably, the fad produced spoofs as well, such as Henry Horn's 1864 collection *Strange Visitors*, which features "new works" by such deceased writers as Poe, Irving, and Margaret Fuller. But Jacob Harshman's *Series of Communications* (1852), in case you hadn't guessed, was very earnestly self-published—and its enclosed printer's slip of errata is perhaps the most hopelessly outgunned copyediting effort in the history of publishing. Maybe it didn't help that, as the author claimed in his introduction, "They [the ghosts] always spelled spirit SPERIT, and stated that it was the proper way."

The fantastical press accounts of images being retained on dead men's retinas are recounted in *Notes and Queries* magazine article "Impressions on the Eye," in its October 3, 1857, issue. As an urban legend, it had legs, for precisely the same press claims were reported again a decade later, under the title "Photographic Miracle," in the *Notes and Queries* issues of June 9 and 23, 1866.

But for an endlessly fascinating pseudoscience, nothing quite beats phrenology. The best glimpse into the daily workings and cultural spread of phrenology can be found simply by leafing through old issues of Fowler's monthly *American Phrenological Journal*, which had a staggering seventy-three-year run from 1838 to 1911. The latest celebrities and reformers of the day are pictured in each issue—along with analysis of their heads, naturally—and the result is a fascinating and forgotten glimpse into both phrenology and popular culture at large. Fowler's own *Practical Phrenology* is another obvious starting point; its sales were so great that there are constantly copies to be found in online auctions, and not uncommonly with Orson's or Lorenzo's signature on the personalized title page. Fowler's *Self-Culture* (1847) is if anything even more valuable, as its goals of progressive phrenology are more explicitly stated.

In describing Fowler's store I found his *Catalogue of Portraits, Busts, and Casts* (n.d.) brochure helpful; many of those masks eventually wound up in the Fowler Mask Collection at the New-York Historical Society, where they can still be seen today. Of Fowler's innumerable other pamphlets and books, I'm especially fond of the *Hydropathic Cookbook*, perhaps because it includes an anti-meat soliloquy delivered in verse by the ghost of a cockroach. The cockroach is the meat, so to speak, that accidentally turns up in a piece of bread:

A cockroach crawled o'er a baker's shelf,
Waving his horns and looking for pelf;
The baker, upon his bread board below,
Was kneading and rolling about the dough.

The board received such terrible thumps,
As the baker's rolling-pin struck the lumps,
The shelf was shaken, the cockroach fell—
Ah, where? the baker he could not tell!

Who says Whitman was Fowler's only poet of importance?

In addition to Fowler's seminal octagon work *Home For All*
(1849), Carl Schmidt's self-published *The Octagon Fad* (1958) is
an invaluable state-by-state compilation of surviving examples of
octagonal architecture. Schmidt also includes many floor plans for
these buildings, and these are quite revealing: ideological fervor
eventually gave way to pragmatism, and many buildings sprouted
naughty rectangular additions to the back in order to house modern
kitchens, pantries, and the like. A later undated book by Schmidt
and Philip Parr, which looks to be from the 1970s, is *More About
Octagons*; both books, though uncommon, can be found at the New
York Public Library. The dire fate of the Octagon settlement can be
read about in Miriam Colt's memoir *Went to Kansas* (1862), which
includes appendices of the venture's charter and other information;
Russell Hickman's article "The Vegetarian and Octagon Settlement
Companies" in *Kansas Historical Quarterly* for November 1933
remains one of the best summaries of this fiasco.

For an inside look at the movement—and such oddities as John
Brown's final communication—Nelson Sizer's 1882 memoir *Forty
Years in Phrenology* is well worth reading.

Jarvis's plaster death mask of Paine proved to be part of a long and curious history of death masks. Aside from the Fowlers, the pre-eminent collector in the 1800s was Laurence Hutton, whose collection is now owned by Princeton University. Hutton is better known today, when he is known at all, as Mark Twain's friend and editor at Harper & Brothers. But death masks were his great hobby, and they are altogether more haunting than any bust or heroic statue. The effect is that of a man sleeping; you realize you are seeing them as perhaps only their spouse and children ever did: unguarded, a little unkempt, and unconscious. "He does not pose; he does not 'try to look pleasant,'" Hutton explained of his unwilling subjects. "In his mask he is seen, as it were, with his mask off." Hutton had masks of Coleridge, Keats, and Wordsworth; he could gaze upon the faces of Lincoln, Webster, Clay, and Calhoun. Grant and Sherman both stared out from Hutton's display cases, the pair vanquished by a more implacable foe than they ever could have imagined. Jonathan Swift cast a baleful eye over Hutton's study; so did the surprisingly brawny head and shoulders of Samuel Johnson and the eternal good-hair-day features of actor David Garrick. The result of Hutton's obsessive pursuit was surely one of the strangest volumes his publishing house ever printed: *Portraits in Plaster*, released by Harper & Brothers in 1894. It is a sumptuous old volume, crammed with smooth photographic plates in black-and-white, face after face of death.

As you might imagine of such a volume upon such a *singular* interest, not many copies were printed. The copy I found, entombed peacefully in the "Sculpture/How-To" section of a used bookstore in Portland, had the sturdy, well-maintained look of a book that nobody has bothered reading in several generations. Inside the front cover, though, a surprise waited. Spidery handwriting spiked and dipped across the creamy paper:

Horace Traubel
His book.
by his friend
Laurence Hutton.

What a curious route this book must have taken, bumping along the currents of the streams of time before coming to rest here among the reeds. Horace Traubel had been Walt Whitman's faithful assistant in the final years of that poet's life. Today Traubel is famous—infamous, really—among Whitman scholars for writing down a nine-volume account, millions of words, of every single detail of Whitman's final years.

Hutton started his collection when a boy found a pile of what were probably George Combe's abandoned death masks in a trash can at the corner of Second Street and Second Avenue; a collector's widow was getting rid of the hideous things. I was first put onto the story of the trash can by Frank Weitenkampf's 1947 memoir *Manhattan Kaleidoscope*. The book is long out of print, but it deserves reissue. Weitenkampf, by then an ancient and retired prints curator at the New York Public Library, offers a wonderfully scattershot stroll through Victorian Manhattan, as when he recalls the time in 1892 that ax-wielding country lumberjacks were brought in by the city to fell the city's old telegraph poles—really, just imagining Irish and Polish immigrants gawking out of their tenements at the burly chaw-chewing lumberjacks makes for a pleasantly off-kilter thought. Weitenkampf is particularly fine at conveying a sense of life as an artist back then; he describes one ramshackle art school on Bond Street where "snow would sift through the roof, to the discomfort of the model posing in the altogether."

As to the eventual fate of Fowler's own building, there were numerous *New York Times* articles in the 1960s about the construction site for the Federal Building, especially during the 1964 evictions. The key pieces are "Vast U.S. Office Building Planned at Foley Square" (11/24/58), "Architects Urge Foley Sq. Delay" (6/14/ 62), "Digging Shifts Foley Sq. Land" (5/1/64), "Evictions Pushed at Foley Square" (5/6/64), and "New Federal Office Building" (8/29/ 68).

The rise of scanned indexes of newspapers from across the country has opened up a wealth of information about the Fowlers and the history of phrenology. One of my favorite minor items turned up in the February 17, 1843, issue of the *Brooklyn Daily Eagle*, recounting a phrenological professor who was entertaining an audience by stimulating the various significant bumps of a slumbering subject: "Finally he touched the organ of Combativeness, when the slumberer gave the professor such a blow in his 'bread basket' as to lay him sprawling upon the floor."

It is mystifying that no comprehensive history of the Fowlers and their phrenological movement has been published for three decades. Madeleine Stern's splendid 1971 account *Heads and Headlines: The Phrenological Fowlers* proved invaluable to me, as did Ms. Stern herself—she still keeps a rare book shop on the Upper West Side. Publishers, will you please do her the courtesy of reprinting this fine work?

Personal Effects

The first thing you must know is that the doorplates are back in box 46, swaddled in their old gauze and ribbon: and my apologies if they fall out on your lap. As anyone who has seen me murder the roll of gift wrap on Chistmas Eve can attest, I am terrible at wrapping things.

There really are some odd things to be found in those boxes of Conway's. In one of them, I came across a framed piece of art: a placid scene of people by a pond and a church. But look closely, and it gets rather strange. The frame is comprised of pieces of rolled-up bits of colored paper, and the illustration itself is made of rolled-up bits of hair and ribbon. A note on the back reads: "Made by one of Napoleon's soldiers when a prisoner—with hair on a piece of ribbon—(England)." God knows where Conway found *that*. But aside from the treasure trove of Conway's papers and possessions at the Rare Book and Manuscript Library of Columbia University, much of this chapter is drawn from Moncure Daniel Conway's invaluable *Autobiography: Memories and Experiences* (2 vols., 1904), and it is worth laying your hands on a copy. The man is a veritable Forrest Gump of the Victorian world; his memoir is one of the great overlooked eyewitness accounts of transcendentalism, abolitionism, and radical politics in both the U.S. and U.K.

The book is full of odd little anecdotes. When he first arrived in Boston, the local historian the Reverend Dr. Alexander Young showed the wide-eyed Southerner around the great city's streets, taking in the sights of buildings which, just barely within living memory, had been the backdrop of revolution. He even met one ancient lady who held among her earliest memories that of the Boston Tea Party—which, historians were always quick to point out, only involved the pointedly political dumping of tea, and not the grubby thievery of it.

Funny—how living memory doesn't always match with what is written down. "The young men in her parents' household had been in the riot," Moncure marveled, "and she told me her recollection of them rushing in, and emptying their shoes of tea which they had preserved from destruction for the benefit of their grandmother." It is a mark of just how valuable tea was back then that tea crammed into someone's sweaty shoes was still deemed palatable.

Conway was a prolific writer in his later years, not least including his *Life of Thomas Paine* (1892) and his *Collected Writings of Thomas Paine* (1894); those interested in Conway himself will find an interesting cross-section of his writings from over the years in *Moncure D. Conway: Addresses and Reprints, 1850–1907* (1909), ranging from his early proslavery writing to the liberal jeremiads against imperialism in his later years. I also found useful information in Edward Walker's eulogistic *A Sketch and Appreciation of Moncure Daniel Conway* (1908), and in a lengthy and genial remembrance published in 1907 by Thomas Wentworth Higginson. The latter, a clipping of which I found pasted inside a copy of Conway's *Autobiography*, bore neither a date nor the name of the publication, though it seems to have run in a Boston newspaper in the days after Conway's death on November 15, 1907.

There are also two books on Conway—Mary Burtis's *Moncure Conway, 1832–1907* (1952), and John D'Entremont's *Southern Emancipator: Moncure Conway, the American Years, 1832–1865* (1987), and both are useful as such things go, particularly if you are trying to save yourself the trouble of reading Conway's weighty autobiography. But don't save yourself that trouble. Plowing through both volumes of Conway's own account is well worth it. Loyd Easton's *Hegel's First American Followers* (1966) provides an additional useful bit of context to Conway's intellectual growth while in Cincinnati.

Gilbert Vale's *Life of Thomas Paine* is still to be found in major libraries, including the New York Public Library, but acquiring your own copy will cost you dearly—unless, of course, you are fortunate enough to rescue a splendidly horrid copy like mine from a rubbish bin. Augustine Birrell's quote on the "villainous" printing of old editions of Paine comes from a review of Conway's *Life of Thomas Paine*, included in Birrell's collection *In the Name of the Bodleian: And Other Essays* (1905). Though not known today, Birrell was esteemed as a belles-lettrist, and his books still have their charms. Discussing the much-loved—though only among very owlish bibliomaniacs—*Life and Errors* of John Dutton (1705), Birrell includes this pricelessly frank bit of advice about reading eighteenth-century memoirs: "[It] may be safely recommended to everyone, except, indeed, to the unfortunate man or woman who is not an adept in the art, craft, and mystery of skipping."

But really: do go and buy Conway's autobiography. And do not skip.

Every once in a while one comes across odd little sideways glances at the great figures of American literature; one other pleasant example of this is Herbert Gleason's *Through the Year With Thoreau* (1917), a book-length photographic essay which revisits the various sites, plants, and animals of Thoreau's writings. Gleason did some wonderful detective work over the years on foot to find the actual coves, clearings, and pastures Thoreau wrote about. And while time had already obliterated some of the vistas Thoreau had seen decades earlier, a surprising number of sights were still to be seen, including the pile of stones that marked the remains of Thoreau's cabin. Gleason also spoke with a number of locals, some of whom still remembered Thoreau and who were not in any awe of him. Meeting an old man who used to drive the butcher's cart from house to house, and thus had known virtually every resident of the area, Gleason asked him if by any chance he'd known Henry David Thoreau:

> "Henry Thoreau?"—with an expression of undisguised contempt—"I knew Henry Thoreau ever since he was a boy, and I never had much of an opinion of him. *And I hain't seen nothing since to change my mind!*"

As Gleason dryly concludes, "It is curious to note how little Thoreau was esteemed by most of his fellow villagers."

Comfort for the Ruptured

For anyone curious about E. B. Foote, there is no better place to start than with the books themselves. Not only was Foote a prolific author, he also frequently excerpted and recycled his material under different titles: anyone trying to amass a comprehensive collection of Footesiana would have a lifetime pursuit on their hands. But the three ur-texts are undoubtedly *Medical Common Sense* (1857), *Plain Home Talk* (1870), and the *Sammy Tubbs* series (1874). Thanks to Foote's popularity, it is relatively easy to track old copies of the first two titles. *Tubbs* was not as popular, but it is now much loved among collectors in the know; consequently, you can easily pay $100 for a single volume from that series. If you know anything of human nature, it will not surprise you to hear that volume 5, *Elimination and Reproduction*, is the most eagerly sought one of all. It is only in the first printing (quite rare indeed) that illustrator Stephens managed to sneak in the infamous tooting vagina.

Curiously, in addition to a great many British and American editions, Foote's works were widely published in German in both Germany and the United States. *Plain Home Talk*, for example, was published as *Offene Volks-Sprache*. Foote himself made a point of advertising that he was available to give private consultations in his Manhattan office in German. This, I think, is a clue for an intrepid scholar. German-Americans appear to have had access to a body of American contraceptive literature *written in German*. I have never heard of anyone publishing in German getting prosecuted by Comstock and his minions. Fortunately for horny immigrants, meddling religious prudes tend toward anti-intellectualism: they can barely read in their own language, never mind someone else's. So there may well have been a substantial hidden contraceptive subculture in America, one that operated under the noses of authorities *simply by being in a different language.*

The first modern account of Foote was Edward Cirillo's articles in volume 25 (1970) of the *Journal of the History of Medicine and Allied Science.* A great many further details of Foote's life and of the contraceptive business can be found in two excellent books, which I cannot recommend highly enough for students of social history: Janet Farrell Brodie's *Contraception and Abortion in 19th Century America* (Cornell UP, 1994), and Michael Sappol's *A Traffic of Dead Bodies: Anatomy and Embodied Social Identity in Nineteenth Century America* (Princeton UP, 2002). Both Janet and Michael were very kind in responding to my inquiries about some of the more arcane bits of this history.

As a tireless self-promoter, Foote also had much written about him in his own lifetime, primarily and rather conveniently by his own hand. *Medical Common Sense* and *Plain Home Talk* both give brief autobiographical accounts, one fleshed out by pamphlets like his *Evidences of Dr. Foote's Success* (1888). Thaddeus Burr Wakeman's elegy and testimonial collection *In Memory of Edward Bliss Foote* (1907) is also quite useful.

Unmentioned in this chapter is one of the great pioneers of earth toilets, the English inventor the Reverend Henry Moule, who in 1861 had published a treatise with the doggedly literal title *National Health and Wealth, Instead of Disease, Nuisance, Expense, and Waste, Caused by Cesspools and Water Drainage.* His Moule Earth Closet never did get much recognition. As our water runs out, his work may prove prophetic yet. And prophesy would not be too strong a word. Moule, being a man of the cloth, viewed the matter in theological terms. He noted the Deuteronomy 23:13 instruction that "With your equipment you will have a trowel, and when you squat outside, you shall scrape a hole with it and then turn and cover your excrement." The Bible has nothing to say, on the other hand, about plungers, S-bends, or chain pulls. To Moule's mind, if water sewage fouled God's creation and wasted perfectly good manure for crops, then surely earth closets treated feces with the respect it deserved.

For those eager to learn more about Victorian toilets—I know you're out there—I recommend Adam Hart Davis's *The Great Stink of London: Sir Joseph Bazalgette and the Cleansing of the Victorian Metropolis* (2001), and his general history *Thunder, Flush, and Thomas Crapper* (1997). Also see Lawrence Wright's *Clean and Decent* (1997) and Wallace Reyburn's *Flushed With Pride: The Story of Thomas Crapper* (1969). Schematics of the Wakefield Earth Toilet are on page 286 of *The Manufacturer and Builder* magazine for December 1871. Details of the 1867 inspection of Britain's rivers, and the sewage and other pollution problems discovered, can be found in *The Life of Frank Buckland*, by George C. Bompas (1886).

Finally, details of August Woehler's attempt upon E. B. Foote's life can be found in the *New York Times* for 1879, on the dates November 2, 7, and 17. As one might have gathered by Woehler's choice of it as a good place to hang himself, Putnam House was not the most happy of boardinghouses. In February 1892, another boarder—this one signing himself in as "J. Davis," and suicidally despondent over racetrack debts—shut himself into his room and tried to blow both himself and the house up with the gas stove. Instead of landing in the Hereafter, though, the gentleman later awoke in the decidedly less tranquil confines of Bellevue Hospital.

The Mornington Crescent Game

Several years ago, when I was still living in Portland, I was sitting in the Periodicals Room of the Multnomah Public Library reading the January 25, 1868, issue of *Notes and Queries* when I came across a letter in it, sent in anonymously by the old customer of John Chennell, and titled "Tom Paine's Bones." I read it in stunned disbelief. I'd vaguely heard once about Paine's body going missing, but—this? What was he doing in the basement of some corn merchant's shop in Guildford? What on earth . . . ?

It was at that moment that this book began.

The Guildford Museum was very helpful in directing me to Mark Sturley's *The Breweries and Public Houses of Guildford* (1990) for more information about the Chennell clan. The hair-raising murder and executions in 1818 are described in the anonymous booklet *Murder and Paricide!!!* (1818) and in the 1841 edition of *The Newgate Calendar.* I also found useful the Guildford Ordnance Survey Map (1895), E. M. Butts's *Guildford Shops & Shopping: 1740–1850* (1989), and *Shops & Shopping: A History of Buying and Selling in Guildford* (2002)—and, of course, John Janaway's splendid *Surrey Privies: A Nostalgic Trip Down the Garden Path* (1999), which reminds us that "The surviving privies of Surrey need all the help they can get."

In addition to the three accounts of Paine's bones cited for "The Bone Grubbers" chapter (Watson, Conway, and Hunns), and Moncure Conway's *Autobiography*, further information can be gleaned from Moncure Conway's exhibition catalogue *Thomas Paine Exhibition at South Place Institute, Finsbury* (1895), which can be found at the British Library. The catalogue contains the first mention of Louis Breeze's ownership of Paine's brain. Breeze's appeals to Parliament over vaccination can be found in the *Times* of London for 21 February 1876 and 20 June 1877; his run-ins with the law are noted in the *Times* for 20 September 1884 and 21 January 1885, and his household members are noted in the United Kingdom Census for 1881.

The British Library has numerous books and pamphlets by Robert Ainslie, including *Is There a God?* (1840). The Darwin Correspondence Online Database (University of Cambridge) also has letters by son Oliver Ainslie to Charles Darwin inquiring about the possibility of buying Trowmer Lodge, most notably his letter of 23 November 1880. But for those tracing Ainslie's steps who find themselves at Mornington Crescent, remember: it's *A Lifetime to Learn, a Minute to Master.* Or so proclaim the devotees of the Mornington Crescent Game, and never was a truer word spoken. Details may be found at the Web site for the radio program *I'm Sorry I Haven't a Clue* (isihac.co.uk). The closing and reopening of Mornington Crescent station, along with a summary of the game's "rules," can be found in the BBC News story "Mornington Crescent: The Legend Is Reborn" (27 April 1998).

Speaking of splendid hoaxes, Tom Paine's appearance among banjo-strumming con men is recounted in *The Scotsman* for 16 November 1876. George Reynolds and his battles with the staged photos and claims of Dr. Barnardo can be found in Gillian Wagner's history *Barnardo* (1979), as well as in two booklets at the British Library, Reynolds's *Dr. Barnardo's Homes: Containing Startling Revelations, Etc.* (1877) and *The Charity Organization and the Reynolds-Barnardo Arbitration* (1878).

The possible fate of Paine's skull can be glimpsed in Richard W. Holloway's eyewitness account of the use of human bones by British chemical manure manufacturers, which he recounted in an April 1917 letter in the *Cairns Post* (compiled online at www.holloways-beach.com by Ian Johnson of Holloways Beach, Australia), as well as in the weirdly compelling October 1871 article "The Art of Utilizing" in *Manufacturer and Builder* magazine, which includes among its many revelations that "fishes' eyes are used for buds in artificial flowers."

Gordon Alexander's account of meeting the Muggletonians can be found in *Ancient and Modern Muggletonians* (1870) at the British Library; more recently, see Ted Underwood's *The Acts of the Witnesses: The Autobiography of Lodowick Muggleton and Other Early Muggletonian Writings* (1999). They survived well into the twentieth century and the last surviving Muggletonian—Philip Noakes, of Matfield, Kent—passed away in 1979. He left behind a trove of early and previously unknown Muggletonian documents to the British Library; he had, in effect, been the last guardian of the sect's legacy.

Laurence Hutton's complaint about not being able to find old landmarks is even truer today than when he first wrote it in *Literary Landmarks of London* (1885). Still, we at least have better maps to work with now. A recent poll of *Time Out London* readers for the "best London book" found their choice to be the *London A–Z* street atlas (1936), which beat out any novelist or historian. This was taken as a rather overly literal answer to the poll's question, but perhaps there's something to that judgment. I trudged around London equipped with a *Dickens's Dictionary of London* (1884), and Karl Baedeker's *Baedeker's London and Its Environs* (1885). If you want to know exactly what a person would see when they walked down a street—what businesses they would patronize, what things cost, what cons and arcane laws they had to watch out for—then old Baedekers and the like are just extraordinary. These were also the last generation of guides to show the dynamic of city life before automobiles overran it.

Forgetting

An account of the Tivoli discovery can be found in the *New York Times* for July 19 ("Paine Tombstone Uncovered Upstate Revives Mystery About Pamphleteer"), and July 20, 1976 ("Thomas Paine Mystery at Tivoli, N.Y., Solved"), both written by James Feron. Feron had previously been a Middle East correspondent for the *Times;* one can only wonder what he made of being dispatched to, as he informed readers, "an object of curiosity and mystery for Jack and Josephine McNeil and their children, as well as for neighbors who live in trailers, frame houses and modest contemporary homes."

The *Times* of London account—Peter Strafford's "Tombstone Is Said to Be Paine's," which ran July 20—was, though filed the same day as the latter Feron story, seemingly unaware of the explanation of the obelisk's origin. Given how often stories from both *Times* are picked up in the foreign media, I imagine the Paine story made its way into other countries and continents; in a conversation with Josephine McNeil, she mentioned to me that back in 1976 she was receiving calls and letters from as far away as Australia.

There was a brief attempt at gathering up Paine's bones in 2001— a "Citizen Paine Restoration Initiative," was profiled in the March 30, 2001, *New York Times*. It seems to have fallen quite silent since then. Among those cited was Hazel Burgess, the Australian owner of the alleged Paine skull bought from a dealer in Sydney. She was trying to raise money for DNA tests on the skull, but has not been heard from publicly since; when I contacted her, she politely declined to give further details on any findings.

Perhaps her story will become rather like that of the McNeils. Cultural forgetfulness is not the same as the individual loss of memory, but the former seems to me largely an accumulation of the latter. When we no longer find something useful, we—individually and collectively—tend to forget it. After all, the too-strong persistence of memory winds up interfering with one's ability to perceive the present moment. The hippocampus and amygdala are constantly throwing away memories—whether by destroying or sealing them off is not clear—though this function notably goes awry in the traumatic memories associated with depression and post-traumatic stress disorder. The best academic introduction to this field of memory studies is Daniel Schecter and Larry Squire's *Neuropsychology of Memory* (3rd ed., 2002) and in Schacter and Elaine Scarry's *Memory, Brain, and Belief* (2002). One promising new area is the use of memory-related drugs, notably in the work of Bryan Strange, Larry Cahill, and Roger Pitman. These are not the old panaceas that promise to improve your memory: quite the opposite. *They help you forget.*

Eternity in a Box

Accounts of the Thirteen Club, an idea surely due for a revival, can be found in abundance in the *Brooklyn Daily Eagle* in the late 1890s; this particular celebration is described in articles that ran on February 6 and 14, 1898.

For more on the fate of phrenology and Orson Fowler, see the histories cited in "The Talking Heads" chapter; the growing disenchantment of both Foote Senior and Junior with it can be found in speeches reported by the *Brooklyn Daily Eagle* for May 11 and 23, 1896. Phrenology really was something of an intellectual tragedy. In retrospect, its basic set of propositions was surprisingly accurate: that different cognitive functions are localized to specific parts of the brain; that the brain has a plasticity that allows it to develop or atrophy at any age, but disproportionately and critically so in one's youth; and that cognition itself is a physical phenomenon. These are now the most fundamental assumptions of neurology. The observation of localized brain function underlies MRI scan research; neural plasticity is the raison d'être of Head Start, special education, and stroke therapies alike; and the chemical basis of cognition has built a multibillion-dollar industry of antidepressants to pull you up, antipsychotics to hold you down, and sedatives to knock you sideways. Phrenology's error was believing these effects could be observed at the level of gross anatomy. Without a serious commitment to scientific methodology, this error grew until phrenology truly became the sham its opponents always said it was.

One of the only newspaper accounts of the 1905 ceremony with Thomas Paine's brain is in the *New York Times* for October 15, 1905. A number of details about Thomas Paine's memorial can also be found in the *News Letter* of the Thomas Paine National Historical Association, and the commemorative booklet *Rededication of the Paine Monument* (1909). *Rededication* contains the 1905 ceremony's speeches by Foote and other locals, some of whom were rather less eloquent than others; one Minuteman reenactor began his remarks with "I find myself somewhat in the position of an old darkey down in Virginia . . ."

Photographs of the preserved cottage, as well as a timeline of the Paine monument, can be found in the *Souvenir Program: Thomas Paine Centennial Celebration* (1909) and the *Memorial Celebration of the Hundredth Anniversary of the Death of Thomas Paine* (1909); both were published by E. B. Foote Jr. and the Thomas Paine National Historical Association, and can be found at the New York Public Library. Accounts of the cottage's near-destruction are in *Leslie's Illustrated Weekly* for January 2, 1908, and the *New York Times* for May 31, 1908, as well as the TPHA booklet *Thomas Paine and New Rochelle, NY* (1951) and the Huguenot and Historical Association of New Rochelle's booklet *Thomas Paine Cottage and Grounds* (1931).

Aside from Paine's body, his grave itself became something of a missing relic. In September 1909, *South Place Magazine* ran "Thomas Paine's Gravestone," which traces a large fragment of the shattered headstone with Cobbett to Liverpool. A reminiscence by William Lowes Rushton, son of the 1820s Liverpool radical Edward Rushton, includes this interesting detail about what else was in Cobbett's luggage: "I understand the gravestone was broken into fragments soon after it was laid down, and long before Cobbett visited America. I do not know how this fragment came into Cobbett's possession, but according to my remembrance of what my father said on the subject, Cobbett brought it to Liverpool with Tom Paine's bones, which he had disinterred, and gave it to my father. This fragment I remember seeing in my father's library when I was a child, and it is now in my possession."

In addition to the sources mentioned in the "Personal Effects" chapter, information on Moncure Conway's final days in Paris can be found in Edward Walker's *A Sketch and An Appreciation of Moncure Daniel Conway, Freethinker and Humanitarian* (1908) and John Robertson's *The Life Pilgrimage of Moncure Daniel Conway* (1914). But perhaps the most charming eulogy on the man came right after his death from his old friend Thomas Wentworth Higginson, who by now was famous as Emily Dickinson's "preceptor." Recalling trips to the theater with Conway, he wrote: "He always chose seats by preference in the very highest gallery, where rough men sat with their hats on, eating sandwiches, among their wives and daughters, and affording, as he always maintained, the best source of appreciation for good acting."

An account of the death and burial of E. B. Foote Sr. can be found in *In Memory of Edward Bliss Foote, M.D.* (1907), a compilation of addresses and newspaper clippings related to his funeral. For E. B. Foote Jr.'s final days, see the posthumous collection *Edward Bond Foote: Biographical Notes and Appreciatives* (1913). One anecdote involves the senior Foote's seventieth birthday, when the old doctor was given a wonderful present by Junior—a collection of fifty newfangled phonograph wax cylinders, each bearing birthday messages from across the country. He set one into his phonograph and out crackled the voice of his old friend Elizabeth Cady Stanton—a *very* old friend, as she was now eighty-four—and the doctor listened appreciatively as her voice spun from the revolving cylinder:

I am glad to tell you that there is no old age but old age of the heart, and if you wish to preserve what health and youth you still have, I will give you three directions: First, sleep all you possibly can. Next, do not worry; whatever you can prevent that's wrong, do so; what you can not, accept. One more: Interest yourself crackle, crackle, crackle *in some great question of reform.*

And indeed he did—they all did.

Acknowledgments

WITHOUT THE LOVE and support of my wife Jennifer, my first reader and editor in all matters, this book could not have been written. For rather like Tom Paine's bones, it has had some unexpected travels and surprises—namely, the birth of our son Bramwell and our family's move from Oregon to Iowa. Those readers of my work about my son Morgan will understand how in watching my two sons grow, history becomes meaningful to me: they remind me of why it is that I write.

Were it not for the immense help of Marc Thomas, this book would have taken me many years longer to write. Thanks are due as well to Michelle Tessler and Colin Dickerman for shepherding it through to publication. There were innumerable libraries and antiquarians essential to the creation of this book, but particular thanks are due to the library at Columbia University and to the Guildford Museum. A tip of the hat, too, to the scholars who were so generous with their knowledge when I contacted them— David A. Wilson, Madeleine Stern, Michael Sappol, and Janet Brodie—and to Olivia Lo and Josephine McNeil for humoring my unaccountable need to see a gravestone sitting in a dog-filled garage.

I am indebted to my fellow authors at the Friday-afternoon

Scrabble game here in Iowa City for their tea, ginger cookies, and sympathy while I went through several sleepless months finishing the book, and . . . okay, *okay*, I'll take my turn now.

Finally, my great appreciation indeed to the many efforts over the years by the staff of the Thomas Paine National Historical Association, from E. B. Foote and Moncure Conway on up to Brian McCartin. New members are always welcome at their Web site:

www.thomaspaine.org

A NOTE ON THE AUTHOR

Paul Collins is the author of *Banvard's Folly, Sixpence House*, and *Not Even Wrong: A Father's Journey into the Lost History of Autism*. He edits the Collins Library for McSweeney's Books, and his work has appeared in *New Scientist* and the *Village Voice*. He lives in Iowa City.

A NOTE ON THE TYPE

The text of this book is set in Adobe Caslon, named after the English punch-cutter and type founder William Caslon I (1692–1766). Caslon's rather old-fashioned types were modeled on seventeenth-century Dutch designs, but found wide acceptance throughout the English-speaking world for much of the eighteenth century until being replaced by newer types toward the end of the century. Used in 1776 to print the Declaration of Independence, they were revived in the nineteenth century, and have been popular ever since, particularly among fine printers. There are several digital versions, of which Carol Twombly's Adobe Caslon is one.